D1154508

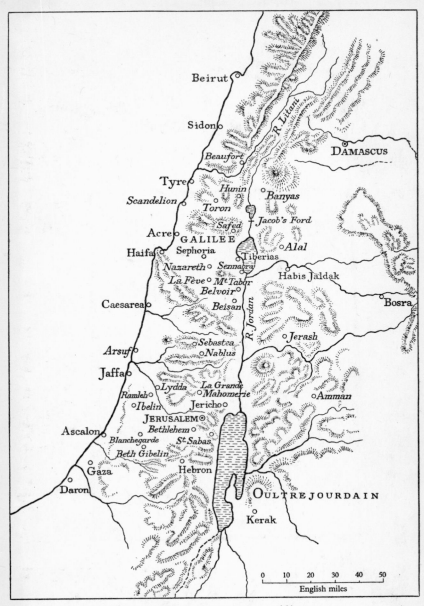

The Kingdom of Jerusalem in the twelfth century.

Maps from Steven Runciman, *History of the Crusades* (3 vols.; Cambridge: Cambridge University Press, 1951-54). Reprinted with permission.

The CRUSADES

A DOCUMENTARY SURVEY

The

CRUSADES

A DOCUMENTARY SURVEY

by JAMES A. BRUNDAGE, Ph.D.

Associate Professor of History
The University of Wisconsin—Milwaukee

THE MARQUETTE UNIVERSITY PRESS

Milwaukee   1962   Wisconsin

D157
B88

940.18
B894

© COPYRIGHT, 1962, THE MARQUETTE UNIVERSITY PRESS,
MILWAUKEE, WIS.

Library of Congress Catalogue Card No.: 62-12897

MANUFACTURED IN THE UNITED STATES OF AMERICA

To

Jamie

Filius Sapiens Laetificat Patrem

JAN 3 0 1963

PREFACE

I first began work on this book in the summer of 1955 in connection with a course of lectures on the history of the Crusades which I was to give during the following academic year in Fordham College. My original design called for the assembly of a group of readings which would serve as an introduction both to the history of the Crusading movement itself and to the major chroniclers and other contemporary Western historians whose narratives underlie all of our fundamental knowledge of the Crusades. I very quickly discovered difficulties. Of some of the authors who should be included, there were no English translations extant. Of several other authors there were translations, indeed, but either they were not satisfactory or (in a few cases) the existing translations were not readily available to me. It was soon evident that I must do a major part of the translating myself. It also became evident quite early that, since in any case brief introductions to each of the translated documents would be necessary, there would be considerable merit in trying to weave the documents together with a connecting narrative account of the Crusades for the reader's benefit. This seemed an especially useful notion since, save for Sir Ernest Barker's rather dated article in the *Encyclopedia Brittanica* (enlarged slightly and published separately as *The Crusades*), there was no brief, single-volume survey of the Crusades available in English. Thus this book has slowly

grown into a documentary survey of the history of the Crusades.

My work on this book has been sporadically pursued in
the midst of many other commitments and distractions, both
academic and domestic. Much of it was written in New
York City and in Bergenfield, New Jersey, while I was
teaching at Fordham College. Other portions were composed
in Provincetown, Massachusetts, and the last five chapters
were finished in Milwaukee, Wisconsin. The accidents of
time and place and the facilities of the various libraries at
my disposal account for some of the minor oddities of this
volume—such as, for example, the way in which various
editions of William of Tyre jostle cheek by jowl with one
another in the notes.

It is both a pleasure and an obligation to acknowledge
the debts which I have incurred while composing this book.
My thanks are due and are here gratefully rendered to the
librarians and staffs of the Fordham University Library, the
New York Public Library, the Newberry Library, the University of Illinois Library, the Marquette University Library,
and the University of Wisconsin Libraries in Madison and
Milwaukee. I further owe a major debt of gratitude to Dr.
Dean L. Towle, who has once again given cheerfully and
generously of his time to read and criticize my wayward
prose. Likewise I should like to acknowledge the helpful
comments of Professor Cyril Smith of Marquette University
and Professor Jeremiah F. O'Sullivan of Fordham University. Mr. Gregory Burke McDonald also read and criticized
the manuscript at an early stage of its development.

Lastly, to my wife I owe the greatest of all my debts for
her constant assistance and patient encouragement throughout the travail of this prolonged literary gestation.

JAMES A. BRUNDAGE

Milwaukee, Wisconsin
June 12, 1961

CONTENTS

Chapter I

pREpARATiON

I

The Crusades were a product of the eleventh century, probably the most decisive period in the history of Western Europe, for it was then that the West was born. The decades following just after 1050 saw the birth of a distinctively Western world, far different from anything which had gone before. The Crusades were a part of that new world.

Western Europe in the period just prior to the launching of the Crusades by the Papacy, was small and narrowly confined, restricted for all practical purposes to central and northern Italy, Gaul, western Germany, and England. On all sides the people of this Western world were hemmed in by foreign and hostile races: some of these neighbors, such as the Byzantine Greeks, were sophisticated and cultured, far more so in fact than the peoples of the West themselves; others, such as the Slavs who inhabited eastern Germany, were crude and primitive. All of Western Europe's neighbors at this period, however, had this in common: all were potential enemies of the West; in addition, they all inhabited potential areas for Western conquest, colonization, and assimilation.[1]

The two hundred years immediately following 1050 witnessed an enormous expansion of the West in every direction. Scandinavia submitted to Christianity. The Slavs in Germany were pushed back relentlessly toward the Russian plains by the press of colonists from Saxony and further west, while those Slavs who remained in Germany, in Poland, in Bohemia, and in the Baltic lands were forced to accept Latin Christianity. The Moslems, defeated time and time again in Spain and Portugal, gradually gave up most of the Iberian peninsula under the attack of Western Christian knights. The Moslem and Byzantine settlements in southern Italy and Sicily were reclaimed for the West by the Normans. During this same two hundred year period, Palestine and Syria were subjected first to Western conquest, then to the establishment of a group of Latin colonies, and finally, at the close of the period, they were to see the annihilation of those remote outposts of a vigorous, expanding, but overextended Western civilization.

The Crusades thus constitute one phase of a vast movement by the peoples of the West to extend their frontiers and to incorporate within the Western European family most of the West's immediate neighbors. The Crusades were, in fact, an integral part of the beginning of European colonialism.

II

To represent the Crusades simply as one phase of the first chapter in the history of European expansion is, however, to tell but a part of the story. For while the Crusades were this, they were much more besides. Basically they were also a religious movement whose principal objective in the eyes of most of their Western European participants was to impose Latin Christian rule upon the Holy Places: upon Jerusalem and Bethlehem and upon Syria and Palestine generally. The Syrian and Palestinian Holy Places, the sites of the major events in the life of Jesus and of many early saints and martyrs of the Christian church, were sacrosanct to European Christians. The very fact that these Holy Places were ruled by and frequented by non-Christians was considered wicked and abominable by most European Christians, for it constituted, they believed, a crime in the sight of God. One aim of the Crusades, therefore, was to wrest the hallowed ground of the Holy Land from the Moslems, to restore the Holy Places to Christian hands.

The Crusades were, furthermore, holy wars—wars sanctioned, it was thought, by God himself, to wreak vengeance upon those who by their presence there had polluted and defiled the Holy Land. The Crusaders saw themselves as the specially commissioned agents of God, sent by him as instruments of his vengeance against the followers of Mohammed.

The Crusaders were treading in the footsteps of generations of their forebears who had come to visit the Holy Places, not as conquerors, but rather as unarmed pilgrims.[2] Pious European Christians had regularly made pilgrimages to Palestine since the earliest days of Christianity. The Moslem conquest of Jerusalem in the seventh century had affected pilgrims only slightly. The Moslems were, for the most part, loath to interfere with pilgrimage traffic, which was, after all, rather profitable for the conquerors of the Holy Land. From the eighth through the eleventh centuries, pilgrimages from the West to Palestine had slowly increased, in frequency and in numbers of pilgrims involved.

One of the largest and most important of the pre-Crusade pilgrimage expeditions was that made by a large group of Germans in 1064-1065. Their trip, which may be taken as fairly typical of the hazards involved in these journeys, is described in these terms by the contemporary annalist of Nieder-Altaich:

THE GREAT GERMAN PILGRIMAGE OF 1064-1065[3]

An almost incredible multitude set out for Jerusalem this year[4] to worship at the sepulcher of the Lord. So many people took part in the pilgrimage and so much has been said about it that, lest its omission seem serious, we should briefly summarize here what transpired.

The leading personages who took part in the pilgrimage were Archbishop Siegfried of Metz, Bishop William of Utrecht, Bishop Otto of Ratisbon, and Bishop Gunther of Bamberg. Bishop Gunther, though younger than the others, was not inferior to the rest in wisdom and strength of spirit. Although now, after his death, we can scarcely record it without sorrowful groans Gunther was at that time the glory and pillar of the whole realm. Those who were acquainted with his secrets used to say that in many virtues he was perfection itself, down to the most minute details.

These leaders were followed by a multitude of counts and princes, rich and poor, whose numbers seemed to exceed twelve thousand.[5] As soon as they had crossed the river known as the Morava, they fell at once into constant danger from thieves and brigands. Prudently avoiding these dangers, they cautiously made their way to the city of Constantinople. There they conducted themselves so honorably in every way that even the imperial arrogance of the Greeks was taken aback by them. The Greeks were so astounded by the noble appearance of Bishop Gunther that they took him to be, not a bishop, but the King of the Romans.* They believed that he had disguised himself as a bishop, because he could not otherwise pass through these kingdoms to the sepulcher of the Lord.

They left Constantinople a few days later and, after passing through various difficulties and tribulations, came to Latakia. Bishop Gunther made their troubles clear when he wrote from Latakia to his people who were still at home. He said, among other things: "Brethren, we have truly passed through fire and water and at length the Lord has brought us to Latakia, which is mentioned in the Holy Scriptures as Laodicea. We have had the Hungarians serve us without faith and we have had the Bulgarians prey secretly upon us; we have fled from the open raging of the Uzes† and we have seen the Greek and imperial arrogance of the citizens of Constantinople; we have suffered in Asia Minor, but worse things are yet to come."

While they were staying for a few days in Latakia, they began to meet each day many people returning from Jerusalem. The returning parties told of the deaths of an uncounted number of their companions. They also shouted about and displayed their own recent and still bloody wounds. They bore witness publicly that no one could pass along that route because the whole land was occupied by a most ferocious tribe of Arabs who thirsted for human blood.

The question before the pilgrims was what to do and where to turn. First of all, they quickly agreed in council to deny their own wishes and to put all hope in the Lord. They knew that, living or dying, they belonged to the Lord and so, with all their wits

* The title taken by the medieval German Emperors prior to their official coronation by the Pope as Holy Roman Emperor.
† The Byzantine name for the fierce Oghuz Turks, 600,000 of whom were reported to have penetrated the Balkan provinces of Byzantium in 1065.

about them, they set out through the pagan territory toward the holy city.

They soon came to a city called Tripoli. When the barbarian commander of the city saw such a multitude he ordered that all of them, without exception, be slaughtered cruelly with the sword; he hoped thereby to acquire an infinite sum of money. Immediately there arose from the sea (which beats against one side of the city) a dark cloud, from which there issued a great many lightning flashes, accompanied by terrifying claps of thunder. When this storm had lasted until noon of the next day and the waves of the sea had reached unusual heights, the pagans, united by the urgency of the situation, shouted to one another that the Christian God was fighting for his people and was going to cast the city and its people into the abyss. The commander, fearing death, changed his mind. The Christians were given leave to depart and at once the disturbance of the sea was calmed.

Harassed by various trials and tribulations, the pilgrims at last made their way through the whole country to the city called Caesarea. There they celebrated Holy Thursday, which fell that year on March 24. They even congratulated themselves on having escaped all danger, since it was reckoned that the journey from there to Jerusalem would take no more than two days.

On the following day, Good Friday,[6] about the second hour of the day,[7] just as they were leaving Kafar Sallam, they suddenly fell into the hands of the Arabs who leaped on them like famished wolves on long awaited prey. They slaughtered the first pilgrims pitiably, tearing them to pieces. At first our people tried to fight back, but they were quickly forced, as poor men, to take refuge in the village. After they had fled, who can explain in words how many men were killed there, how many types of death there were, or how much calamity and grief there was? Bishop William of Utrecht, badly wounded and stripped of his clothes, was left lying on the ground with many others to die a miserable death. The three remaining bishops, together with a considerable crowd of various kinds of people, occupied a certain walled building with two stone towers. Here they prepared to defend themselves, so long as God allowed it.

The gate of the building was extremely narrow and, since the enemy was so close, they could not unload the packs carried by their horses. They lost, therefore, their horses and mules and everything that the animals were carrying. The enemy divided these things among themselves and soon hastened to destroy the owners of the wealth. The pilgrims, on the other hand, decided to take up arms[8] and with weapons in hand they courageously fought back. The enemy, more indignant than ever, pressed the attack more vigorously, for they saw that the pilgrims, who they had thought would not attempt anything against them, were resisting manfully. For three whole days both sides fought with full force. Our men, though handicapped by hunger, thirst, and lack of sleep, were fighting for their salvation and their lives. The enemy gnashed their teeth like ravening wolves, since it seemed that they were not to be allowed to swallow the prey which they had grasped in their jaws.

At last, on Easter Sunday,[9] about the ninth hour of the day,* a truce was called and eight pagan leaders were allowed to climb up into the tower, where the bishops were, to find out how much money the bishops would pay for their lives and for permission to leave.

As soon as they had climbed up, the one who seemed to be their chief approached Bishop Gunther, whom he took to be the leader of the pilgrims. The sheik removed the linen cloth with which his head was covered[10] and wrapped it around the neck of the seated bishop. "Now that I have taken you," he said, "all of these men are in my power and I shall hang you and as many of the others as I wish from a tree." Gunther acted as he did because the just man was fearless as a lion.[11] As soon as the interpreter made known what the sheik had done and said, Gunther, who was not at all terrified by the numerical strength of the surrounding enemy, immediately leaped up and knocked the pagan to the ground with a single blow of his fist. The venerable man brought his foot down on the sheik's neck; then he said to his men: "Quick now! Set to and cast all these men into chains and put them out naked to ward off the missiles which their men are throwing at us." There was no delay; as soon as he had spoken his orders were carried out. Thus the assault of the attacking pagans was quelled for that day.

On the following day, about the ninth hour, the governor of the King of Babylon,[12] who ruled the city of Ramla, came at last

* That is, the ninth hour of the Roman day, i.e., in the mid-afternoon.

with a large host to liberate our men. The governor, who had heard what the Arabs, like heathen, were doing, had calculated that if these pilgrims were to perish such a miserable death, then no one would come through this territory for religious purposes and thus he and his people would suffer seriously. When the Arabs learned of his approach, they dispersed and fled. The governor took charge of those who had been captured and tied up by the pilgrims and opened the gate so that our men could leave. They made their way, after leaving, to Ramla, where, at the invitation of the governor and townspeople, they rested for two weeks. They were finally allowed to leave and on April 12 they entered the holy city.

One cannot describe with words the fountain of tears which was shed there, the number and purity of the prayers and consecrated hosts which were sacrificed to God, or the joyful spirit with which, after many sighs, the pilgrims now chanted: "We shall now pay reverence at his footstool."[13]

After they had spent thirteen days there, fulfilling with intimate devotion their vows to the Lord, they finally returned in exultation to Ramla. Large numbers of Arabs gathered together at many places along the route, lying in ambush at all the entrances to the road, for they still sorrowed over the prey which had been snatched from their jaws. Our men, however, were not unaware of this. They presently gave passage money to the merchants. When they saw a favorable wind they boarded the ship. After a prosperous voyage they landed on the eighth day at the port of the city of Latakia. Leaving there a few days later, they joyfully arrived at last, though not without great difficulty and travail, at the Hungarian border and the banks of the Danube river. [*Trans. James A. Brundage*]

III

At the very time when Bishop Gunther and his pious German pilgrims were making their way to Jerusalem, momentous changes were afoot in the eastern Mediterranean area. For generations the Near East had been dominated by three great powers: the Abbasid Caliphs of Baghdad had controlled Iran, Mesopotamia, and Turkestan; the Fatimid Caliphs of Cairo had controlled Egypt, Palestine, and southern Syria; and the Christian Byzantine Empire, the descendant and successor of the East Roman Empire of antiquity, had controlled northern Syria, Asia Minor, and the Balkans.

In 1055, however, a new power had suddenly appeared in this area. The Seljuk Turks, fierce and powerful tribesmen from Central Asia, took Baghdad. From there the Seljuk Sultan, Tughril Bey, loosed a formidable attack upon the Byzantine provinces in Syria and Asia Minor. The death of Tughril Bey in 1063 brought only a short interruption to the Seljuk attacks. Under Tughril Bey's nephew and successor, Alp Arslan, Byzantium was again menaced by the swift, formidable Seljuk armies.

To meet this Turkish threat, the Byzantine Emperor Romanus Diogenes set out in the spring of 1071 to reconquer Lesser Armenia. Near Manzikert on August 26, the Byzantine army fell into a trap set by the Turks and was massacred. This disaster opened the way for general and nearly unopposed Turkish conquest of central Asia Minor.

With Byzantium reeling from the blows inflicted by the Seljuks at Manzikert and with the Empire nearly torn apart by the chaotic events of the years immediately following that disaster, the Emperor Michael Dukas was led in desperation to appeal for military aid to the great reforming Pope, Gregory VII. Gregory greeted the Byzantine appeals with enthusiasm. The Pope attempted to arouse general interest in the West for the Byzantine cause and even considered leading an army in person to relieve Byzantium and also to liberate the Holy Land from its Moslem rulers. Although Gregory's plans never came to fruition (owing largely to the Papacy's involvement in a desperate struggle for the control of the Western church itself), three of the Pontiff's letters reveal the stage which his plans reached. The similarity of these plans to the Crusade which was preached twenty-one years later is striking:

POPE GREGORY VII PROPOSES MILITARY AID FOR BYZANTIUM[14]

Bishop Gregory, servant of God's servants, to Count William of Burgundy—Greeting and the apostolic benediction.

Your Prudence must remember with how great an outpouring of affection the Roman church has already received Your Mightiness and with what special love she enjoys your friendship. Neither can you rightly have forgotten the promise made to God before the body of Peter, Prince of the Apostles, in the presence of our venerable predecessor, Pope Alexander . . . that whenever necessary your strength would not be lacking if called upon for the defence of St. Peter's possessions. Remembering Your Honor's noble promise, therefore, we beseech and admonish your sagacious zeal that you make ready the strength of your military forces to aid the liberty of the Roman church and that, if necessary, you come hither with your army in the service of St. Peter.

We do not intend to assemble this multitude of soldiers in order to shed Christian blood. . . . For we hope . . . that when the Normans have been pacified we may cross over to Constantinople to help the Christians who have suffered exceedingly from the oft-inflicted stings of the Saracens and who have vainly besought us to lend our hand to help them. . . . You may be certain that you and all those who shall exert themselves with you in this expedition will be given a double—rather, a multiple—reward, as we believe, by Peter and Paul, the Princes of the Apostles. (Rome, March 1, 1074)

Bishop Gregory, servant of God's servants, to all those willing to defend the Christian faith—Greeting and the apostolic benediction.

We would have you know that the bearer of these presents, upon his recent return from overseas, has visited us at the apostolic court. We have learned from him, as we have from many others, that a pagan people has prevailed strongly against the Christian Empire, that they have already cruelly laid waste and occupied with tyrannical violence everything, almost to the walls of the city of Constantinople, and that they have slain many thousands of Christians, as if they were herds of beasts. On this account, if we love God and call ourselves Christians, we should grieve deeply over the sad fate of such an Empire and of so many Christians. In this affair it is not enough to grieve with fitting solicitude. Rather, the example of our Redeemer and the obligation of brotherly love demand that we lay down our lives for the liberation of our brethren, just as he "laid down his life for us and we ought to lay down our lives for our brethren. . . ."[15]

We beseech you, therefore, by the faith in which you are united through Christ in the adoption of the Sons of God,[16] and we admonish you by the authority of the blessed Peter, Prince of the Apostles, that you be moved to fitting compassion by the wounds and blood of your brethren and by the peril of the aforesaid Empire and that your strength be brought, in Christ's name . . . to the aid of your brethren. . . . (Rome, March 1, 1074)

Bishop Gregory, servant of God's servants, to the glorious King Henry*—Greeting and the apostolic benediction.

If God were in some way to make it possible for my mind to be opened to you, I know beyond doubt that, through his bountiful grace, no one could separate you from my sincere affection. I have confidence, however, in his mercy, that some day he will make it clear that I love you with sincere charity. . . .

Let me point out to Your Greatness, moreover, that the Christians overseas, the greater part of whom have been destroyed with unheard of slaughter and who are being daily butchered like herds of cattle, have humbly sent to me . . . begging that I succor these brethren of ours in whatever way I can, lest—God forbid!—the Christian religion perish completely in our times. I have been touched, therefore, with great grief . . . and I have taken steps to rouse and stir up certain Christians who long to lay down their lives for their brethren by defending the law of Christ. . . . By the inspiration of God, the Italians and the ultramontaine peoples, as I hear, or rather, as I can fully affirm, have freely accepted this command. Already more than fifty thousand men have prepared themselves so that, if they can have me as their Pontiff and leader, they may raise up their mailed fist against God's enemies and, under his leadership, go all the way to the Lord's sepulcher.

I am especially anxious to undertake this mission because the church of Constantinople, which differs from us over the Spirit,[17]

* The German King, and Emperor, Henry IV, soon to become Gregory's bitter opponent in the struggle between Empire and Papacy.

hopes for an understanding with the Apostolic See. The Armenians, almost all of whom have strayed from the Catholic faith, and nearly all the Easterners are awaiting the decision of the apostle Peter's faith about their various opinions. . . .

But, since great undertakings call for great counsel and the help of the great, if God allows me to begin this, I shall seek your counsel and, if it please you, your aid. For, if through God's favor, I do go, I shall leave the Roman church (after God) to you, that you may care for her, as for a holy mother, and that you may defend her honor. Inform me as soon as possible of your wishes in these matters. . . .

May almighty God, from whom all good things proceed, absolve you, by the merits and authority of the blessed apostles Peter and Paul, from all your sins and may he cause you to walk in the paths of his commandments[18] and lead you to life everlasting. (Rome, December 7, 1074) *[Trans. James A. Brundage]*

Abbreviations used in the notes:

AHR	American Historical Review
Grousset, Croisades	René Grousset, Histoire des Croisades et du Royaume franc de Jérusalem (3 vols.; Paris: Payot, 1934-1936).
MGH	Monumenta Germaniae Historica
SS	Scriptores
SSRG	Scriptores Rerum Germanicarum
Munro, Essays	The Crusades and Other Historical Essays Presented to Dana C. Munro by His Former Students (New York: F. S. Crofts, 1928).
PL	J. P. Migne (ed.) Patrologiae cursus completus, series Latina, 221 vols., (Paris, 1844-1855)
RHC, Occ	Recueil des historiens des Croisades, Historiens occidentaux
Runciman, Crusades	Steven Runciman, A History of the Crusades (3 vols.; Cambridge: Cambridge University Press, 1951-1954).
Setton, Crusades	A History of the Crusades, Kenneth M. Setton (ed.), (to be completed in 5 vols.; Philadelphia: University of Pennsylvania Press, 1955-).

CHAPTER I

[1] More detailed treatments of the background of the Crusades may be found in Steven Runciman, A History of the Crusades (3 vols.; Cambridge: Cambridge University Press, 1951-1954), I, 3-100: Kenneth M. Setton (ed.), A History of the Crusades (to be completed in 5 vol.; Philadelphia: University of Pennsylvania Press, 1955-), I, 3-219; René Grousset, Histoire des Croisades et du royaume franc de Jérusalem (3 vols.: Paris: Payot, 1934-1936), I, i-lxii. See also the extensive treatment of the Crusading idea by Carl Erdmann, Die Entstehung des Kreuzzugsgedankens (Stuttgart: Kohlhammer, 1935). There are six studies of the same topic in Relazioni del X Congresso Internazionale di Scienze Storiche (Firenze. G. C. Sansoni, 1955), III, 543-652.

[2] On the subject of pre-Crusade pilgrimages, see Runciman, Crusades, I, 38-50; Runciman is also the author of the section, "The Pilgrimages to Palestine Before 1095," in Setton, Crusades, I, 68-78; see also Ludovic Lalanne, "Des pèlerinages en terre sainte avant les croisades," Bibliothèque de l'École des chartes, VII (1845-1846), 1-31. Eng-

lish translations of the accounts of some pre-Crusade pilgrimages are contained in the thirteen volumes published by the Palestine Pilgrims Text Society (London: 1896-1897), and also in Thomas Wright, (ed.), *Early Travels in Palestine* (London: Bohn, 1848).

3 *Annales Altahenses Maiores, s. a.* 1065, *MGH, SS,* XX, 815-17.

4 The annalist of Nieder-Altaich recorded these events under the year 1065, although the pilgrims actually began their journey about the middle of November 1064. See Einar Joranson's study of this pilgrimage, "The Great German Pilgrimage of 1064-1065," in Dana C. Munro, *The Crusades and Other Historical Essays Presented to Dana C. Munro by His Former Students* (New York: F. S. Crofts, 1928), pp. 3-43.

5 Another contemporary chronicler estimated their numbers at only seven thousand (Sigibert, *Chronica, MGH, SS,* VI, 361); see also Joranson, in Munro, *Essays,* p. 11. Medieval estimates of large numbers are notoriously inaccurate, and all that can reasonably be inferred from the figures given for this group of pilgrims is that there were a great many of them.

6 March 25, 1065.

7 Another contemporary chronicler indicates that the incident took place about the third hour of the day (Lambert of Hersfeld, *Annales,* O. Holder-Egger, (ed.), *MGH, SSRG,* p. 94). By our method of reckoning time, the attack must have begun at some time between 6:30 and 8:00 in the morning; see Joranson, in Munro *Essays,* p. 20.

8 As was normal for pilgrims, the party had up to this point traveled unarmed.

9 March 27, 1065.

10 His *kufiyah,* the flowing Arab headdress.

11 Cf. Prov. 28:1.

12 Al-Mustansir, the Fatimid caliph of Cairo.

13 Ps. 131:1.

14 Erich Caspar (ed.), *Das Register Gregors VII.* (Berlin: Weidmann, 1920), I, 46, 49; II, 31 (*MGH, Epistolae Selectae,* II¹, 70-71, 75-76, 165-68).

15 I John 3:16.

16 Rom. 8:23.

17 A reference to the *Filioque* controversy. The teaching of the Western church was that the Holy Spirit proceeds from the Father and the Son; the Eastern church held that the Spirit proceeds from the Father only.

18 Ps. 118:32.

Chapter II

pROCLAMATiON OF THE CRUSADE

I

The fruitless efforts of Pope Gregory VII to secure military forces to fight in the East failed in stemming the Turkish threat to Byzantium. Turkish advance into Byzantine territory in Asia Minor continued apace after 1074 and the consequences for Byzantium were nearly disastrous. Provincial governors and army commanders, one after another, revolted against the governments of successive emperors at Constantinople, while the Normans, who had already ousted the Byzantines from their colonies in southern Italy and Sicily, added to the difficulties of the Greek emperors by invading the Empire's Balkan provinces. Chaos threatened to overwhelm the only powerful Christian government in the eastern Mediterranean when, in 1081, as the result of still another revolt, the most promising of Byzantium's military leaders, the youthful Alexius Comnenus, seized the throne.[1]

The thirty-seven years of Alexius' reign were to see a gradual stabilization of the Empire's frontiers, the expulsion of the Normans from the Balkans, a halt put to the Turkish invasions, and a regeneration of the internal administration of the Empire. But Alexius, for all his great ability and administrative capacity, could not undertake, unaided, a counteroffensive against the Turks. He was able to stabilize the empire's frontiers, but he was unable to advance back into the territories which the Turks had captured in the decades prior to his accession to the Byzantine throne. Alexius had perforce to endure, since he could do nothing else about it, the presence of a Turkish sultan at Nicaea, less than a hundred miles from Constantinople itself.

The military commitments of Byzantium were heavy: there was a long Danube border which must be guarded against persistent threats by various enemies, including Oghuz, Kuman, and Pecheneg Turks, Bulgars, and Slavs. The Norman invasion of the Balkans, although successfully repulsed after more than five years of fighting, made it imperative for the Empire to remain on guard against further aggression from that quarter. And in Asia Minor, where Byzantium had already lost all but a handful of coastal towns, there was a long, ill-defined frontier to guard against a treacherous, ever threatening foe.

In 1095 Alexius determined to appeal again, as Michael Dukas had done twenty years before, for military aid from Western Christendom. His petition was prompted by his hope of securing from the West the troops he needed so badly, both to guard his present positions and to take the offensive against the Seljuk Turks who now controlled Asia Minor. One obvious avenue of approach for a Byzantine emperor searching for Western assistance was through the Pope, the spiritual leader of the West.[2] Accordingly, Alexius dispatched ambassadors to seek out the reigning Pontiff, Pope Urban II, a former disciple and colleague of Pope Gregory VII.

In March of 1095, Rome was held by the anti-Pope, Clement III, while Pope Urban II was presiding over an ecclesiastical council at Piacenza, in northern Italy. It was there that the Byzantine ambassadors caught up with him and presented their messages. Urban seems to have been greatly impressed by the urgency of the Byzantine requests. The ambassadors were called upon to address the council, which is said to have numbered 4,000 clerics and more than 30,000 laymen.[3] The Emperor's envoys urged upon their auditors the fearful picture of a Moslem conquest of all the East, up to the very walls of Constantinople. There is good reason to believe that they stressed to their audience the fact that Jerusalem and the Lord's Sepulcher were being defiled by pagan hands. This latter fact was presented to the council as one of the principal reasons why united Christian efforts against the Turks were of major importance and of great urgency.[4] Pope Urban II was apparently as impressed by the envoys' personal pleas as he was by the message they bore and he is said to have addressed the council himself in support of their claims.[5]

II

The claims and arguments advanced at Piacenza for Western intervention in the East doubtless led the Pope to ponder the situation there and to reflect upon the part the Papacy might play in channeling military aid to Byzantium. We have no record of Urban's thoughts during the spring and summer of 1095 as he journied through northern Italy from Piacenza to Vercelli, to Milan, Como, and Asti,[6] but the lines along which his mind travelled are fairly obvious.

For decades the papacy had been on uneasy terms with the patriarchs of the East. Could Western response to these recent Eastern pleas for military aid be turned to good account in strengthening papal discipline over the churches of that area? For decades, too, the papacy had encouraged the Christian reconquest of Spain and to that end had granted spiritual privileges to those who took part in the wars against the Moslems. Could this technique also be applied to abate the peril which was taking shape in the East? For nearly a century the papacy had encouraged efforts to promote civil peace in Europe, to limit private feudal warfare in the West. Could a Western military expedition to the East contribute in some way to the achievement of these ends? Perhaps most pressing of all, there was the history of the past twenty years in Europe, the record of a consuming internecine strife between Empire and Papacy. Would not a successful military venture in the East, under papal auspices and papal leadership, tend to bolster papal prestige and power against the Western enemies of the Papacy? And if such a military expedition were to be organized, when, where, and how should the work begin? These and similar questions may well have occupied the pontiff's attention in the months between the closing of the Council of Piacenza and August 1095, when he entered France.

By August 15, when he was at Le Puy, Urban must have settled on some tentative plans, for from there he dispatched a summons to the French hierarchy to meet with him in council at Clermont on November 18. Urban spent the month of September travelling in Provence; October saw him in Burgundy, consecrating the high altar of the new basilica at the monastery of Cluny where he had once been a monk. By November 14, Urban had reached Clermont, in company with the bishop of that city, who had worked so strenuously preparing for the meetings of the council that he died on the night of Urban's arrival.

The sittings of the Council of Clermont opened formally on Sunday, November 18, 1095. The membership of the council is variously estimated. Whatever the exact figures may have been, it is clear that the council was attended by several hundred archbishops, bishops, abbots, and other ecclesiastical dignitaries, drawn mainly from southern France. Ten days were devoted to purely ecclesiastical business, concerned for the most part with disciplinary reforms within the church. Finally it was announced that on Tuesday, November 27, the Pope would address a general gathering of both the clergy and the laity. At this meeting Pope Urban announced publicly for the first time the details of the plan which had been maturing in his mind for six months or more. An eyewitness reports his words[7] as follows:

THE SERMON OF POPE URBAN II AT CLERMONT[8]

In the year of the Incarnation of our Lord 1095, a great council was held in the Auvergne region of Gaul, in the city of Clermont. Among those present at the council were the Roman bishops and cardinals and Pope Urban II. This famous council was also attended by a great number of bishops and princes from both Gaul and Germany. When the ecclesiastical business of the gathering had been disposed of, the lord Pope went out to a wide and spacious field, since the crowds could not easily be accommodated in any building. There the pope addressed the whole gathering in these words:

"Frenchmen! You who come from across the Alps; you who

have been singled out by God and who are loved by him—as is shown by your many accomplishments; you who are set apart from all other peoples by the location of your country, by your Catholic faith, and by the honor of the Holy Church; we address these words, this sermon, to you!

"We want you to know the melancholy reasons which have brought us among you and the peril which threatens you and all the faithful. Distressing news has come to us (as has often happened) from the region of Jerusalem and from the city of Constantinople; news that the people of the Persian kingdom,* an alien people, a race completely foreign to God, 'a generation of false aims, of a spirit that broke faith with God,'[9] has invaded Christian territory and has devastated this territory with pillage, fire, and the sword. The Persians have taken some of these Christians as captives into their own country; they have destroyed others with cruel tortures. They have completely destroyed some of God's churches and they have converted others to the uses of their own cult. They ruin the altars with filth and defilement. They circumcize Christians and smear the blood from the circumcision over the altars or throw it into the baptismal fonts. They are pleased to kill others by cutting open their bellies, extracting the end of their intestines, and tying it to a stake. Then, with flogging, they drive their victims around the stake until, when their viscera have spilled out, they fall dead on the ground. They tie others, again, to stakes and shoot arrows at them; they seize others, stretch out their necks, and try to see whether or not they can cut off their heads with a single blow of a naked sword. And what shall I say about the shocking rape of women? On this subject it would, perhaps, be worse to speak than to keep silent. These Persians have so dismembered the kingdom of the Greeks and have sequestered so much of it that it would be impossible to cross the conquered territory in a two month journey.

"Who is to revenge all this, who is to repair this damage, if you do not do it? You are the people upon whom God has bestowed glory in arms, greatness of spirit, bodily agility, and the courage to humble the 'proud locks'[10] of those who resist you.

"Rise up and remember the manly deeds of your ancestors, the prowess and greatness of Charlemagne, of his son Louis, and

advocates war tradition

* That is, the Seljuk Turks who had taken over the Baghdad caliphate.

of your other kings, who destroyed pagan kingdoms and planted the holy church in their territories. You should be especially aroused by the fact that the Holy Sepulcher of the Lord our Savior is in the hands of these unclean people, who shamefully mistreat and sacreligiously defile the Holy Places with their filth. Oh, most valiant knights! Descendants of unconquered ancestors! Remember the courage of your forefathers and do not dishonor them!

"But if your affection for your beloved children, wives, and parents would hold you back, remember what the Lord says in the Gospel: 'He who loves father or mother more than me is not worthy of me.'[11] 'Everyone who has left house, or brothers, or father, or mother, or wife, or children, or lands, for my name's sake, shall receive a hundredfold, and shall possess life everlasting.'[12] Do not allow any possession or any solicitude for family affairs to detain you.

"This land in which you live, surrounded on one side by the sea and on the other side by mountain peaks, can scarcely contain so many of you. It does not abound in wealth; indeed, it scarcely provides enough food for those who cultivate it. Because of this you murder and devour one another, you wage wars, and you frequently wound and kill one another. Let this mutual hatred stop; let these quarrels abate; let these wars cease; and let all these conflicts and controversies be put to rest. Begin the journey to the Holy Sepulcher; conquer that land which the wicked have seized, the land which was given by God to the children of Israel and which, as the Scripture says, 'is all milk and money.'[13]

"Jerusalem is the navel of the world, a land which is more fruitful than any other, a land which is like another paradise of delights. This is the land which the Redeemer of mankind illuminated by his coming, adorned by his life, consecrated by his passion, redeemed by his death, and sealed by his burial. This royal city, situated in the middle of the world, is now held captive by his enemies and is made a servant, by those who know not God, for the ceremonies of the heathen. It looks and hopes for freedom; it begs unceasingly that you will come to its aid. It looks for help from you, especially, because, as we have said, God has bestowed glory in arms upon you more than on any other nation. Undertake this journey, therefore, for the remission of your sins, with the assurance of 'glory which cannot fade'[14] in the kingdom of heaven."

Proclamation of the Crusade

When Pope Urban had said these and many similar things in his urbane sermon, those who were present were so moved that, as one man, all of them together shouted: "God wills it! God wills it!" When the venerable pontiff heard this, he turned his eyes toward heaven and gave thanks to God. He then waved his hand for silence, and said:

"Dearly beloved brethren! We have seen today that, as the Lord says in the Gospel, 'Where two or three are gathered together in my name, I am there in the midst of them.'[15] If the Lord God had not been present in your minds, you would not all have cried out the same thing, for although all of you shouted, your cries had but one origin. I tell you, therefore, that God placed this shout in your breasts and that God brought it out. Since this shout came from God, let it be your battle cry. When you make an armed attack on the enemy, let all those on God's side cry out together, 'God wills it! God wills it!'

"We do not ask or advise that elderly or feeble persons or those who are unable to bear arms should undertake this journey. No women should set out unless they are accompanied by their husbands, brothers, or legal guardians. Such persons are more a hindrance than an aid, more burdensome than useful. Let the rich help the poor; let them also, as their means allow, bring experienced soldiers with them to the war. Priests or clerics of whatever kind are not to come without the permission of their bishops, for the journey will be of no profit to them if they go without their bishops' authorization.* Nor, indeed, should laymen begin the pilgrimage without their priest's blessing.

"Whoever shall decide to make this holy pilgrimage and shall take a vow to God, offering himself as 'a living sacrifice, consecrated to God and worthy of his acceptance,'[16] shall wear the sign of the Lord's cross, either on his forehead or on his breast. When, after fulfilling his vow, he shall wish to return home, let him place the cross on his back, between his shoulders. By this twofold action such men will fulfill that command of the Lord which he uttered in the Gospel: 'He who does not take up his own cross and follow after me is not worthy of me.' "[17]

---

*The Pope's meaning is that priests who went on Crusade without the approval of their bishops would not receive the indulgence which they would otherwise gain.

When all these things were done, one of the Roman cardinals, Gregory by name, said the "confiteor" for the whole crowd, which now knelt on the ground. All of them, beating their breasts, begged absolution for their misdeeds. When the absolution had been given, the blessing followed; when the blessing was finished, the crowd was given leave to go home. *[Trans. James A. Brundage]*

On the day following this scene, a final conference of the council was held at Clermont. At this meeting the details of the organization of the expedition were arranged. The Bishop of Le Puy, Adhemar, whom Urban had visited the previous August, was selected as Papal legate to lead the Crusade as Urban's personal representative. It was probably also at this meeting that arrangements were made to set August 15, 1096 as the official starting date for the expedition. This would give the bishops time to preach and to enlist recruits for the expedition; it would also give the knights who were to take part sufficient time to settle their affairs at home before setting out on the journey.

Pope Urban spent the next eight months in France, attending to ecclesiastical business[18] there and, probably, gathering recruits himself for the glorious expedition which he had announced at Clermont. On August 15, 1096, the date set for the official beginning of the expedition, Urban was crossing the Alps on his way back to Italy, secure in the knowledge that the Crusade was well under way.

CHAPTER II

[1] The fundamental source for the history of the reign of Alexius Comnenus (and, incidentally, for the Greek view of the First Crusade) is the *Alexiad,* by Alexius' daughter, Anna Comnena. The best edition is that by Bernard Leib, which includes the Greek text with a French translation and copious notes in three volumes (Paris: Les Belles Lettres, 1937-1945). There is an English translation by E. A. S. Dawes (London: Kegan Paul, French, Trubner and Co., 1928). The best general treatment of the reign of Alexius is that by Ferdinand Chalandon, *Essai sur le règne d'Alexius I Comnène (1081-1118)* (Paris: A. Picard, 1900). There is an interesting study by Georgina Buckler entitled *Anna Comnena* (Oxford: Oxford University Press, 1929), which treats of a great many aspects of eleventh and twelfth century Byzantine life. There are also numerous short treatments in English of Alexius'

life and work in the several general histories of Byzantium, e.g., Norman H. Baynes and H. St. L. B. Moss, *Byzantium: An Introduction to East Roman Civilization* (Oxford: Clarendon Press, 1948); Charles Diehl, *Byzantium, Greatness and Decline* (New Brunswick: Rutgers University Press, 1957); Jack Lindsay, *Byzantium into Europe* (London: The Bodley Head, 1952); George Ostrogorsky, *History of the Byzantine State* (New Brunswick: Rutgers University Press, 1957); A. A. Vasiliev, *History of the Byzantine Empire, 324-1453,* (2d English edition; 2 vols; Madison: University of Wisconsin Press, 1958).

[2] The relationship between Byzantium and the Papacy at this period was complex and often is rather puzzling. The "schism" of 1054 is regarded by most recent writers as a much less clear-cut and decisive break between Rome and Constantinople that it had been considered in the past. Certainly the ties between the Eastern and Western churches were tenuous in 1095, but there is little reason to believe that Alexius and Urban II regarded one another as hopeless heretics or irretrievable schismatics. Cf. George Every, *The Byzantine Patriarchate* (London: Society for Promoting Christian Knowledge, 1947); Peter Charanis, chapter, "The Byzantine Empire in the Eleventh Century," in Setton, *Crusades,* I, 177-219; Runciman, *Crusades,* I, 93-105; Yves Congar, "Neuf

cents ans après; notes sur le 'schisme oriental,' " in *1054-1954, L'Église et les églises* (2 vols.; Chevetogne: Editions de Chevetogne, 1954-1955), I, 3-95.

[3] If these figures were divided by ten or fifteen, they would probably represent the council's numbers more accurately. The figures quoted are those given by Bernold of Constance, *Chronicon, MGH, SS,* V, 462.

[4] See Peter Charanis, "A Greek Source on the Origin of the First Crusade," *Speculum,* XXIV (1949), 93.

[5] Bernold of Constance, *Chronicon, MGH, SS,* V, 462; cf. D. C. Munro, "Did the Emperor Alexius I. Ask for Aid at the Council of Piacenza, 1095?" *AHR,* XXVII (1921-1922), 731-33.

[6] Urban's travels between Piacenza and Clermont are summarized in C. J. Hefele and H. Leclercq, *Histoire des Conciles* (11 vols. in 22; Paris: Letouzey et Ané, 1907-1952), V[1], 396-99. For Urban's plans for the Crusade, see Frederick Duncalf, "The Pope's Plan for the First Crusade," Munro, in *Essays,* pp. 44-56; A. C. Krey, "Urban's Crusade—Success or Failure?" *AHR,* LIII (1947-1948), 235-50; Augustin Fliche, "Les origines de l'action de la papauté en vue de la Croisade," *Revue d'Histoire Ecclésiastique,* XXXIV (1938), 765-75.

[7] Urban II's address at Clermont was reported by four contemporary writers: Fulcher of Chartres, Baldric of Dol, Guibert of Nogent, and Robert

the Monk. Of these four, Robert the Monk, whose report is translated here, was the only one to make a definite claim that he was present, although it is reasonable to assume that the others were there also. There are numerous discrepancies between the various accounts of the sermon; these have been analyzed by D. C. Munro, "The Speech of Pope Urban II. at Clermont, 1095," *AHR*, XI (1905-1906), 231-42. English translations of the four accounts have been printed by Munro in *Translations and Reprints from the Original Sources of European History* (Philadelphia: University of Pennsylvania Press, n.d.). I, no. 2.

8 Robert the Monk, *Historia Hierosolimitana*, I, 1-3 (*RHC, Occ.*, III, 727-730).

9 Ps. 77:8.

10 77:22.

11 Matt. 10:37.

12 Matt. 29:29.

13 Exod. 3:8.

14 I Peter 5:4.

15 Matt. 18:20.

16 Rom. 12:1.

17 Luke 14:27; Matt. 10:38.

18 The Pope's business in France was mainly concerned with routine administrative affairs. The seventy-five letters which he wrote during the eight months following the Council of Clermont are principally concerned with confirming grants to monasteries, dedicating churches, awarding privileges, and deciding appeals which were referred to him as chief arbiter of the ecclesiastical courts. Setton, *Crusades*, I, 250-52; P. Jaffé *et al.* (eds.,) *Regesta pontificum Romanorum ab condita ecclesia ad annum post Christum natum MCXCVIII* (2 vols.; Graz: Akademische Druck-und Verlagsanstalt, 19-56), No. 5592-5667.

Chapter III

THE POPULAR CRUSADE

I

Pope Urban II and the bishops who attended the Council of Clermont were not, however, the only preachers of the Crusade, nor were the nobility of the West the sole participants in the Crusade, as Pope Urban had probably expected they would be. The movement which Urban began at Clermont quickly grew far beyond the Pope's wishes and expectations, for the Crusade which Pope Urban inaugurated was taken up and preached to the Western world at large, not only by the official hierarchy, but also by a number of popular preachers and demagogues. The expedition of Western knights and noblemen which Urban had planned and inspired quickly spawned a heterogenous progeny of popular expeditions, whose participants were drawn in the main from the lower classes of Western society. These various popular expeditions, five in number, are usually taken together as the "Popular Crusade" or the "Peasants' Crusade,"[1] in contrast to the "Seigneurial Crusade," as the more official expeditions of knights and nobles are called. What Pope Urban may have thought of these spontaneous and unplanned-for popular expeditions must be left to the imagination. No record of the Pope's thoughts on the matter has survived.

The most famous figure of the Popular Crusade was Peter the Hermit, who was for long credited with being the originator of the Crusades as a whole.[2] Peter was certainly the central figure and the leader of the two popular expeditions which actually got to Constantinople and Asia Minor.

Contemporary descriptions of Peter the Hermit sound remarkably unattractive to modern ears. Short of stature, Peter had a long, lean, swarthy face which, like the rest of his person, was customarily filthy. An ascetic, he usually went barefoot and rode from place to place astride a donkey. Peter limited his diet to fish and wine and was ordinarily attired in a hermit's cloak, from which he derived his nickname. By any standards, however, Peter must be accounted an eloquent and persuasive preacher, able to stir up an apocalyptic enthusiasm among vast crowds of people who forthwith abandoned their homes, friends, and many of their possessions, piled their moveable belongings in carts, and set out to join Peter and his company on the journey to Jerusalem.

Peter the Hermit's preaching of the Crusade began before the end of 1095. During the winter and spring of 1095-1096, he travelled through northern France preaching the Crusade as he went and collecting followers by the hundreds. By April 12, 1096, when he reached Cologne, Peter had with him a band of followers whose numbers were estimated in the thousands. Peter's recruits were a motley group: they included peasants in large numbers, some townsmen, a number of noblemen (landness knights and younger sons of noble families, for the most part), brigands and criminals, too, as well as women and children.

members

Cologne greeted the would-be Crusaders with scorn and derision. Peter imperturbably settled down to preach and gather further recruits from among the derisive townsmen. The proposed delay, however, was distasteful to many of those who had already joined him. Eager to reach their destination, several thousand of Peter's recruits set out directly from Cologne on April 15 to proceed to the Holy Land at once. This advance party was committed to the care of Walter the Penniless, one of the landless knights in Peter's entourage.

Peter himself remained in Cologne until April 20, when, having successfully persuaded a good many of the Germans to join his party, he set out to follow the group led by Walter. Both parties, five days apart, marched overland toward Hungary and Constantinople. Some of their adventures en route are described by Albert of Aachen, who got his information from one of the participants:

WALTER THE PENNILESS AND PETER THE HERMIT
JOURNEY TO THE EAST[3]

In the year of our Lord's incarnation 1096 . . . on the eighth day of March,[4] Walter, known as the Penniless, a distinguished knight, entered the kingdom of Hungary, having begun the journey to Jerusalem at the urging of Peter the Hermit. Walter was accompanied by a large body of French foot soldiers, but there were only eight knights in his group.

Coloman, the most Christian King of the Hungarians, received him kindly. When Coloman had heard and learned of Walter's intentions and the reason for his journey, he granted him leave to pass through the kingdom and permission to buy provisions. The army came, with no misfortunes or untoward incidents, through Semlin, where the Hungarian frontier ends. Here they peacefully crossed the Save River to the Bulgarian city of Belgrade. Sixteen of the men remained behind at Semlin to buy weapons, without the knowledge of Walter who had already crossed the river. Some perversely minded Hungarians, who were aware that Walter and his army had gone, laid hands on these sixteen individuals. They despoiled them of their weapons, clothes, gold, and silver and then allowed them to depart, naked and empty-handed. These grieving men, who now lacked both goods and weapons, quickly made their way to the aforesaid city of Belgrade, where Walter and all hands had pitched camp outside the walls. The robbed men reported to Walter what had befallen them. Walter, however, received the news calmly and would not consider returning to take revenge.

On the same night on which the naked and empty-handed brethren rejoined the group, Walter petitioned the Bulgarian governor and the magistrate of the city for permission to buy necessary supplies. The Bulgarian officials, who considered Walter's mission a fraud and his army a group of spies, forbade any sales to them. As a result of this, Walter and his whole army were much distraught and they began to seize and take away by force the herds of oxen, cattle, and sheep which had been put out to pasture and which were wandering hither and yon. The serious quarrel which had arisen between the Bulgarians and the pilgrims who were trying to drive away the flocks grew heated and became an armed conflict. When the ranks of the Bulgarians had increased to the number of a hundred and forty men, some members of the pilgrim army were cut off from the main group and took refuge in a chapel. Walter, meanwhile, lost confidence and his army dispersed, while the strength of the Bulgarians was still growing. The Bulgarians laid siege to the chapel and burned alive sixty of the men who were in it. When the others, in order to save their lives, tried to escape from the church, a great many of them were seriously wounded.

After this calamity and loss of men, Walter and the rest of his companions fled as fugitives into the Bulgarian forests. Eight days later he took refuge in the extremely wealthy city called Nish, in the midst of the Bulgarian kingdom. There Walter informed the duke and prince of the territory of the injuries and damage which had been done to his forces. The prince dealt justly with all these claims; he also gave weapons and money to Walter, as reparations. The lord of the region furthermore gave Walter safe conduct through the Bulgarian cities of Sternitz, Philippopolis, and Adrianople. He also gave Walter permission to buy supplies. Walter and his group proceeded peacefully to Constantinople, the capital of the whole Greek realm. When they arrived, the most humble possible petition was drawn up in which Walter begged the emperor to allow him to encamp peacefully and to give him permission to buy the necessities of life while he awaited the arrival of Peter the Hermit at whose urging and direction he had begun the journey. When Peter arrived and Walter was joined by his forces, they would then sail across the Arm of St. George. In this fashion they would be better able to fight off the Turks and all the other heathen. What they asked was done. The Emperor, Alexius by name, replied obligingly and granted all their requests.

Not long after this, the aforesaid Peter and his sizeable army, as numerous as the sands of the sea, likewise continued on the road to Jerusalem. Peter's army was made up of men who had assembled from various kingdoms to join him: they included Frenchmen, Swabians, Bavarians, and men from Lorraine.

In the course of his journey, Peter came to the Hungarian Kingdom, where he and the Christian army which he led set up their tents before the gate of Oedenburg. As soon as they were settled, Peter sent messengers to the Hungarian ruler to ask that he and his associates be allowed to enter and pass through the Hungarian Kingdom. The request was granted on condition that no looting take place in the King's territory and that the army stay peacefully on its way. Whatever the army needed it was to purchase, without quarrels or fighting. Peter was delighted when he heard of the King's benevolence toward him and his men. He crossed Hungary peacefully, carrying on a just and fair exchange with the inhabitants for necessary articles. Thus Peter and the whole army approached Semlin without any disturbance.

As Peter approached the boundaries of Semlin, reports reached him and his men that the count of this region, a man named Guz,[5] who was one of the leading men of the Hungarian Kingdom, was tainted with greed and had collected a force of armed knights. It was further reported that Guz had entered into an evil plot with the aforementioned Duke Nicetas, the prince of the Bulgarians and governor of the city of Belgrade. The plan was for Nicetas to collect the forces of his satellites and with them to attack and kill Peter's first battalions, while Guz was to follow behind and lop off the rear guard. In this manner they could seize and divide between them the booty of the whole army: horses, gold, silver, and clothes.

Peter heard of all this, but since the Hungarians and Bulgarians were both fellow Christians, he refused to believe they would plot such a crime. When Peter came to Semlin, however, he saw hanging from the battlements and walls the weapons and belongings of the sixteen men from Walter's group, whom the Hungarians had presumed to despoil a short while earlier. When Peter became aware of the injuries which had been inflicted upon his associates, and when he saw their weapons and belongings, he urged his men to take revenge. The signal was sounded stridently on the horns, the standards were set up, and they advanced rapidly toward the walls. They shot a hail of arrows at the walls. The shower of arrows was so thick and persistent that the Hungarians on the ramparts were unable to remain at their posts and retired into the town to see if they might perchance be able to hold out there against the strength of the attackers.

When Geoffrey Burel, an infantryman, a native of Etampes, and the master and standard-bearer of two hundred powerful foot soldiers, heard of the Hungarians' flight from the battlements, he hastened up the walls on a ladder which he had by chance discovered there. Reginald of Bray, a distinguished knight, with his head covered by a helmet and wearing a coat of mail, likewise scaled the wall after Geoffrey. Then everyone, both knights and infantry, strove to enter the town.

Nearly seven thousand Hungarians, spurred on by their distressed condition and the imminence of danger, had assembled to defend the town. Now they fled through another gate, which opened to the east. This gate led onto the pinnacle of a lofty crag. On one side flowed the Danube, while on the other there was an insurmountable fortification. Most of the Hungarians were unable to get through the gate, which was extremely narrow. The Crusaders slaughtered these people with swords in front of the gate. The others were pitched from the top of the mountain and were swallowed in the waves of the Danube. Many of these men, however, were able to escape by boat.

About four thousand[6] Hungarians were killed there, while only a hundred of the pilgrims were killed, in addition to those who were wounded. After Peter had gained this victory, he and his men remained for five days in Semlin, because of the abundance of supplies which were discovered there: grain, flocks of sheep, herds of cattle, an abundance of potables, and an endless number of horses. *[Trans. James A. Brundage]*

After this irresponsible though auspicious beginning at Semlin, Peter's expedition built rafts to ferry themselves across the Save River to the opposite Byzantine town of Belgrade. At the news of the Crusaders' imminent arrival, the citizens of Belgrade, quite understandably, forsook their town and fled to the woods. The Byzantine governor, seeing that he had insufficient troops to cope with the unruly pilgrims, withdrew his forces to Nish. The Crusaders were thus left a free hand in Belgrade, which they promptly pillaged and burned. Pushing onward, they arrived at Nish on July 3, where the Byzantines furnished them with supplies and food only after the Crusaders had given hostages to guarantee their future good conduct. On July 4, the pilgrim band started on its way to Sofia but ran into further trouble when the Byzantine troops, who were keeping an eye on the Crusaders, tried to arrest some of the men who were accused of setting fire to a mill. A riot ensued, Nicetas turned his troops loose on the Crusaders, and Peter's company suffered a humiliating rout. Peter with five hundred of his men fled to the woods where he attempted to reorganize his scattered forces. Several thousand other pilgrims eventually rejoined Peter and on July 12 they arrived at Sofia. From this point onward, so long as they were in Byzantine territory, the Crusaders were carefully escorted by organized bodies of Byzantine soldiers, who succeeded in maintaining order among the quarrelsome, ill-organized Crusading party.

The expedition finally reached Constantinople on August 1, 1096. Emperor Alexius, after an interview with Peter, arranged to have the whole body of Crusaders, both those in Walter the Penniless' party and those with Peter the Hermit, transported across the Bosporus to Asia Minor at the earliest possible opportunity. The crossing took place, under close Byzantine supervision, on August 6.

II

The lack of organization and of discipline, so characteristic of the Popular Crusade, showed up once again as soon as the Crusaders had landed in Asia Minor and were free from Byzantine control. The arduous journey through Central Europe had taken some of the edge off the Crusaders' enthusiasm. They were now eager to exploit their opportunities for looting and pillaging. They were also eager to defeat the Turks, of whose military prowess the Popular Crusaders seem to have been quite ignorant. Parties of Crusaders roamed recklessly along the coast of the Sea of Marmora, stopping first at the deserted city of Nicomedia and then wandering further along the coast to a fortified camp site at Civetot. Here they settled down to await the arrival of the main Crusading armies from Europe.

As the expedition settled at Civetot to await further developments, however, the morale of the army deteriorated and Peter's ephemeral authority over his men disappeared. The Crusaders quarrelled among themselves and separated into small cliques. They also took to raiding, in small, unorganized groups, such nearby villages and settlements as they could find. In mid-September, one group, mainly French in origin, raided the suburb of Nicaea, the capital of the Turkish sultan of Asia Minor, Kilij Arslan. Not to be outdone, a group of German pilgrims late in September 1096 captured a fort called Xerigordon and settled down there, intending to make it a center from which to plunder the countryside round-about.

These raids had the unfortunate effect of calling the presence of the Crusaders to the attention of Kilij Arslan. The sequel was disastrous for the Popular Crusade.

MASSACRE OF THE CRUSADERS[7]

The Turkish prince and leader Suleiman,* when he heard of the arrival of the Christians and of their plundering and looting, gathered together fifteen thousand of his Turks from all over Asia Minor and Khurasan.[8] His troops were highly skilled in warfare and were extremely dextrous archers, using bows made either of horn or bone. Two days after they had assembled, a considerably exaggerated report of the German victories was brought from afar to the city of Nicaea. Kilij Arslan's sorrow and wrath were further magnified by the stories about the Germans, by the loss of his fortress, and by the defeat and expulsion of his garrison.

At sunrise on the third day,[9] therefore, Kilij Arslan and all his forces set out from their encampment at Nicaea for the fort which the Germans had attacked. The first groups of the Turkish force assailed and beat down the Germans so decisively that the Germans, who fought back ferociously, were unable to hold their defensive positions and were forced from the walls and battlements by a heavy hail of arrows. The poor unprotected Germans then took shelter in the stronghold from the Turkish missiles. When the Turks saw that they had forced the Germans back from the walls and battlements, they prepared to make their way over the walls. The Germans within the fort, however, were still striving anxiously to save their own lives. Some of the Germans brought up their lances to stave off the entering Turks, while others fought them back with swords and double-edged axes. In the face of this resistance the Turks dared not continue the assault.

---

* The Seljuk Sultan of Rum, Kilij Arslan ibn-Suleiman, sometimes called Suleiman II. For the sake of uniformity, he is hereafter referred to in this translation as Kilij Arslan.

Since they had not cowed the Germans by showering them with a hail of arrows, the Turks now assembled all kinds of wood at the gate of the fort. They kindled it and it burst into flames. A number of buildings within the compound were also ignited. At length the flames and heat grew so intense that some of the Germans were consumed, while others, hoping for safety, leaped from the walls. The Turks outside the walls slaughtered the fugitives with swords. They took captive about two hundred whose youthful features and bodies made them attractive. All the rest were killed by arrows or by the sword.

When Kilij Arslan and his men had withdrawn with their German captives, following this dreadful fray, the news of the slaughter of the Germans reached Peter's camp. The spirits of the group were greatly dampened by the defeat of their comrades. Moved by the misfortunes of their companions, they took frequent counsel with one another to decide whether to set out immediately to revenge their comrades' slaughter or to wait for Peter, who had left some time before to journey to the Emperor at Constantinople, where he sought better marketing conditions for his men.

In their councils with one another, Walter the Penniless held out against a foray to avenge their brethren until the situation was clarified and until the return of Peter, on whose advice they would act. Walter's plan quieted the people for eight days, while they awaited Peter. Peter, however, was unable to secure the Emperor's permission to return.

On the eighth day a hundred Turkish soldiers, men illustrious in the art of war, set out from Nicaea. They wandered through the countryside and the hill towns, seeking to ascertain and find out about the loot and booty which the Franks had stolen. These Turks took it upon themselves that day to behead a great many Crusaders who were roving hither and yon in groups of ten or fifteen or a few more. When the rumor reached Peter's camp that the Turks were near and that they had beheaded the roaming Crusaders, the men refused to believe that the Turks had come so far away from Nicaea. Some of the Crusaders advised, however, that they give chase to the Turks, were any discovered in that vicinity.

Meanwhile, when the truth became known, a tumult arose among the people. All the infantrymen called together Walter the Penniless, Rainald of Breis, Walter of Breteuil, and Fulk of Orleans, who were the leaders of Peter's army. They asked the leaders whether they should all rise up against the insolence of these Turks, but the leaders forbade any attacks until they could consult Peter upon his return. The master of the infantry, Geoffrey Burel, listened to their replies and then asserted that the timid were scarcely worth as much as brave knights in battle. He made a harsh speech in which he repeated his charges and rebuked the men who forbade the troops to follow the Turks and to revenge their brethren. The army leaders, on the other hand, were unable to bear any longer the charges and insults of Geoffrey and of their own followers. Deeply moved by wrath and indignation, the leaders agreed to set out against the Turkish snares and plots, no matter what the cost. There was no delay. All the cavalry and infantry troops throughout the camp were ordered to arise at the first light of dawn on the fourth day.[10] They were then to sound on their horns the signals to assemble for battle. Only the sick and those without weapons were left in the camp, together with a countless number of women. Twenty-five thousand armed infantrymen and five hundred armored knights were assembled and started on their way to the city of Nicaea in order to avenge their comrades by provoking Kilij Arslan and the other Turks to battle. The army was divided and was arranged in six divisions, with the standard bearers marching on the right and left flanks of the group. Peter was still absent and his wishes were unknown.

The army marched barely three miles from the gate of the stronghold at Civetot, making its way noisily with loud boasts and much shouting through mountain and forest. Suddenly Kilij Arslan and his whole reprehensible army entered the forest from the other side. The enemy were coming from Nicaea to make a surprise attack upon the Frankish camp and thus to slaughter and annihilate with swords those who were unprepared and unwary. When Kilij Arslan heard the noise made by the advancing Christians he was very anxious to know who was responsible for the uproar, for he was quite unaware of the Christians' intentions. As soon as he learned that the Crusaders were there, he addressed his men:

"The Franks, whom we were going to trap, are here. Undoubtedly they are on their way to attack us. Let us, therefore, withdraw from the forest and the mountains into the open plains. There we can engage them freely in battle, while they can find no place of refuge." Kilij Arslan's directions were carried out without delay, and in deep silence they left the forest and mountains.

The Franks, of course, were unaware of Kilij Arslan's arrival. They came out of the forest and mountains with much shouting and noise-making. Then, for the first time, they gazed in amazement at Kilij Arslan's forces standing in battle formation in the midst of the plain, covering them for battle. When the Franks caught sight of them, they began to comfort one another in the name of the Lord. They sent on ahead two divisions, which included five hundred knights.

Kilij Arslan, when he saw the two divisions advance, at once loosened the reins of his horse and unleashed his men. Their unheard-of shouting terrified and stupified the Catholic knights. Then the Turks sent a shower of arrows into the midst of the two divisions. As a result of this, the scattered survivors of those divisions were separated from the multitude which followed them.

The rest of the Crusading army had not yet marched out of the forest when they heard the clash of arms and the cruel attack of the shouting Turks. The Crusaders assembled in one group on the narrow path by which they were travelling and tried to block and hold the path through the mountains. Meanwhile, the two divisions which the Turks had broken up and divided from their Christian companions, found that they could not return to the forest and mountains and so began to take the road to Nicaea. All at once, they turned around and, shouting loudly, they flew back into the midst of the Turks. Knights and foot soldiers encouraged one another and in a short time, they had killed two hundred Turks. The Turks saw that the force of the Christian cavalry was grinding down their men. Accordingly, they shot arrows which wounded the horses of the Crusaders. Thus the strongest of Christ's athletes were turned into foot soldiers.

Walter the Penniless was struck by seven arrows through his mail coat and belly and was laid to rest there. Rainald of Breis and Fulk of Chartres—men famous in their own country—suffered a similar martyrdom when they were destroyed by the enemy and died, though not without a great slaughter of Turks. Walter of Breteuil, the son of Waleran, and Geoffrey Burel, the master of the infantry, escaped by taking flight through the bramble and bush. This whole group withdrew from the fight, assembled, and fled by a narrow path. When it became known that they had fled and forsaken the rest, all the men took flight, speedily hurrying back toward Civitot on the same road by which they had come, but now they were scarcely able to defend themselves from the enemy.

The Turks, accordingly, rejoiced in the good fortune of their success and victory. They beheaded the piteous handful of Crusaders, whom they followed for three miles, killing them as they went along, all the way into Peter's camp. They entered the camp and found there the feeble and the sick, clerics, aged women, monks, and infants. All of these they destroyed with swords, irrespective of age. They took alive only those delicate girls and nuns whose appearance and figures appealed to them, as well as some beardless youths of attractive appearance. They carried off to Nicaea the money, clothing, mules, horses, and all the other valuables, along with the tents.

On the seashore, alongside the aforementioned town of Civitot, there was an old deserted fort and to this place three thousand of the Crusaders took flight, entering the crumbling fort in the hope of defending themselves there. Since there were no gates or defensive works, they used their shields for a gate, while they cleverly piled up rocks at the entrance for they were afraid and bereft of help. They fought for life itself, defending themselves from the enemy only with spears, the wooden bow, and stone missiles. The Turks, since they were able to accomplish only a part of their plan to kill those within the fort, surrounded the structure, which was roofless, and shot arrows into the air. When the arrows dropped down out of the sky, they hit the defenders, killing the poor wretches. The rest of the men, when they saw this, were forced to consider surrendering, for a great many are reported to have been wounded and killed there in this fashion. They feared even crueler treatment from these godless men, however, and so neither arms nor force would bring them to leave the fort.

Now the sun had marked midday when the three thousand men had entered the fort and had been besieged by the Turks. They defended themselves vigorously, not by the cleverness of their strategy, but because they were fighting for life itself. At last, during the night, a loyal, Catholic, Greek messenger was able to sail across the sea to find Peter, who was in the royal city. The messenger reported the dangers besetting the Crusaders and the devastation and destruction of the rest. When Peter learned of the dangers to his men and of the tragedy of those who had been annihilated, he went, weeping and grieving, to beseech the Emperor in Christ's name to assist those wretched Crusaders, the few who were left out of so many thousands. He begged the Emperor not to allow his anguished men to be destroyed and consumed by such executioners.

The Emperor heard Peter's report of the defeat and besieging of the Crusaders and was moved to pity. He summoned his Turcopoles* and all the nations of his realm and ordered them to cross the straits to assist the fugitive and besieged Christians and to drive the assaulting Turks from the siege. When the Turks got wind of the Emperor's command, they marched away from the fort, taking their Christian captives and much booty with them. And so the surrounded and besieged Crusading soldiers were freed from these godless men. [*Trans. James A. Brundage*]

The rescue of these remnants of Peter the Hermit's expedition marked the end of the Popular Crusade as a distinct force. Peter himself, together with some of those who had escaped the destruction of most of Peter's army, remained at Constantinople under Alexius' protection, to await the arrival of the other Crusading expeditions from the West.

The whole episode of the Popular Crusade illustrates forcefully and dramatically both the major merits and defects of the Crusading movement as a whole: the fierce zeal and piety which impelled so many thousands to participate in this ill-starred expedition combined with the lack of discipline and organization as the major causes of its ultimate failure. The combination of selfless devotion and of selfish ambition which appeared in this expedition of the humbler classes was to appear and reappear among the knights, lords, and barons of the Seigneurial Crusade.

* Troops of mixed, non-Byzantine origin, serving as mercenaries in the Byzantine army.

CHAPTER III

[1] The most important contemporary source of information about the Popular Crusade is Albert of Aachen. Two selections from his *Historia Hierosolymitana* (*RHC, Occ,* IV, are translated below. Among the modern treatments of these expeditions, see especially Frederick Duncalf's article, "The Peasants' Crusade," *AHR,* XXVI (1920-1921), 440-53; also Ferdinand Chalandon, *Histoire de la première croisade* (Paris: Auguste Picard, 1925), pp. 50-110; Reinhold Röhricht, *Geschichte des ersten Kreuzzuges* (Innsbruck: Wagner, 1901), pp. 33-58; Runciman, *Crusades,* I, 113-41; Setton, *Crusades,* I, 258-66, 280-84. See also H. Hagenmeyer, *Peter der Eremite* (Leipzig: Otto Harrassowitz, 1879). The five expeditions which made up the Popular Crusade were: (1) that led by Peter the Hermit in person; (2) the group led by Walter the Penniless, an offshoot of Peter the Hermit's Crusaders; (3) the band led by a certain Fulk. This company was responsible for the anti-Semitic riots and massacres at Magdeburg and Prague. This was also the group of Crusaders destroyed by the Hungarians at Nitra, late in June 1096; (4) the group led by one Gottschalk, which was also massacred by the Hungarians, and (5) the expedition led by Count Emicho of Leiningen. This latter group was responsible for Jewish massacres at Speyer, Worms, Mainz, Cologne, and Trier. They, however, were subsequently dispersed in the course of an unsuccessful attempt to break through the Hungarian frontier, but some of its members later joined other groups of Crusaders and eventually reached the Holy Land.

[2] Following the account given by William of Tyre, most modern historians prior to the last decades of the nineteenth century credited Peter with inspiring the whole Crusading movement. Hagenmeyer's *Peter der Eremite,* and a book of H. von Sybel, *Geschichte des ersten Kreuzzuges* (2d. ed.; Leipzig: R. Oldenbourg, 1881) were largely responsible for reducing Peter's role to its proper proportions in modern historical writing on the Crusades.

[3] Albert of Aachen, *Historia Hierosolymitana,* I, 6-7 (*RHC, Occ,* IV, 274-77).

[4] The date given by Albert is undoubtedly incorrect; modern writers assign these events variously to May 8 or May 21; Röhricht, *Geschichte der ersten Kreuzzuges,* pp. 36-37; Runciman, *Crusades,* I, 122; Setton, *Crusades,* I, 259, n. 13.

[5] Runciman, *Crusades,* I, 124, suggests that Guz may have been a Ghuzz (or Oghuz) Turk.

[6] The figure given here by Albert of Aachen is almost certainly a gross exaggeration. On Medieval estimates of large numbers generally, see above, Chap. I, n. 5.

[7] Albert of Aachen, *Historia Hierosolymitana,* I, 17-22 (*RHC, Occ,* IV, 285-89).

8 Northeastern Persia. The Chroniclers of the Crusades use this term indiscriminately to indicate almost any area occupied by the Turks.

9 September 29, 1096.

10 October 21, 1096.

Chapter IV

The Seigneurial Crusade

I

In August 1096, as the members of the Popular Crusade settled down at Civetot to await their fate there, the first parties of European noblemen to respond to Pope Urban's plea were setting out for the East.[1] The army of the First Crusade, as had been agreed at Clermont, was to make its way under various leaders to Constantinople. There the army was to assemble under the leadership of the Papal Legate, Bishop Adhémar of Le Puy. The various expeditions which assembled at Constantinople would, it was expected, march forward from there as a single fighting force, and battle its way through Asia Minor, thus reestablishing Christian rule in that area by eventually capturing the Holy Land and the Holy City of Jerusalem.

The Crusaders made their way to Constantinople in five main groups. Each of these parties of feudal knights, together with their servants, priests, monks, pilgrims, and other non-combatants, was led by one or more feudal barons. Characteristically, each group was made up in large part of the vassals and friends of the individual leader. The Crusading army had, from the beginning, something of the character of an agglomeration of separate feudal forces.

The first group to begin the journey to the East on the Seigneurial Crusade was made up mainly of knights from the Ile de France, led by Hugh of Vermandois, the haughty, empty-headed brother of King Philip I of France. King

Philip might have led this army himself, since it was composed in large part of his own vassals and followers, had it not been for the fact that he was excommunicated.[2] The King had, therefore, committed his group to Crusaders to his younger brother, Hugh. Hugh and his party left on the Crusade in late August 1096, journeyed south through France to Italy, and down the Italian peninsula to Bari where they arrived in early October. Hugh and his soldiers crossed the Adriatic Sea from Bari to Dyrrachium on the Balkan coast, there to be welcomed by John Comnenus, the brother of the Emperor Alexius. Under close Byzantine surveillance, the French knights marched through the Balkans to Constantinople, where Hugh was immensely flattered by the gracious welcome accorded him and his knights by the Emperor.

Alexius Comnenus was genuinely interested in giving such help as he could to the Europeans on Crusade. At the same time, he was well aware that the presence of large bodies of armed European soldiers within his Empire constituted a potential threat to his own best interests. Alexius was also eager to use the Crusading armies, if he could, to better his own position in Asia Minor. This, after all, had been the reason for his appeal to the Papacy for aid in the first place. Alexius, though no doubt anxious to see the Holy Land in Christian hands, was even more anxious to recapture the Byzantine territories in Asia Minor which had recently fallen to the Turks.

For all of these reasons, therefore, Alexius demanded that each Crusade leader, as he arrived at Constantinople, swear an oath. The oath involved a pledge by the leaders of the Crusade: (1) not to endanger Byzantine interests; (2) to restore to Byzantine rule any formerly Byzantine cities which the Crusaders might capture; and (3) to acknowledge the Byzantine Emperor as overlord of any other cities which the Crusaders might capture and keep for themselves. Alexius was aware that European noblemen were accustomed to seal their obligations to their Western overlords with an oath. He saw no reason why they should not take a similar oath to respect the territorial rights of Byzantium.

To the demand for an oath, Hugh of Vermandois, overcome by Alexius' graciousness, made no objection. After

Hugh had complied with the Emperor's wishes, he was forthwith housed quite comfortably, though still under vigilant Byzantine surveillance, in a monastery at Constantinople, while his troops camped in the suburbs.

II

The second division of the Crusading army was led to the East by Godfrey of Bouillon, the blond, bearded Duke of Lower Lorraine. Godfrey, accompanied by his two brothers, Count Eustace III of Boulogne and Baldwin of Boulogne, a former cleric, led his large, heavily armed expedition to Constantinople via the route taken six months earlier by the expeditions of the Popular Crusade. Godfrey's army, in contrast to the earlier expeditions which took this route, was well disciplined throughout the march until it arrived in the vicinity of Constantinople, in mid-December, 1096. There was a minor riot near Selymbria, on the coast of the Sea of Marmora. After a week of fighting, Godfrey was able to restore his men to order. They then proceeded to Constantinople. When the Emperor Alexius demanded that Godfrey take an oath, as Hugh of Vermandois had already done, there was further trouble. Godfrey refused; the Emperor insisted; and Godfrey again refused to subscribe to the pledge. Godfrey feared to take the required oath lest it be construed as an oath of fealty to Alexius, and thereby possibly compromise Godfrey's position in the West as Duke of Lower Lorraine.[3] Godfrey still persisted in his refusal to take the oath in March of 1097, when Alexius, anxious to secure Godfrey's promise, began to cut off the supplies of food to Godfrey's force. The Emperor's action caused another riot by the duke's formidable army. On Holy Thursday, April 2, 1097, Godfrey's forces attacked Constantinople and on Good Friday Alexius threw the full weight of his troops against the Crusaders, who were quickly routed. After this humiliating defeat, Godfrey was forced to take the hated oath. As soon as this had been done, Alexius had Godfrey's men transported across the Bosporus to a camp at Pelecanum in Asia Minor, where they awaited the arrival of the other Crusading forces.

III

The third expeditionary force to take part in the Seigneurial Crusade was comprised mainly of Norman nobles and adventurers from southern Italy. They were led by Bohemund, the tall, slim, blond Prince of Taranto, and by Tancred, Bohemund's nephew. Bohemund's forces sailed from Bari, across the Adriatic to Dyrrachium in October 1096. From Dyrrachium, they travelled along an irregular course through the mountains of Macedonia toward Constantinople. Bohemund, who had journeyed on in advance of the main body of his troops, arrived at Constantinople on April 9, 1097, just a week after Godfrey's troops had begun to riot against the Byzantines. Bohemund, upon request, took the oath which had been demanded of the other Crusaders and did so without protest. Doubtless, Bohemund hoped to gain favors for himself from Alexius as a result of his eager cooperation with the Emperor. Alexius' daughter, Anna Comnena, relates that Bohemund did, in fact, request her father to appoint him Grand Domestic, a position which would have made Bohemund potentially the most powerful of the Crusading leaders. Alexius, however, bypassed the request with his customary diplomatic tact. He did so because he thoroughly distrusted Bohemund, and with good reason, considering Bohemund's earlier participation in the Norman attacks upon Byzantium.[4] After Bohemund had taken the oath, his army (which had meanwhile arrived upon the scene) was escorted across the straits, to join Godfrey's forces at Pelecanum.

IV

The largest of the five main forces to join in the First Crusade was that led by the rich, elderly, and pious Count of Toulouse, Raymond of St-Gilles. Raymond's force, which was accompanied also by the Papal Legate, Bishop Adhémar of Le Puy, left southern France in October 1096, travelled across the Alps, through northern Italy, and marched thence down the east coast of the Adriatic Sea. The route was ill-chosen and the journey was thoroughly dismal. It was thus described by Count Raymond's chaplain:

THE ARMY OF RAYMOND OF ST-GILLES
IN THE BALKANS[5]

When they entered Sclavonia[6] they suffered many annoyances on the road, especially because by this time it was winter.

Sclavonia is a forsaken, unfrequented, and mountainous region where for three weeks we saw neither beasts nor birds. The natives of the place are so rustic and rude that they were unwilling either to trade with us or to furnish us with guides. Rather, they fled from their settlements and forts.

But when they found a chance they killed a great many of the feeble, sick, and poor people who, because of their infirmities, followed at a distance behind our armies; these they slaughtered like sheep. Nor was it a simple matter for our armed knights to follow those impoverished bandits, familiar as they were with the lay of the land, through steep mountains and thick woods. Nonetheless, the knights kept continuous watch over them, although our men were neither eager to fight nor able to avoid it. We must not pass over one of the Count's* illustrious acts. When the Count and some of his knights were surrounded by a few of the Slavs, he charged at them and captured six of them. And when, on account of this, the Slavs threatened him more forcefully and compelled him to follow the army, he had the eyes of some of the Slavs torn out. He also ordered that the feet of some of the others be cut off and commanded that still others have their hands and noses removed, in order thus to deter the remaining Slavs and so to occupy them with their suffering friends that the Count and his companions could escape. Thus by the grace of God he was freed from the threat of death and the perils of this situation. It is not easy, in fact, to report how much courage and prudence the Count evidenced there.

We were in Sclavonia for almost forty days and during this time were bothered by fog so thick that we could grasp it and push a bit of it aside. Amidst all this, the Count fought continually against those who followed us. He was forever fighting for his people. He was never the first, but always the last to encamp. While some went to rest at noon and others at sundown, the Count frequently did so at midnight or at sunrise. Finally by God's grace, the Count's labor, and the Bishop's† advice, the army passed through Sclavonia without our having lost anyone[7] either in open combat or from hunger.

I believe that God wished his army to pass through Sclavonia so that those savages, who knew not God, might, after ob-

* Count Raymond of St-Gilles.
† Bishop Adhémar of Le Puy.

serving the virtue and patience of his knights, either moderate their savagery somewhat or else be brought without excuse before God's judgment. At length we came, after many labors, to the King of the Slavs[8] at Scutari.[9] The Count made a brotherly agreement with him and gave him many things as tribute so that the army could trade in safety and get whatever was necessary.

This agreement, however, was one in name only, for the King made us sorry enough for seeking peace from him. On his account, the Slavs, as was their custom, began their usual raging and killed some of our men. They also seized whatever they could take from the poor. We sought some place of refuge rather than trying to take revenge. So much for Sclavonia.

We next came to Dyrrachium[10] where we thought we were in safe territory, since we believed that the Emperor Alexius and his retinue were our brothers and coworkers. But, like lions, they thirsted for blood and attacked our peaceful men, who were giving less attention to their weapons than to anything else. They slaughtered them secretly in groves and in villages far from the camps, where they could attack secretly during the night. They went to such mad lengths that their leader promised us peace and then, on pretext of peace, they killed Rainald of Pons and mortally wounded his brother Peter. Both of them were most noble princes. When a chance for revenge was offered to us, it was decided to continue on the journey rather than take revenge for injuries.

We took up the journey. We had letters sent to us by the Emperor about peace, fraternity, and, I may also say, alliance. But these were mere words, for in front of us and behind us, on our right and on our left, we were watched by Turks, Kumans, Hungarians, Turcopoles, Pechenegs, and Bulgarians.[11] [*Trans. James A. Brundage*]

Raymond finally arrived at Constantinople on April 21, 1097. There he found himself confronted, as the other Western leaders had been, by the demand that he take an oath, to which he was unwilling to agree. As the others had been, however, so Raymond was finally led by argument and by pressure to make the required promises. Having done so, his army was, like the others, shipped straightway across the Bosporus to join the rest of the Crusaders in Asia Minor.

V

The last of the major forces on the Crusade was a powerful force composed chiefly of Norman knights, drawn from Brittany, Flanders, and Normandy and commanded by three princes. The leaders were Duke Robert of Normandy, the eldest son of William the Conqueror; Stephen of Blois, the henpecked husband of William the Conqueror's daughter Adele; and Count Robert of Flanders, a cousin of Duke Robert of Normandy. The three leaders and their respective forces met at Pontarlier in Burgundy in October 1096. They marched together across the Alps, down to Rome, and into the Norman duchies of southern Italy. There Duke Robert of Normandy and Count Stephen of Blois spent most of the winter of 1096-1097. Count Robert of Flanders, more anxious than his two companions to hurry on to the Crusade, took his force directly across the Adriatic to Dyrrachium and marched quickly to Constantinople, arriving there early in April 1097. He took the famous oath with no significant protest.

The other two Norman leaders, after a leisurely winter in Calabria, where part of their forces deserted, finally embarked from Brindisi in April 1097. They landed at Dyrrachium and marched to Constantinople, where they arrived in May 1097, only to discover that the other Crusaders had gone on ahead and were by this time besieging Nicaea. The Count of Blois and the Duke of Normandy, after taking the necessary oath to Alexius, lingered for two more weeks in Constantinople, enjoying the sights of the city. Finally they too crossed the straits and hurried on to join the main Crusading army.[12]

VI

Once most of the troops and leaders of the Crusading army had arrived in Asia Minor, the military operations of the Crusade began. The first objective of the Crusaders was to capture the Turkish stronghold of Nicaea. This important center had to be taken before any other large scale operations in Asia Minor could commence. Left in Turkish hands, Nicaea would jeopardize the lines of communication between the Crusaders and Constantinople.

The Seigneurial Crusade

45

In late April 1097, preparations for an attack on Nicaea began, even though the forces of Robert of Normandy and Stephen of Blois had not yet arrived. The moment was propitious, for the Turkish Sultan Kilij Arslan was campaigning far from Nicaea and, after his experience with Peter the Hermit's rabble, was scornful of any possible Western attack.

About April 26, 1097, Godfrey of Bouillon led the way on the march out of the Crusaders' camp at Pelecanum. The army of Crusaders was joined very shortly thereafter by Peter the Hermit and some stragglers who had survived his ill-fated expedition. Byzantine troops also accompanied the Crusaders, to act as guides and advisors and to give technical assistance as engineers. The Crusaders passed by Civetot, where the Popular Crusade had met its end, climbed through a rugged and difficult mountain range, and arrived at Nicaea on May 6.

The Crusaders' first sight of Nicaea must have been anything but reassuring. The city was heavily fortified, with its four miles of walls and its 240 towers manned by a strong garrison. The city was pentagonal in shape and its western walls rose straight up out of the waters of Lake Ascanius.

The first detachments of the Crusading army took up positions on the north and east sides of the city, and as other groups arrived on the scene the army gradually surrounded Nicaea. The forces were in place and the siege began in earnest on May 14.

THE SIEGE AND CAPTURE OF NICAEA[13]

On Ascension Day[14] we began to attack the town on all sides and to erect wooden towers and war machines with which we could knock down the towers on the walls. In two days of bitter fighting we managed to pierce a wall. The Turks within the town sent messengers to other Turkish forces,[15] which were coming to relieve the town, to advise them that they could approach Nicaea boldly yet safely by entering the town through the south gate, since no one would attack or harass them on that side of the town.[16]

Now the Count of St-Gilles and the Bishop of Le Puy had occupied positions near this gate on that same day, that is on the Saturday after the feast of the Ascension.[17] The Count, protected by the power of heaven and glittering with arms of the world, was coming from the other direction with his powerful army when he came across the advance guard of the approaching Turkish forces. Armed on all sides with the sign of the cross,[18] the Count rushed violently upon the enemy, defeating them and putting them to flight. In the fray, the greater part of the enemy force was killed. Meanwhile, the rest of the Turks, gleefully rejoicing over what they believed would be a certain victory, came up to assist their advance guard. They had even brought along ropes, with which they were going to tie us up when they captured us and take us to Khurasan.[19] As they came joyfully along, they began to descend one by one from the summit of the mountain. But, as the Turks came down the mountain, their heads were struck off by our men. Our troops, using a sling, hurled the heads of the dead Turks into the town and thereby greatly terrified the Turkish garrison.

The Count of St-Gilles and the Bishop of Le Puy then took counsel together about how to undermine a certain tower, located opposite their camp. Arrangements were made for the men to do the excavating and archers and crossbowmen were posted to guard them. The men dug down to the foundations of the wall and propped it up with wooden posts and beams. In the evening they set fire to the wooden props. The tower collapsed during the night, but since it was dark, an attack on the Turks was not feasible. Meanwhile, the Turks arose during the night and speedily set to work rebuilding the wall. They worked so effectively that by dawn a breakthrough at that point was no longer possible.

At this juncture, Count Robert of Normandy,[20] Count Stephen,[21] and many others, including Roger of Barneville, arrived.[22] Bohemund occupied the first position, with Tancred next to him.

Next came Duke Godfrey and then the Count of Flanders, with Robert the Norman next to him; then came the Count of St-Gilles and the Bishop of Le Puy. Now the whole army was brought together here and this region was so thoroughly beset that no one could enter or leave it. The army of Christ was innumerable and I think that no one had ever previously seen or will ever see again so many distinguished knights.

On one side of the city there was a large lake[23] across which the Turks sailed ships which could enter or leave the town, bringing in fodder, wood, and many other supplies. Our leaders met

The
Seigneurial
Crusade

together and agreed to send representatives to Constantinople to ask the Emperor to send ships to Civetot, where there is a harbor. They also asked the Emperor to collect oxen, so that the ships could be dragged over the mountains and through the woods to the lake. These requests were promptly complied with. The Emperor also ordered his Turcopoles to accompany the ships. When the ships arrived at the lake it was decided to wait for a time before launching them. When night had fallen, the ships, filled with well-armed Turcopoles, entered the lake. At daybreak the ships were in the lake, sailing in formation toward the city. The Turks were astonished to see them, but they were at first doubtful whether the ships contained their own soldiers or the Emperor's. When the Turks discovered that the ships belonged to the Emperor, however, they wept and shrieked, and were fearful unto death. The Franks, on the other hand, rejoiced and glorified God.

When the Turks realized that it was no longer possible to get help from any of their forces, they sent an ambassador to the Emperor. They offered to turn their city voluntarily over to the Emperor if he, for his part, would allow them to leave with their wives and children and all their possessions. The Emperor, filled with vain and wicked thoughts, ordered that the Turks be allowed to retire unharmed from the town and with great solicitude he had them brought to Constantinople. He cared for them diligently so that he might have them ready to injure and obstruct the Franks.[24]

We spent seven weeks and three days in that siege[25] and there many of our men became martyrs. With joy and gladness they gave their fortunate souls back to God. A great many of the poorer classes starved to death for Christ's name. Their souls were triumphantly carried to heaven, where they received martyrs' robes and cried out together, saying: "O Lord, revenge our blood which was shed for You, who are blessed and worthy of praise, world without end. Amen."[26] *[Trans. James A. Brundage]*

VII

The capitulation of Nicaea provided the Crusaders with a chance to rest and to take stock of their resources. For a week the army relaxed in the vicinity of Nicaea before it began to move on. A council of the Crusading princes decided

to divide the army into two groups for the next stage of the
expedition, with one division following a day's march behind
the other. The advance division was composed of Normans,
including those from southern Italy as well as those from
Normandy, Brittany, and Flanders. The second division was
composed of French knights, including those from Provence,
from Lorraine, and from the Ile de France. Thus arrayed, the
army set out toward Dorylaeum, with the first division commanded by Bohemund and the second division under Raymond of St-Gilles.

Meanwhile, Kilij Arslan and his army had learned of the
fate of Nicaea and had determined to take vengeance for their
losses there. Having reorganized his forces and secured new
allies, the Turkish Sultan and his army had taken up positions
in a valley near Dorylaeum. There they lay in wait to ambush
the unwary Western knights.

On July 1, 1097, the first division of the army, led by
Bohemund, fell into the Turkish trap.

THE BATTLE OF DORYLAEUM[27]

On the third day,[28] the Turks made a violent assault on Bohemund and his companions. The Turks began unceasingly to shout,
babble, and cry in a loud voice, making some devilish sound, I
know not how, in their own tongue.[29] When the wise Bohemund
saw from afar the innumerable Turks shouting and crying a dia-
bolical sound, he straightway ordered all the knights to dis-
mount and pitch the tents immediately. Before the tents had been
erected, he spoke to all the soldiers: "My lords and strongest of
Christ's soldiers! A difficult battle is now building up around us.
Let everyone advance against them courageously and let the infantry put up the tents carefully and quickly."

By the time all this had been done, the Turks had already
surrounded us on all sides. They attacked us, slashing, hurling, and
shooting arrows far and wide, in a manner strange to behold.
Although we could scarcely hold them back or even bear up under the weight of such a host, nevertheless we all managed to
hold our ranks. Our women were a great blessing to us that day,
for they carried drinking water up to our fighting men and comforted the fighters and defenders. The wise Bohemund at once
commanded the others, namely the Count of St-Gilles, Duke God-

frey, Hugh of France, the Bishop of Le Puy, and all the rest of Christ's soldiers to make speed and to march quickly to the battle scene. He said: "If they wish to fight today, let them come on with full force." The strong and courageous Duke Godfrey and Hugh of France both came on ahead with their forces. The Bishop of Le Puy followed with his troops, and the Count of St-Gilles with a large force came after him.

Our people were very curious about where such a multitude of Turks, Arabs, Saracens, and others whom I cannot name, had come from. Indeed this excommunicated race filled all the mountains, hills, valleys, and plains on all sides, both inside and outside of the battlefield. We had a secret parley among ourselves and, after praising God and taking counsel, we said: "Let us all unite in Christ's faith and the victory of the Holy Cross, for, God willing, today we shall all be made rich."

Our forces were drawn up in one continuous battle line. On the left there were Bohemund, Robert the Norman, the prudent Tancred, Robert of Ansa,[30] and Richard of the Principate.[31] The Bishop of Le Puy approached by way of another mountain and thus the unbelieving Turks were surrounded on all sides.* Raymond of St-Gilles also fought on the left side. On the right there were Duke Goddfrey, the Count of Flanders (a most valiant knight), and Hugh of France, together with many others whose names I know not.

As soon as our knights arrived, the Turks, Arabs, Saracens, Angulans,[32] and all the barbarian tribes speedily took flight through the byways of the mountains and plains. The Turks, Persians, Paulicians,[33] Saracens, Angulans, and other pagans numbered 360,000,[34] besides the Arabs, whose numbers are known only to God. With extraordinary speed they fled to their tents but were unable to remain there long. Again they took flight and we followed, killing them as we went, for a whole day. We took many spoils: gold, silver, horses, donkeys, camels, sheep, cattle, and many other things of which we know not. Had the Lord not been with us in the battle and had he not suddenly sent us the

* Bishop Adhémar of Le Puy had, in other words, led a company of southern French knights through the mountains, around and behind the Turkish lines. The sudden appearance on the field of the Bishop and his knights, who came up behind the Turkish flanks, threw the Turks into panic and assured victory for the Crusaders.

other force, none of our men would have escaped, for the battle lasted from the third to the ninth hour.[35] But Almighty God is merciful and kind. He did not allow his troops to perish, nor did he deliver them into the hands of the enemy; rather he sent help to us quickly. Two of our honored knights were killed, namely Godfrey of Monte-Scaglioso and William the son of the Marquis and the brother of Tancred. Some other knights and infantrymen whose names I do not know were also killed.

Who will ever be wise or learned enough to dare to describe the prudence, prowess, and valor of the Turks? They believed they could terrify the Frankish race by threatening them with their arrows, as they had terrified the Arabs, Saracens, Armenians, Syrians, and Greeks. But, please God, they will never be as powerful as our men. Indeed, the Turks say that they are related to the Franks and that no man ought by nature to be a knight save the Franks and themselves. I speak the truth, which no one can deny: that if they had always been steadfast in Christ's faith and in Christianity, if they had wished to confess one triune Lord, and if they had honestly believed in good faith that the Son of God was born of the Virgin, that he suffered and rose from the dead and ascended into heaven in the presence of his disciples, that he has sent the perfect comfort of the Holy Spirit, and that he reigns in heaven and on earth; if they had believed all this, it would have been impossible to find a people more powerful, more courageous, or more skilled in the art of war. By the grace of God, however, we defeated them. The battle took place on the first of July. [Trans. James A. Brundage]

VIII

The Christian army rested for two days at Dorylaeum, rejoicing in their victory and in the spoils they had taken. July 3 saw them again on the march, this time headed to the southeast, so as to skirt the edges of the great salt desert along the road to Heraclea. Here the bitter fruits of their previously lackadaisical progress caught up with them: they were forced to cross this desolate and arid terrain in midsummer. Water supplies were meager at best, at worst nonexistent. The heat was oppressively intense and the heavily armored knights were nearly cooked in their metal trappings. Horses and pack animals dropped dead from hunger and thirst, so that a great many knights were reduced to marching on foot or riding oxen.

By mid-August the army had reached Iconium, which the Turks had deserted. Here the weary troops were able to rest and replenish their supplies before moving on to Heraclea, which they reached on September 10.

At Heraclea the army again divided. The venturous princelings, Tancred and Baldwin of Boulogne, with their respective forces, separated themselves from the main Crusading army. They chose to march through the narrow, difficult passes of the Cilician Gates. The remainder of the army took a more roundabout route which led them across the Anti-Taurus Mountains, through Marash and the Amanus Gates to the Antiochene Plain, where they arrived about October 20.

Tancred and Baldwin, meanwhile, took the opportunity afforded by their separation from the main host to capture for themselves a number of towns and hamlets in Cilicia. Their intention in this venture was to establish private feudal states for themselves in the East and they took this opportunity to make the first steps toward that goal.

Baldwin of Boulogne, after taking Tarsus, moved on to an even more lucrative field of operations in the Tigris-Euphrates Valley. There, during the winter of 1097-1098, he managed to secure for himself the major city of Edessa and several minor Armenian towns. With the cooperation of Armenian friends, who looked upon him as a liberator and protector, Baldwin was able to carve out for himself a sizeable principality, the county of Edessa, the first of the Latin States in the East.

IX

While Baldwin was creating the Latin county of Edessa, Tancred, having seized a number of towns in Cilicia, rejoined the main Crusading army in northern Syria, before the walls of the venerable city of Antioch. The capture of this ancient and prosperous city was necessary before making an attack on Jerusalem, the Crusaders' goal. Unless Antioch were in friendly hands, no Christian army in Palestine or Syria could be considered safe.

But the capture of Antioch was a formidable problem. The city was ancient, built upon rugged terrain and splendidly fortified. The main part of the city was located upon the plains at the very foot of Mount Silpius. A full thousand feet above the city proper towered the citadel, built on the peak of the mountain. The whole city was girded by walls, intersected at regular intervals by 360 towers. When the Crusaders arrived before Antioch in October 1097, the city was in the hands of a Turkish governor, Yaghi-Siyan, who possessed a sizeable garrison. The wily Turk had long since taken the precaution of collecting supplies against a prolonged siege.

The stupendous size of Antioch at first deterred the Crusaders from a massed assault against its walls, but at the same time there was no immediate alternative to such tactics for the city was far too large to be surrounded by the forces which the Crusaders had at their command. The Crusaders settled down to pitch their camp on the plains in front of the city, while Antioch and its garrison likewise settled down to wait out the siege.

The weeks wore on, without either side gaining any major advantage over the other. Both besiegers and besieged made minor sorties against the other without gaining ground. Winter came, bringing near famine to the Crusaders, who sent out foraging parties far and wide to find sufficient food to feed their multitudes. The besiegers were likewise troubled by cold, torrential winter rains, by earthquakes, and by desertion. Two major Turkish relieving forces approached the city during the winter to try to beat off the Christians. Both times, however, the Turks were forced back and the siege continued. In the spring of 1098, after receiving reinforcements and supplies by sea through the convenient seaport of Saint Simeon twelve miles from Antioch, the Crusaders began to build a number of fortified towers of their own. These structures helped to seal off the front of the city and thus made it difficult for the Turkish defenders to sortie and attack the Crusaders.

Bohemund, meanwhile, had designs on Antioch for himself. By the terms of the oaths which he and the other Crusading princes had sworn to the Byzantine emperor, Antioch,

The Seigneurial Crusade

53

as a former Byzantine possession, would have to be turned over to the Emperor when taken. Constantinople was far away, however, and there seemed no immediate possibility that Byzantium would be able to make good its claims by force. By June 1098 Bohemund had made contact with a traitor within Antioch and began to set into motion the plan by which he might be able to get the city for himself.

THE CAPTURE OF ANTIOCH[36]

There was a Turkish emir named Firuz[37] who became a close friend of Bohemund. In the messages which they frequently exchanged Bohemund promised that if Firuz would receive him in a friendly fashion within the city and would freely embrace Christianity, Bohemund, for his part, would make him rich and greatly honored. Firuz was amenable to these words and promises and said: "I have charge of three towers. I promise them freely to Bohemund and, whenever he wishes, I shall let him into them."

Now Bohemund thereby had a sure entrance into the city. He came joyfully with quiet mind and calm countenance to all the leaders. Gleefully he said to them: "Most illustrious knights! You are aware that all of us, great or small, are here in extreme poverty and misery. We know not from what quarter an amelioration of our situation may come. I propose, therefore, if you deem it good and honest, that one of us should volunteer before the others. If he can, by any means or device, take or reduce the city, either by himself or with the help of others, we should give the city to him by common consent."

The leaders were opposed and spurned this course, saying: "The city shall be given to no one; rather we shall all share in it equally. As we have shared the labor equally, so we should, as a result, share equally in the honor."[38] When Bohemund heard these words, he smiled slightly and left shortly thereafter.

Not long afterward we heard reports concerning the enemy's army, composed of Turks, Paulicians,[39] Azymites,[40] and many other nations.[41] The leaders assembled at once and took counsel,[42] saying: "If Bohemund can take the city himself or through others, we shall freely and unanimously turn it over to him, on this condition, however, that if the Emperor should come to help us and should fulfill all his commitments to us, as he promised and swore he would do, then we shall give him the city by right; if not, however, Bohemund shall have the city."

Shortly thereafter Bohemund began humbly to beseech his friend with daily requests. Abjectly he promised the best of everything: "The right time is now at hand for securing the good things we want. Let my good friend Firuz help me now." Firuz was pleased and declared that he would help Bohemund in proper fashion. The following night Firuz secretly sent his own son as a hostage to Bohemund, so that Bohemund might feel more secure about entering the city. He also sent a message to this effect: that on the next day Bohemund should have all the Franks summoned and he should go off as if to raid the land of the Saracens. Then he should feint and return quickly by way of the right-hand mountain.* "I shall be observing the troops attentively," he said, "and shall be watching for them and I shall let them into the towers which are in my power and custody."

Bohemund at once ordered one of his sergeants,[43] namely Male Couronne, to come to him. Bohemund ordered him as herald to summon a great number of the Franks in order to prepare them for a journey into the land of the Saracens. And so it was done. Bohemund confided his plan to Duke Godfrey, the Count of Flanders, the Count of St-Gilles, and the Bishop of Le Puy. He said: "With the help of God's grace, Antioch will be ours tonight!"

Things were arranged in this way: the knights held the plains, the infantry, the mountains. They marched and rode through the night until dawn. Then they began to approach the towers which the watchman† had guarded all night. Bohemund dismounted at once and gave orders to everyone, saying: "Go on, securely and tranquilly. Climb the walls by the ladder and enter Antioch, which, please God, we shall soon have in our keeping."

They went to the ladder which was already set up and firmly tied to the city's battlements. About sixty of our men climbed up and were dispersed among the towers which Firuz guarded. Firuz, seeing that so few of our men had climbed up, began to tremble, fearing that he and our men might fall into the hands

---

* In other words, the army was to move out to the east or southeast of Antioch, then swing around through the mountains, and double back to the city from the west.
† Firuz.

of the Turks. He exclaimed:"*Mikrous Frankous, echomen!*" (that is: "We have only a few Franks!") "Where is fierce Bohemund? Where is the invincible one?" One of the Lombard sergeants descended at once and ran hurriedly to Bohemund, saying, "Why are you standing here, skilled sir? Why did you come here? We already have three towers!" He went off with the others and, rejoicing, they all came to the ladder.

Those who were already in the towers saw them and began to shout in glad tones: "God wills it!" and we took up the same cry. Then, those who were there began to climb up with dexterity. They climbed all the way and began running hastily to the other towers. They massacred those whom they found there and also killed the brother of Firuz.

Meanwhile, the ladder on which we had made our ascent broke and, for this reason, we were troubled and saddened. Although the ladder had broken, there was, on our left, a certain gate near us which was unknown to some people. It was still night, but by searching and feeling our way we found it. We all ran at it and, when it was broken, we entered through it.

A terrible noise resounded throughout the town. Bohemund gave his men no rest. He ordered his honored banner to be set up on a certain peak near the citadel. In the city everyone was shouting together. At daybreak those who were outside in the tents heard the strident noise in the city, hurried out, and saw Bohemund's banner flying from the peak. They all came running hastily and entered the city through the gates. They killed the Turks and Saracens whom they found there, except for those who fled up to the citadel.[44] Other Turks left through the gates and, by fleeing, escaped alive.

Yaghi-Siyan, their lord, took to headlong flight, together with many of his attendants. While fleeing he came to Tancred's territory, not far from the city. Their horses were exhausted and they made their way into a peasant village where they took refuge in a house. The Syrian and Armenian inhabitants recognized him, however, and seized him at once. They beheaded him and brought his head to Bohemund so that they might thereby obtain their liberty. His belt and scabbard they sold for sixty besants.

These events occurred on Thursday, June 3 [1098], the third day before the nones of June. All the squares of the city were filled with the bodies of the dead and no one could stay there

whomever he pleased to rule over the others and govern the city. They ordered that all the dead Saracens should be cast out of the city because of the great stench, since the city was filled with their corpses. The living Saracens dragged the dead outside the gates and made heaps of them, as large as houses. No one ever saw or heard of such a slaughter of pagan peoples, for funeral pyres were formed of them like pyramids and no one knows their number save God alone. [Trans. James A. Brundage]

CHAPTER IV

[1] The literature dealing with the Seigneurial Crusade is enormous. Some important treatments of the subject are: Runciman, *Crusades,* I, 142-288; Setton, *Crusades,* I, 253-341; Grousset, *Croisades,* I, 11-163; Chalandon, *Histoire de la première croisade;* Röhricht, *Geschichte des ersten Kreuzzuges.* A. C. Krey's *The First Crusade* (Princeton: Princeton University Press, 1921) is a convenient compilation of translations from the original source. Some more detailed studies of particular leaders and special aspects of the Crusade are: C. W. David, *Robert Curthose, Duke of Normandy* (Cambridge, Mass.: Harvard University Press, 1920); M. M. Knappen, "Robert II of Flanders in the First Crusade," in Munro, *Essays,* pp. 79-100; J. H. Hill, "Raymond of Saint Gilles in Urban's Plan of Greek and Latin Friendship," *Speculum,* XXVI (1951), 265-76; Walter Porges, "The Clergy, the Poor, and the Non-Combatants on the First Crusade," *Speculum,* XXI (1946), 1-21.

[2] Philip I of France (1060-1108) had repudiated his wife, Bertha, in 1092 and had taken as his mistress Bertrade de Mont-

fort, the wife of Fulk of Anjou. The King's subsequent demand that the French bishops sanction his connubial ventures was met with an excommunication which was imposed upon him in 1094 by a papal legate, Hugh of Die, Archbishop of Lyons. The excommunication was ratified by the Council of the Clermont in 1095. As an excommunicate Philip was debarred from participation in the Crusade and as an enemy of Pope Urban II he was in any case unwilling to enlist in an enterprise proclaimed by the Pope. Augustin Fliche, *La Chrétienté médiévale (394-1254)* ("Histoire du monde," ed. M. E. Cavaignac Vol. VII[2] [Paris: E. de Boccard, 1929]), pp. 308-09.

[3] By becoming a vassal of the Byzantine Emperor, Godfrey might have been held to have broken the oath of allegiance he had previously sworn to the Holy Roman Emperor upon becoming Duke of Lower Loraine. For a discussion of the issues involved in such agreements see Marc Bloch, *Feudal Society,* L. A. Manyon (trans.), (Chicago: University of Chicago Press, 1961), pp. 146-47, 211-18; J. H. and L. L. Hill, "The Convention of Alexius

Comnenus and Raymond of Saint Gilles," *AHR*, LVIII (1953), 322-27.

4 For the Norman attacks on Byzantium prior to the First Crusade see A. A. Vasiliev, *History of the Byzantine Empire*, II, 380-81; Runciman, *Crusades*, I, 69-72; Setton, *Crusades*, I, 214; Anna Comnena, *Alexiad*, V, i, 1 - V, vii, 5, II, 7-32.

5 Raymond of Aguilers, *Historia Francorum qui Ceperunt Iherusalem, I* (*RHC, Occ,* III, 235-36).

6 By Sclavonia Raymond means Dalmatia, whose inhabitants he calls "Slavs" (*Sclavi*).

7 Raymond here seems to contradict his earlier statement (above), that the Slavs "killed a great many of the feeble, sick, and poor people" who accompanied Count Raymond's forces. Possibly the chronicler means to indicate here that none of the armed men of the force had been lost on the journey.

8 A local Serbian prince named Bodin.

9 The modern Albanian town of Shkodër.

10 The modern Albanian town of Durrës, known also by its Italian name, Durazzo.

11 These Byzantine mercenaries had been sent by the imperial authorities to keep guard over the Crusaders and to escort them to Constantinople.

12 At this point, then, the army of the First Crusade was composed of six major forces, as follows:

1. Hugh of Vermandois and a group of knights from the Ile de France.
2. Godfrey of Bouillon and a force of knights from Lorraine.
3. Bohemund leading a force of Normans from southern Italy.
4. Raymond of St-Gilles and a group of Provençal troops accompanied by
5. Bishop Adhémar of Le Puy, the papal legate, who brought a small force of his own.
6. The Norman, Breton, English, and Flemish troops who travelled together under several leaders, of whom Robert of Normandy, Robert of Flanders, and Stephen of Blois were the most important.

13 Louis Bréhier (ed.), *Histoire anonyme de la première Croisade* [Gesta Francorum et Aliorum Hierosolymitanorum] (Paris: Les Belles Lettres, 1924), II, 8 (pp. 36-42).

14 May 14, 1097.

15 The armies of Kilij Arslan, who was on campaign elsewhere in Asia Minor.

16 The Crusaders had not yet gathered sufficient troops at Nicaea to surround the city completely.

17 May 16, 1097.

18 A reference to the crosses which were the characteristic insignia of the Crusaders.

19 See above, Chap. III, n. 7.

20 Robert Curthose, Duke of Normandy.

21 Stephen, Count of Chartres and Blois.

22 These additional forces arrived at Nicaea on June 3, 1097.

23 Lake Ascanius.

24 This account reflects the anti-Byzantine bias of the author of the *Gesta*, whose suspicious attitude toward Byzantium is reflected by many other Western writers who deal with the Seigneurial Crusade.

25 Five weeks and two days elapsed from the beginning of the siege (May 14) to the capitulation of the city (June 20). The reference here is doubtless to the period from the first arrival of the advance units of the army (May 6) to the final departure of the Crusaders (June 26).

26 Apoc., VI, 9-11.

27 Bréhier, *Gesta Francorum*, III, 9 (pp. 44-52).

28 July 1, 1097.

29 They were probably shouting the traditional Moslem battle cry, *Allahu akbar* ("God is great").

30 A Norman nobleman from southern Italy, a member of Bohemund's army.

31 Bohemund's nephew, the Count of the Principate.

32 A force of heavily armored Moslem swordsmen.

33 Christian dualist heretics who had been driven from the Byzantine Empire because of their unpopular religious beliefs and had subsequently taken refuge among the Moslems. See Steven Runciman, *The Medieval Manichee* (Cambridge: Cambridge University Press, 1955), pp. 26-62.

34 An estimate which is not to be taken literally.

35 That is from mid-morning to mid-afternoon.

36 Bréhier, *Gesta Francorum*, VIII, 20 (pp. 100-10).

37 "Pirrus" in the text. The form used here is that adopted in Setton, *Crusades*.

38 "Honor" is used here in the technical sense of "a possession or piece of property." Cf. the discussion of the word's meaning in J. H. and L. L. Hill, "The Convention of Alexius Comnenus and Raymond of Saint Gilles," 322-27.

39 Christian heretics.

40 A term used by the Greeks to refer to Christian groups who used unleavened bread in the eucharistic liturgy. Possibly the "Azymites" referred to here were cooperating with Kerbogha in his planned attack upon the Crusaders.

41 Kerbogha, the *atabeg* of Mosul, in cooperation with other Turkish princes (notably the Sultan of Baghdad and the Sultan of Persia) had raised an enormous army to attack the besiegers at Antioch and thus relieve the city.

42 The meeting probably took place on May 29, 1098.

43 A medieval military term meaning, generally, an infantryman.

44 The citadel and its garrison continued to hold out on Mount Silpius until June 28, 1098.

45 See, for comparison, the account of an Armenian eyewitness of the Crusaders' capture of Antioch given by P. Peeters, S.J., in *Un Témoignage autographe sur le siège d'Antioche par les croisés en 1098* (Lou-

ain: Bibliothèque de l'Université, 1946; offprinted from *Miscellanea historica Alberti de Meyer,* (Louvain: Bibliothèque de l'Université, 1946), pp. 373-90).

46 Raymond of Aguilers, *Historia Francorum,* X-XI (*RHC, Occ,* 253-57).

47 December 30, 1097.

48 To Antioch.

49 March 20, 1098.

50 Antioch.

51 Raymond of Aguilers, the author of this account.

52 June 15, 1098.

53 Raymond of St-Gilles was the commander of the fortified tower of La Mohamerie, near the Gate of St. George, just outside of Antioch.

54 Adhémar had good grounds for his skepticism: he had probably noticed, when he was in Constantinople. that one of the major relics on view there was the Holy Lance. In the eighteenth century Cardinal Lambertini (later Pope Benedict XIV) officially repudiated the Lance found at Antioch; see Steven Runciman, "The Holy Lance Found at Antioch," *Analecta Bollandiana,* LXVIII (1950), 197-209.

55 Probably an outbreak of typhoid fever.

56 He burned down Maarat an-Numan as he left.

57 Bréhier, *Gesta Francorum,* X, 38-39 (pp. 200-06).

58 July 13-14, 1099.

59 July 15.

60 The crucifixion began at the third hour of the day (Mark 15:25), i.e. between 9:00 in the morning and noon; this attack probably took place in the late morning.

61 Count Eustace III of Boulogne, Godfrey of Bouillon's elder brother.

62 Possibly the same Lethold, a knight from Tournai, mentioned by Albert of Aachen, *Historia Hierosolymitana,* VI, 11 (*RHC, Occ,* IV, 472).

63 The modern el-Aksa mosque.

64 Iftikhar ad-Daula, the Egyptian governor of the city and the commander of its garrison.

65 The citadel of Jerusalem, located on the west side of the city.

66 Raymond of St-Gilles.

67 The Jaffa gate, through which pilgrims had entered the city and the place where they had paid the toll and tribute levied upon visitors by the Turks.

68 On July 16.

69 Probably on July 17.

Chapter V

Tϩᴇ Lᴀᴛïɴ Sᴛᴀᴛᴇs

I

Once Jerusalem had been captured, the first consideration of the Crusaders was how to keep it. It was generally
acknowledged among the soldiers that this could best be
done by the creation of a permanent government modeled
after the type of government with which the Crusaders were
familiar: a feudal kingdom. This type of state would enable
those Crusaders who wished to settle in the East to enjoy the
quasi-independent position of feudal lords within the kingdom; at the same time, it would provide for a more or less
centralized government, capable of coordinating the defense
against armed attack upon the new Western colonies.[1]

There was, however, some discordant sentiment, both
among the laity and among the clergy who had accompanied
the army. It was thought by some that the only proper government for the Holy City would be an ecclesiastical one in
which purely secular officials, such as a king, would be clearly and permanently subordinated to a clerical ruler.

The Crusaders, in other words, found themselves drawn
in two opposite directions by the same sentiments and feel-
ings which were dividing their contemporaries in Europe:
the notion, on the one hand, that a strong secular ruler was
necessary to deal with civil problems and to preserve peace
and order within the state conflicted with the notion, on the
other hand, that the clergy and the church, as God's specially consecrated servants on earth, were preëminently quali-

fied to exercise secular as well as ecclesiastical authority. As in Europe, so also in the East, eleventh and twelfth century Europeans were caught between two swords.

The imminent and evident dangers to the newly acquired Eastern territories, however, were sufficient for the moment to convince most of the Crusading princes that strong secular rule was absolutely essential there. The princes therefore proceeded, a week after taking Jerusalem, to elect a monarch:

GODFREY OF BOUILLON BECOMES "DEFENDER OF THE HOLY SEPULCHER"[2]

When the Holy City had, by the superabundant grace of the Lord, been restored and affairs had returned to a more or less tranquil state, the army spent seven days rejoicing greatly, with spiritual gladness and fear of the Lord. On the eighth day,[3] the princes gathered in order that, after calling on the grace of the Holy Spirit, they might deal with the business of electing one of their group to rule over the area and take charge of the royal duties in the province. While they were gathered, some of the clergy assembled. The latter were puffed up with spiritual pride. They sought their own ends, not those of Jesus Christ.[4] They professed to have a secret message which they wished to convey to the princes who were participating in the conclave. The clergy's representatives, when admitted, said: "It has been announced to the clergy that you have assembled in order to elect one of yourselves as king. Your proposal seems to us a just and useful one and worthy to be carried out if only the proper order in this matter be observed. For it is certain that spiritual matters are of greater dignity than secular affairs and, truly, what is of greater dignity ought to have precedence. It seems to us, therefore, that unless a backward order be followed, a religious person, a man pleasing to God,[5] ought first to be chosen, who will know how to preside and rule over the Church of God. This, rather than the election of a secular power, ought to be done first. If you will follow this procedure, we shall indeed be pleased and we shall be with you body and soul. If you do not, however, we shall judge and decree that whatsoever you have ordained out of our order is invalid and without force among men. . . ."

The princes, however, considered the aforementioned message frivolous and without weight. . . . Some say that in order to proceed to an election which was pleasing to God and which took account of individual merits, the princes called in some of the household of each of the great leaders, made them take a solemn oath, and questioned them about the conduct and habits of their lords so that they would tell the truth without any admixture of falsehood. This was done so that the electors might thus be more fully and more faithfully informed of the merits of the candidates. Those who were later very closely questioned under the required oath by the electors were forced to confess in secret the vices of their lords and likewise to enumerate their virtues, so that it might be made plain just what sort of men their lords were. When the Duke's[6] household were questioned among the others, they replied that, among all the Duke's actions, the one which most irritated his servants was this: that when he entered a church, even after the celebration of the liturgy had been finished, he could not be drawn out. Rather, he demanded of the priests and those who seemed experienced in such matters an account of each picture and statue. His associates, who were interested in other things, found this boring, even nauseating. Further, his meals, which had been prepared for a certain and appropriate hour, grew cold and most unappetizing because of these long and vexing delays. The electors who heard these things said: "Blessed is the man to whom are ascribed as faults those traits which would be called virtues in another." At length, after consulting with one another and after many deliberations, they unanimously elected the lord Duke. They brought him to the Holy Sepulcher of the Lord most devoutly, chanting hymns and canticles.

It is said, however, that most of the nobles had agreed upon Lord Raymond, Count of Toulouse. When they learned, however, that if the kingdom were not given to Raymond he would immediately return home, they were led by their desire for their native land to invent reasons to hold him unfitted, and they even went against the dictates of their consciences to do so. Count Raymond, nonetheless, spurned his native land and did not return home, but, instead, most devoutly followed Christ. He extended further the pilgrimage upon which he had embarked and followed it in voluntary poverty to the end. . . .

After the oft-mentioned Lord Duke had, by God's grace, been confirmed as the head of the Kingdom and after all the quarrels

The
Latin
States

71

which had arisen had abated, the Kingdom in his days grew more secure and well established. He reigned but one year,[7] for, because of men's sins, the Kingdom was deprived of the continued consolation of such a prince. He refreshed the newly planted Kingdom and gave it protection against the molestations of attackers. He was wrenched away in mid-career, lest his heart be affected by evil; as it is written: "The men of mercy are taken away and there is none that understandeth."[8]

Duke Godfrey was born in the French kingdom, in the province of Reims, in the city of Boulogne by the English Sea. He was descended from illustrious and religious forebears. His father was the elder Lord Eustace, the famous and splendid Count of that region, whose many and memorable works are still recalled by the old men of the neighboring provinces and his memory as a religious and God-fearing man is like a blessing[9] in the pious recollection of men. Duke Godfrey's mother was well-known among the noble matrons of the West, as much for her way of life as for her noble generosity. She was named Ida and was a sister of the exalted Duke Godfrey of Lorraine who was known as Struma. That Duke Godfrey, since he had no children, adopted his nephew Godfrey as his own son and bestowed his entire patrimony upon young Godfrey as his heir. Thus, when the elder Duke Godfrey died, the young Godfrey succeeded him as Duke.

The younger Duke Godfrey had three brothers who, by reason of their worthy lives and their distinguished virtues, were true brothers to such a prince. They were the Lord Baldwin, Count of Edessa, who succeeded Godfrey in the kingdom; and the Lord Eustace, Count of Boulogne, who was his father's namesake, successor to his father as Count and inheritor of the paternal estate. . . . The third was Lord William, a famous man, no less virtuous and energetic than his father and brothers. Of these three, the first two followed their lord and brother, Duke Godfrey, on the expedition, while the third remained at home.

Godfrey was the eldest of them by birth and the foremost in his inner qualities as well. . . . He was a religious man, mild mannered, virtuous, and God-fearing. He was just, he avoided evil, he was trustworthy and dependable in his undertakings. He scorned the vanities of the world, a quality rare in that age and especially among men of the military profession. He was assiduous in prayer and pious works, renowned for his liberality, graciously affable, civil, and merciful. His whole life was commendable and pleasing to God. His body was tall and although he was shorter than the very tall, yet he was taller than men of average height. He was a man of incomparable strength, with stout limbs, a manly chest, and a handsome face. His hair and beard were a medium blond. He was considered by everyone to be most outstanding in the use of weapons and in military operations.

[*Trans. James A. Brundage*]

The election of Godfrey of Bouillon as King of Jerusalem, or, rather, as he styled himself, "Advocate of the Holy Sepulcher," was followed shortly by the election of a Latin Patriarch of Jerusalem as the chief ecclesiastical officer of the newly founded state. Godfrey and the patriarch, a few days after their election, proceeded to lead the Crusading army on its last expedition: a surprise attack on an Egyptian army which had been hastily summoned by al-Afdal, the Grand Vizier of Egypt, to repel the Western soldiers.

The Crusaders' attack on the Egyptian forces near Ascalon at sunrise on August 12, 1099 was a complete success. The invading army was routed and the Crusaders returned from their foray laden with loot and glory. The new state was safely in Latin hands, at least for the moment. By the end of August 1099, the Crusaders were beginning to depart for home, save for a comparatively small minority who had decided to settle permanently in the East.

II

Those who remained behind to man the defenses of Jerusalem and the other Latin states were faced with a serious problem. They were encircled by a large and potentially hostile population, while the number of Western fighting men available for defense was small indeed.[10] Fortunately, the Moslem neighbors of the new Western states were not immediately anxious to match forces with the new settlers. Indeed, the divisions among the Moslems themselves were at least as great and as serious as those between the Moslems and their new Western neighbors. Just as Moslem disunity had made it possible for the Crusade to reach its objective, so too Moslem disunity now made it possible for the new Latin states to establish themselves in comparative quiet.

The Latin States

73

The problem of establishing a firm government in the newly conquered territories of the East during the twelfth century was of a fundamentally different character than the problems involved in establishing a new state in modern times. The Crusaders and other settlers in the East were not principally engaged during the period of settlement in establishing definite frontier lines to divide themselves from their neighbors as, for example, a new state such as Israel must be today. Rather, among the Crusaders, the problem of establishing their rule was essentially the problem of building and outfitting fortresses and capturing towns from which they could dominate the immediate neighborhood. Walled towns and castles were the military bases upon which the Latin states depended for their continued existence. Consequently, the history of the Latin kingdom is very largely the history of continued warfare, first to seize and later to retain these indispensable fortified centers.

To defend themselves the Latin states had to rely on many and diverse sources of manpower. The bedrock foundation of Latin military strength was the corps of knights who had decided to settle permanently in the East as feudal vassals of the King of Jerusalem or of some other Latin prince. At the end of the First Crusade there were only about three hundred such vassals available, in addition to some two thousand Latin foot soldiers.[11] These were the career Crusaders. They not only settled down in the East, but also, at least to a superficial degree, assimilated themselves into their new environment and new neighbors, learning the native languages, adopting native dress, and following the dietary and social customs of the peoples among whom they settled. These orientalized Crusaders were thus described by Raymond of St-Gilles' chaplain:

TRANSFORMATION OF LATIN SETTLERS IN THE EAST[12]

I pray you, consider and reflect on how God has in our times changed West into East. For we, who were occidentals, have now become orientals. The man who was a Roman or a Frank has, in this land, been turned into a Galilean or a Palestinian. He who was once a citizen of Reims or of Chartres has now become a citizen of Tyre or of Antioch. We have already forgotten the places where we were born; many of us either do not know them or have never even heard of them. One among us now has his own houses and retainers, just as if he possessed them through hereditary or family right. Another takes as his wife, not a woman of his own stock, but rather a Syrian or Armenian, or even, occasionally, a Saracen who has obtained the grace of baptism. . . . One man may possess vineyards, while another has farms. Men address one another in turn in the speech and idiom of various languages. The several languages of various nations are common here and one joins faith with men whose forefathers were strangers. For it is written: "The lion and ox shall eat straw side by side."[13] He who was a foreigner is now just like a native. The interloper has been made into a resident. We are followed here, from day to day, by our neighbors and parents, who abandon, though reluctantly, all their possessions. Those who were needy have here been enriched by God. Those who had a few pennies, here possess countless bezants. He who had not a village, here possesses a God-given city. Why should one who has found the East to be like this return to the West? Nor does God wish to burden with poverty those who have vowed to follow (or, rather, pursue) him with their crosses. You see, therefore, that this is a great miracle, most astonishing to the whole world. Who has ever heard of such a thing? For God wishes to make us all rich and to draw us to himself as the dearest of friends. Since he desires this, we also willingly desire it. We shall do what pleases him with a humble and benign heart, so that we may reign happily with him forever. *[Trans. James A. Brundage]*

If the continued existence of the Latin states had rested upon the members of this group alone, however, those states would probably have been short-lived in the extreme. Fortunately for the Latins, the ranks of the resident Europeans were swelled annually by pilgrims who came from the West. Some of the members of these pilgrim groups settled permanently in the East. Most of them, however, even though they did not intend to stay permanently, were willing to lend assistance to the armies of the Latin states for brief periods of time and thus served to provide a fluctuating but important reserve of manpower.

Some help for the Latins of the East could also be expected from natives of the area itself who were willing to serve in the Latin armies as mercenaries. Some Western knights and foot soldiers could also be recruited to defend the Latin settlements on a mercenary basis.

After 1118 there slowly emerged still another military bulwark to Latin rule in the East. The military orders of the Temple and the Hospital[14] gradually grew to positions of great strength within the Latin states, providing large, stable, well-equipped, and highly trained forces. The military orders were strange combinations of monasticism and chivalry. They were composed principally of knights who took temporary or perpetual vows of poverty, chastity, and obedience and who lived a common life under a rule as did monks. The members of the military orders, however, unlike monks, devoted the major part of their energy and time not to contemplation, devotion, and prayer, but rather to military exercises.

THE FOUNDATION OF THE ORDER OF
KNIGHTS TEMPLAR[15]

In this same year,[16] certain noble men of knightly rank, religious men, devoted to God and fearing him, bound themselves to Christ's service in the hands of the Lord Patriarch.[17] They promised to live in perpetuity as regular canons, without possessions, under vows of chastity and obedience. Their foremost leaders were the venerable Hugh of Payens and Geoffrey of St. Omer. Since they had no church nor any fixed abode, the king[18] gave them for a time a dwelling place in the south wing of the palace, near the Lord's Temple.[19] The canons of the Lord's Temple gave them, under certain conditions, a square near the palace which the canons possessed. This the knights used as a drill field. The Lord King and his noblemen and also the Lord Patriarch and the prelates of the church gave them benefices from their domains, some for a limited time and some in perpetuity. These were to provide the knights with food and clothing. Their primary duty, one which was enjoined upon them by the Lord Patriarch and the other bishops for the remission of sins, was that of protecting the roads and routes against the attacks of robbers and brigands. This they did especially in order to safeguard pilgrims.

For nine years after their founding, the knights wore secular clothing. They used such garments as the people, for their soul's salvation, gave them. In their ninth year there was held in France, at Troyes, a council at which the Lord Archbishops of Reims and Sens and their suffragans were present, as well as the Bishop of Albano, who was the legate of the apostolic see, and the Abbots of Cîteaux, Clairvaux, Pontigny, with many others. This council, by command of the Lord Pope Honorius and the Lord Stephen, Patriarch of Jerusalem, established a rule for the knights and assigned them a white habit.

Although the knights now had been established for nine years, there were still only nine of them. From this time onward their numbers began to grow and their possessions began to multiply. Later, in Pope Eugene's time,[20] it is said that both the knights and their humbler servants, called sergeants, began to affix crosses made of red cloth to their mantles, so as to distinguish themselves from others. They have now grown so great that there are in this Order today[21] about 300 knights who wear white mantles, in addition to the brothers, who are almost countless. They are said to have immense possessions both here and overseas, so that there is now not a province in the Christian world which has not bestowed upon the aforesaid brothers a portion of its goods. It is said today that their wealth is equal to the treasures of kings. Because they have a headquarters in the royal palace next to the Temple of the Lord, as we have said before, they are called the Brothers of the Militia of the Temple. Although they maintained their establishment honorably for a long time and fulfilled their vocation with sufficient prudence, later, because of the neglect of humility (which is known as the guardian of all virtues and which, since it sits in the lowest place, cannot fall), they withdrew from the Patriarch of Jerusalem, by whom their Order was founded and from whom they received their first benefices and to whom they denied the obedience which their predecessors rendered. They have also taken away tithes and first fruits from God's churches, have disturbed their possessions, and have made themselves exceedingly troublesome. [Trans. James A. Brundage]

III

The three Latin states—Jerusalem, Antioch, and Edessa—were increased to four after 1108, when Raymond of St-Gilles and his successors took Tripoli and established a Latin county there. Leading a precarious existence much of the time, these

The Latin States

four states found it difficult to learn the delicate art of co-
öperating with one another, even in the face of serious outside threats.

Jerusalem, the largest and most important of the Latin
states, gradually worked out a satisfactory, if not exemplary,
system of government. The power of the Kings of Jerusalem
—for so they styled themselves after Godfrey's demise—was
based upon the land they controlled, which was exploited
by native peasants under the Latin kings, much as it had been
under earlier conquerors. However, since Palestine was, for
the most part, not very productive agriculturally, trade and
commerce with the Moslem neighbors of the Kingdom and
of the other Latin states was an absolute economic necessity.
Thus it was that a constant stream of caravans of merchants
and traders from Damascus and the other cities of the hinterland found their way to and through the Latin states. Thus
it was, too, that the commercial cities of the West, principally
Genoa and Pisa, came to establish quarters and marts for
their traders in the coastal cities of the Latin East. Here commerce from East and West met in a continual stream of exchange and trade which was profitable both to the merchants
and also to the Latin Kings and princes as well as their feudal
vassals. The basic political organization of the Latin states
was feudal, but feudalism in the East increasingly became
not a feudalism based upon the agricultural exploitation of
manors, as in the West, but rather a feudalism based upon
the taxation and profits which accrued from trade in the cities
of the East.

War, which interrupted trade and cut off communications
with the Moslem merchants, was avoided when possible, but
occasional conflicts were inevitable and necessary to states
so meager and so exposed to hostile powers as were the Crusading principalities. So long as the wars of the Latin states
were confined to minor conflicts with one or two petty Moslem princes, no grave danger was entailed. But when major
combinations of Moslem powers appeared, then the situation
could become perilous indeed. On such occasions, the safety of the Kingdom of Jerusalem and the other principalities
absolutely demanded that they cooperate for mutual defense.
As has often happened in more modern times, however, the

necessity for common action against a common foe was uncommonly difficult for kings and princes to appreciate. And even when the necessity for common action was perceived by the leaders of the Latin East, petty domestic quarrels between them frequently made their combinations with one another tenuous and halfhearted affairs. Thus it was that when the first concerted Moslem attack upon one of the Latin states occurred, the other states were diffident and disinclined to lend assistance to the one attacked.

The occasion arose in 1144, when the easternmost of the Latin states, Edessa, fell prey to Zengi. Zengi, whose rise to power had begun at Mosul in 1127, had gradually acquired authority through war, intimidation, and treaty over a whole host of Moslem principalities in Syria. When his large and powerful army turned its unwelcome attention upon Edessa in 1144, Zengi found the Latins divided. The count of Edessa, Joscelyn II, was at odds with the prince of Antioch. The count of Tripoli was only vaguely interested in events so far to the east, and in Jerusalem, King Fulk had just died, leaving the government in the hands of Queen Melisende as regent for their thirteen year old son, Baldwin III.

Consequently, Zengi found his attack opposed only by the negligible forces of Edessa itself.

THE FALL OF EDESSA[22]

In that same year,[23] during the time which elapsed between the death of King Baldwin's father and Baldwin's elevation to the throne, one Zengi, a vicious man, was the most powerful of the Eastern Turks. His city, formerly called Nineveh, but now known as Mosul, is the metropolis of the region which was earlier called Assur. Zengi, its lord and governor, at this time laid siege to the city of Edessa, more commonly called Rohas, the greatest and most splendid city of the Medes. Zengi did this, relying on the numbers and strength of his men and also on the very dangerous strife which had arisen between Prince Raymond of Antioch and Count Joscelyn of Edessa. The city of Edessa lies beyond the Euphrates, one day's journey from the river. The aforesaid Count of Edessa, contrary to the custom of his predecessors, had ceased to live in the city and made his constant and perpetual abode in a place called Turbessel. He did this both because of the richness of the spot and because of his own laziness. Here, far from the tumult of the enemy and free to pursue his pleasures, the count failed to take proper care of his noble city. The population of Edessa was made up of Chaldeans and Armenians, unwarlike men, scarcely familiar with the use of arms and accustomed only to the arts of trade. The city was only rarely visited by Latins and very few of them lived there. The safekeeping of the city was entrusted solely to mercenaries and these were not paid according to the type of service they performed or the length of time for which they were engaged—indeed, they often had to wait a year or more for the payment of their stated wages. Both Baldwin and the elder Joscelyn, when they held the county, made their home permanently and customarily in Edessa and took care to have the city supplied with food, arms, and other necessary items from nearby places. They had thus been able both to maintain themselves in safety and also to overawe the neighboring towns with their strength.

There was, as we have said before, bad feeling between Count Joscelyn and the Prince of Antioch—a feeling that was not hidden, but rather had become an open hatred. For this reason, each of them took little or no care if the other were attacked or suffered misfortune. Rather they rejoiced at the other's catastrophes and were made glad by the other's mishaps.

The aforesaid great prince, Zengi, took the opportunity offered by this situation. He gathered innumerable cavalry forces throughout all of the East; he even called up the people of the cities neighboring Edessa and brought them with him to lay siege to the city. He blockaded all of the entrances to the city, so that the besieged citizens could not get out and so that those who wished to help them could not get in. The resulting shortage of food and provisions caused great suffering for the besieged. The city, however, was surrounded by a formidable wall. In the upper town there were high towers and down below there was the lower town where the citizens could take refuge, even if the city itself were taken. All these defenses could be of use against the enemy only if there were men willing to fight for their freedom, men who would resist the foe valiantly. The defenses would be useless, however, if there were none among the besieged who were willing to serve as defenders. Towers, walls, and earthworks are of little value to a city unless there are defenders to man them.

Zengi found the town bereft of defenders and was much encouraged. He encircled the town with his forces, assigned the officers of his legions to appropriate stations, and dug in. The catapults and siege engines weakened the fortifications; the continual shooting of arrows tormented the citizens incessantly; and the besieged were given no respite. It was announced, meanwhile, and the news was also spread by rumor, that the city of Edessa, a city faithful to God, was suffering the agonies of a siege at the hands of the enemy of the faith and the foe of the Christian name. At this news the hearts of the faithful, far and wide, were touched and zealous men began to take up arms to harass the wicked.

The Count, when he heard of it, was stricken with anguish. Energetically he assembled his forces. . . . He went around admonishing his faithful friends. Humbly he besought his lord, the Prince of Antioch and, through messengers, he forcefully urged the prince to assist him in his labors to free Edessa from the yoke of future servitude.[24] Messengers bearing news of this sinister event came even to the kingdom of Jerusalem, bearing witness to the siege of Edessa and to the misfortunes suffered by its citizens. The queen, who had charge of the kingdom's government, on the advice of the council of the nobles which she consulted, sent her kinsman, Manasses, the royal constable, Philip of Nablus, and Elinander of Tiberius, together with a great multitude of soldiers with all speed to Edessa that they might give the Lord Count and the suffering citizens the comfort which they desired.

The Prince of Antioch, however, rejoiced in Edessa's adversity and paid small attention to his duties for the common welfare. He was little concerned that personal hatred ought not cause public harm and made excuses, while he put off giving the aid which had been requested.

Zengi, meanwhile, pressed continual assaults on the city. He ran the gamut of attacks and left nothing untried which could harass the citizens and aid him in gaining control of the city. He sent sappers through trenches and underground tunnels to undermine the walls. As they dug passages beneath the walls, they buttressed these with posts, which were afterward set on fire. A great part of the wall was thus broken down. This breach in the wall, more than 100 cubits wide, gave the enemy an entrance into the city. The enemy now had the approach they had desired.

Their forces rushed together into the city. They slew with their swords the citizens whom they encountered, sparing neither age, condition, nor sex. Of them it might be said: "They murder the widow and the stranger, they slay the orphan, the youth, and the virgin, together with the old man."[25] The city, therefore, was captured and delivered to the swords of the enemy.

The more prudent or more experienced citizens rushed to the citadel which, as we have said, was in the city. This they did so that they might at least preserve their lives, their children, and their wives, if only for a short time. At the gate there was such a crush of people trying to enter that, because of the press of the crowd, many were suffocated and died miserably. Among these was the most reverend Hugh, the Archbishop of the city. He is said to have expired in this fashion together with several of his clerics. Some of those who were present would blame his miserable end on the Archbishop himself, for he is said to have collected a vast sum of money. Had he used this for soldiers, it would have been helpful to the city, but he preferred to heap up his treasure like a miser rather than to consider his dying people. Thus it happened that he received the reward of his greed by perishing with his people. . . .

Thus while the Prince of Antioch, overcome by foolish hatred, delayed rendering the help he owed to his brothers and while the count awaited help from abroad, the ancient city of Edessa, devoted to Christianity since the time of the Apostles and delivered from the superstitions of the infidels through the words and preaching of the Apostle Thaddeus, passed into an undeserved servitude.[26] [Trans. James A. Brundage]

Luckily for the other Latin states, the force with which Zengi attacked and took Edessa could not be kept in the field for very long periods of time.[27] As a result it was not turned at this time against the other Crusading principalities. The Latins were lucky again in that, before Zengi could muster another sizeable army to commence a new attack, he was killed by one of his own slaves and the empire he had established was momentarily eclipsed.

The lesson implicit in the fall of Edessa was not altogether lost on the other Latin princes. Steps were soon taken to find military aid and one source from which help was anticipated was from the fabulous Prester John.

We also saw there at that time[29] the aforesaid Bishop of Jabala in Syria. . . . He said, indeed, that not many years since, one John, a king and priest* living in the Far East, beyond Persia and Armenia, and who, with his people, is a Christian, but a Nestorian, had warred upon the so-called Samiards,[30] the brother kings of the Medes and Persians. John also attacked Ebactanus . . . the capital of their kingdom. When the aforesaid kings advanced against him with a force of Persians, Medes, and Assyrians, a three-day struggle ensued, since both sides were willing to die rather than to flee. At length, Prester John—so he is usually called —put the Persians to flight and emerged from the dreadful slaughter as victor. The Bishop said that the aforesaid John moved his army to aid the church of Jerusalem, but that when he came to the Tigris and was unable to take his army across it by any means, he turned aside to the north, where he had been informed that the stream was frozen solid during the winter. There he awaited the ice for several years, but saw none because of the temperate weather. His army lost many men on account of the weather to which they were unaccustomed and he was compelled to return home. He is said to be a descendant of the Magi of old, who are mentioned in the Gospel.[31] He governs the same people as they did and is said to enjoy such glory and such plenty that he uses no scepter save one of emerald. Fired by the example of his forefathers, who came to adore Christ in the manger, he proposed to go to Jerusalem, but he was, they say, turned back for the aforementioned reason. *[Trans. James A. Brundage]*

This semilegendary prince, fortunately, was not the only source from which help for the Latin states was anticipated. The princes of the Latin East were not slow to announce to the Pope and to the Western world at large the news of Edessa's fall, in the expectation that military assistance would also be forthcoming from that quarter.

CHAPTER V

[1] By far the best general treatment in English of the Crusader's states is D. C. Munro, *The Kingdom of the Crusaders* (New York: D. Appleton-Century, 1935). A recent monograph is that by Jean Richard, *Le Royaume Latin de Jérusalem* (Paris: Presses universitaires de France, 1953). A more spe-

---

* Hence the name "Prester," from *presbyter*.

The Latin States

cialized study, and an invaluable one, is by J. L. LaMonte, *Feudal Monarchy in the Latin Kingdom of Jerusalem, 1100-1291* (Cambridge, Mass.: Mediaeval Academy of America, 1932); see also LaMonte's article, "The Significance of the Crusaders' States in Medieval History," *Byzantion*, XV (1940-1941), 300-15. Other studies of importance include: M. W. Baldwin, "Ecclesiastical Developments in the Twelfth Century Crusaders' State of Tripolis," *Catholic Historical Review*, XXII (1936-1937), 149-71; Eugene H. Byrne, "The Genoese Colonies in Syria," in Munro, *Essays*, pp. 139-82; Charles Kohler, *Melanges pour servir à l'histoire de l'Orient Latin et des Croisades* (2 vols.; Paris: Ernest Leroux, 1906); Jean Longnon, *Les Français d'-Outre-Mer au moyen âge* (Paris: Perrin, 1929); R. L. Nicholson, *Joscelyn I. Prince of Edessa* (Urbana, Ill.: University of Illinois Press, 1954); Wilhelm v. Heyd, *Geschichte des Levantehandels im Mittelalter* (2 vols.; Stuttgart: J. G. Cotta, 1879); E. G. Rey, *Les Colonies franques de Syrie aux XIIme et XIIIme siècles* (Paris: A. Picard, 1883). See also the treatments in the general histories of the Crusades, especially, Runciman, *Crusades*, I, 289-326, II, 1-225, and III, 351-86; Grousset, *Croisades*, I, 164-678, II, 1-225.

2 William of Tyre, *Historia rerum in partibus transmarinis gestarum*, IX, 1-2, 5 (*P.L.*,

CCI, 433-35, 437-38). William of Tyre, although he was born nearly thirty years after Godfrey's death, was acquainted as few people have ever been with the Latin East. His account of the history of the Crusading states was based upon extensive experience and a vast familiarity with the government and the records of the Latin Kingdom. His account is based, in part, upon records long since lost or destroyed. For an estimate of William's reliability as an historian, see A. C. Krey, "William of Tyre," *Speculum*, XVI (1941), 149-66, and the introduction to E. A. Babcock and A. C. Krey's translation of William of Tyre, *A History of Deeds Done Beyond the Sea* (2 vols.; New York: Columbia University Press, 1943).

3 July 22, 1099.

4 Cf. I cor. 10:24.

5 Cf. I Thess. 2:4.

6 Godfrey of Bouillon, Duke of Lower Lorraine.

7 From July 22, 1099 to July 18, 1100.

8 Isa. 57:1.

9 Eccles. 45:1.

10 For the military situation of the Latin States, see the excellent study by R. C. Smail, *Crusading Warfare* (Cambridge: Cambridge University Press, 1956).

11 William of Tyre, *Historia*, IX, 19 (*P.L.* CCI, 451).

12 Fulcher of Chartres, *Historia Iherosolymitana*, III, 37 (RHC, Occ, III, 468).

13 Isa. 65:25.

14 The Order of Knights Templars took its name from its first headquarters, which was located near the so-called "Temple of Solomon" in the royal palace of the Latin Kings of Jerusalem. For their origin and early history see below. The Knights Hospitallers grew out of a nursing order which served the Hospital of St. John in Jerusalem. Raymond of Le Puy, the Master of the Order, in about 1118 (the date is uncertain), transformed the original nursing order into a military establishment with the purpose of safeguarding the roads leading to Jerusalem and escorting pilgrims through hostile territory.

15 William of Tyre, *Historia*, XII, 7 (*P.L.*, CCI, 526-27).

16 1118.

17 They thus made a solemn religious profession to the Patriarch.

18 King Baldwin I.

19 The present al-Aqsa mosque.

20 Pope Eugenius III, 1145-1153.

21 William wrote this sometime between 1170 and 1174.

22 William of Tyre, *Historia*, XVI, 4-5 (*P.L.*, CCI, 642-45).

23 1144.

24 Gal. 5:1.

25 Ps. 93:6.

26 The city proper fell on December 23, 1144; the citadel capitulated on Christmas Day.

27 The basis of the military organization of Zengi's army was the military *iqta'*, which, like the European fief, was a military and administrative area whose ruler, the *amir*, mustered levies of troops from his lands to fight in campaigns. Since the *amirs* in Zengi's army needed to supervise their domain closely and since their men were needed for agricultural labor as well as for fighting, it was difficult to keep the forces drawn from the *iqta'* in the field for more than a few months at a time. During the summer and especially as the harvest season approached the pressure to allow the men to return home was very great. See Smail, *Crusading Warfare* (Cambridge: Cambridge University Press, 1956), pp. 64-75, and *The Encyclopedia of Islam* (4 vols.; Leiden and London: Brill, 1908-1938), s.v. *Ikta'*.

28 Bishop Otto of Freising, *Chronicon*, G. H. Pertz (ed.), *MGH, SSRG* (Hannover: Hahn, 1867), VII, 33 (pp. 334-35).

29 At Vetralla, a few miles south of Viterbo, in early December 1145.

30 Probably the Seljuk Sultan Sanjar and his nephew. The Sultan and his nephew were defeated by Qatwan near Samarkand on September 9, 1141, by the Gur Khan of Qarā Kithāy, Yeh-lü Ta-shih, with whom Prester John has been convincingly identified by Charles E. Nowell, "The Historical Prester John," *Speculum, XXVIII* (1953), 435-45.

31 Matt. 2:1-16.

Chapter VI

pREACÞING TÞE SECONÐ CRUSAÐE

The news of Edessa's fall reached the West in the late summer of 1145. The astounding news from the East horrified Western Europeans generally, but the situation caught the papacy at an awkward moment. A communal government had been formed in Rome itself and, amid revolutionary fighting, the Pope had been expelled from the city. The reigning pontiff, Eugene III, a Cistercian monk and a disciple of the great and saintly Abbot Bernard of Clairvaux, although alarmed by the situation in the East, could do little personally to alleviate the situation there. What he could do, however, was to appeal for aid for the Latin East from the young French king, Louis VII, and from the French nobility. Accordingly, on December 1, 1145, the Pope addressed to the French monarch a bull, proclaiming a new Crusade:[1]

THE PROCLAMATION OF THE SECOND CRUSADE[2]

Bishop Eugene, Servant of God's Servants, to his dearest son in Christ, Louis, the illustrious and glorious King of the Franks, and to his beloved sons, the princes and all of God's faithful established in Gaul—Greeting and the apostolic benediction.

How much the Roman pontiffs, our predecessors, have labored for the liberation of the Eastern Church, we have learned from the accounts of the ancients and have found written in their acts. For our predecessor, Pope Urban of blessed memory, sounded, as it were, the heavenly clarion and took care to rouse up from the various parts of the world the sons of the Roman Church for the liberation of the East. At his voice the ultramontaine peoples, and especially the very powerful and brave warriors of the French Kingdom, as well as those of Italy, were inflamed by the fire of love. They assembled and, having gathered a very large army, with the help of divine aid they liberated from the defilement of the pagans (not without much shedding of their own blood) that city in which our Savior was willing to suffer for us and in which he left to us, as a memorial of his passion, his glorious sepulcher. . . .

Now, however, because of our sins and those of the people— we cannot speak of it without much grief and lamentation—the city of Edessa, called Rohais in our language . . . has been captured by the enemies of Christ. They have occupied many Christian castles and they have killed the Archbishop of the city, his clergy, and many other Christians there. The relics of the saints, too, have been given over to be trampled upon by the infidel and have been dispersed. We are well aware (and we assume that it is not hidden from your wisdom) how much danger thereby threatens the church of God and all of Christendom. . . .

We therefore beseech, admonish, and command all of you, and we enjoin it for the remission of sins, that those who are on God's side—and especially the more powerful and noble men— that they gird themselves manfully and attack the pagan multitudes . . . liberate the Eastern church, and strive to wrest many thousands of our captive brethren from their hands. . . .

We also . . . decree and confirm by the authority given to us by God, the remission of sins (which our aforesaid predecessor, Pope Urban, established) for those who, prompted by devotion, shall undertake and accomplish such a holy and necessary task. We decree, also, that the wives and sons, goods and possessions of these men shall remain under the protection of Holy Church, of ourselves, and of the archbishops, bishops, and other prelates of the Church of God. We forbid, also by the apostolic authority, that any suit be brought concerning those things which they possessed peacefully at the time they took the cross until such time as there shall be certain tidings of their return or of their death. Since, moreover, those who fight for the Lord ought in no way to concern themselves with costly garments, bodily appearance, dogs, hawks, or other things which are signs of licentiousness, we admonish your prudence in the Lord that those who undertake such holy work shall not be taken up with these things, but shall, with all their strength, devote their attention and diligence to arms, horses, and other things with which they may war on the infidel. Those who are laden with debt to another and who shall, with pure heart, begin the holy journey, shall not pay interest for time past. If they, or others for them, are bound by oath or pledge for the payment of interest, we absolve them by the apostolic authority. It shall be allowed to them also that when, after their relations or the lords to whom their fiefs belong, have been warned, if these people either can not or do not wish to lend them money, then they may freely and without contradiction pledge their lands or other possessions to churches, to churchmen, or to any of the other faithful.

By the ordinance of our aforesaid predecessor and by the God-given authority of Almighty God and of Blessed Peter, prince of the apostles, we grant absolution and remission of sins in such wise that he who shall devotedly undertake so holy a journey and shall persevere in it or shall die therein shall obtain absolution for all of his sins which he shall have confessed with contrite and humble heart and he shall obtain the fruits of eternal reward from him who rewards all.

Given at Vetralla, December the first.

[Trans. James A. Brundage]

The French King's response to the proclamation of the Second Crusade was immediate and enthusiastic. At Christmas time 1145, Louis VII revealed to his courtiers his designs to go to the aid of the Latins in the East. The King met, however, with considerable opposition from his advisors, who believed that the welfare of the kingdom required that the King remain at home. It was agreed, therefore, to defer any action on the project until the following Easter. In the meantime, the King sought the advice of the powerful and renowned Bernard of Clairvaux, who agreed to preach on behalf of the Crusade to the King's court during Easter time at Vezelay:

SAINT BERNARD AT VEZELAY[3]

In the year of the Incarnation of the Word one thousand one hundred forty-six, Louis, the glorious king of the Franks and duke of Aquitaine, the son of King Louis, came to Vezelay at Easter[4] so that he might be worthy of Christ by bearing his cross after him. Louis was twenty-five years old.

When the same pious King held his court at Bourges on the preceding Christmas, he had first revealed the secret in his heart to the bishops and barons of the kingdom, whom he had purposefully summoned for his coronation in greater numbers than usual. The devout Bishop of Langres[5] had at that time preached in his capacity as a bishop about the slaughter and oppression of the Christians and the great insolence of the pagans in Rohais, known in antiquity as Edessa. He had roused many to tears by this lamentable tale and he had admonished them all that they should fight together with their king for the King of all in order to help the Christians. Zeal for the faith burned and glowed in King Louis. He held luxury and temporal glory in contempt and set an example which was better than any sermon. The King, however, could not immediately harvest by his example what the Bishop had sown by his words. Another day was appointed, therefore, namely Easter at Vezelay, when all were to assemble on Passion Sunday. Those who had received the heavenly inspiration were to take on the glory of the cross on the feast of the Resurrection.

The King, meanwhile, continued to press the undertaking and sent emissaries on this matter to Pope Eugene at Rome. They were joyfully received and were sent back with gladness: they brought back a letter sweeter than any honeycomb.[6] The letter enjoined the King to be obedient and prescribed moderation in weapons and clothing. It also contained a promise of the remission of sins for those who took the sweet yoke of Christ[7] as well as a promise of protection for their wives and children and instructions on certain other matters which seemed useful to the holy wisdom and prudence of the Supreme Pontiff. The Pope hoped that he could be present in person so as to be the first to lay his hands on such a holy enterprise, but he could not, since he was hindered by the tyranny of the Romans.[8] He therefore delegated this task to Bernard, the holy Abbot of Clairvaux.

At last the day which the King hoped for arrived. The Abbot, armed with the apostolic authority and with his own sanctity was there at the time and place appointed, together with the very great multitude which had been summoned. Then the King received the insignia of the cross which the Supreme Pontiff had sent to him and so also did many of his nobles. Since there was no place in the fortress which could hold such a multitude, a wooden platform was built for the Abbot in a field outside of

Vezelay, so that he could speak from a high place to the audience standing around him. Bernard mounted the platform together with the King, who wore the cross. When the heavenly instrument had, according to his custom, poured out the dew of the Divine Word, the people on all sides began to clamor and to demand crosses. When he had sowed, rather than passed out, the parcel of crosses which had been prepared, he was forced to tear his clothing into crosses and to sow them too. He labored at this task as long as he was in the town. I shall not attempt to write about the miracles which occurred there at that time and by which it appeared that the Lord was pleased, since if I write about a few of them, it will not be believed that there were more, while if I write about many of them, it may seem that I am overlooking my subject. Finally it was decided that they would start out in a year and everyone returned home rejoicing.

The Abbot indeed covered his robust spirit with a frail and almost moribund body. He flew everywhere to preach and in a short time the number of those who wore the cross had multiplied manyfold. The King took an almost childlike joy in spreading the faith and sent ambassadors to King Roger in Apulia concerning the large army which he hoped to raise. Roger wrote back willingly on all these matters. He also sent back noblemen who pledged his Kingdom as security for the food, shipping, and all other necessities. They further promised that either Roger or his son would go along on the journey. Louis sent other messengers to the Emperor at Constantinople—I do not know his name, for it is not written in the book of life. The Emperor replied with a long and wordy scroll filled with flattery and in which he called our King his holy friend and brother and promised many things which he did not in fact carry out. But these things belong elsewhere! Louis also asked the Hungarian and German kings for market rights and the right of passage and he received letters and messengers from them granting what he desired. Many of the dukes and counts of those areas were inspired by his example and wrote asking to take part in his expedition. Thus everything went along favorably. Meanwhile the news flew. It crossed over to England and reached the remote parts of the other islands. The people of the maritime areas prepared ships so as to accompany the King by sea. [Trans. James A. Brundage]

St. Bernard had become, in fact, the official preacher and the guiding spirit of the Second Crusade. In addition to preaching the Crusade before the French King and his court at Vezelay, Bernard also undertook an ambitious stint of personal preaching before other European kings and clerics. Bernard's eloquence soon secured the enrollment in the Crusade of another monarch, the German King and Emperor, Conrad III.

The abbot's work on behalf of the Crusade was so effective that soon he could report to the Pope that the cities and castles of the West were deserted and that seven women could scarcely find one man to keep them company, since so many able-bodied males had taken the cross and joined the Crusade.

To those areas where he could not travel to preach the Crusade in person, Bernard sent letters urging participation, as he did, for example, in his letter to the people of the English Kingdom:

ST. BERNARD SEEKS ENGLISH PARTICIPATION
IN THE SECOND CRUSADE[9]

I address myself to you, the people of England, in the cause of Christ, in whom lies your salvation. I say this so that the warrant of the Lord and my zeal in his interests may excuse my hardihood in addressing you. I am a person of small account, but my desire for you in Christ is not small. This is my reason and motive for writing, this is why I make bold to address you all by letter. I would have preferred to do so by word of mouth had I but the strength to come to you as I desire.

Now is the acceptable time, now is the day of abundant salvation. The earth is shaken because the Lord of heaven is losing his land, the land in which he appeared to men, in which he lived amongst men for more than thirty years; the land made glorious by his miracles, holy by his blood; the land in which the flowers of his resurrection first blossomed. And now, for our sins, the enemy of the cross has begun to lift his sacrilegious head there, and to devastate with the sword that blessed land, that land of promise. Alas, if there should be none to withstand him, he will soon invade the very city of the living God, overturn the arsenal of our redemption, and defile the holy places which have been adorned by the blood of the Immaculate Lamb. They have cast their greedy eyes especially on the holy sanctuaries of our Christian religion, and they long particularly to violate that couch on which, for our sakes, the Lord of our life fell asleep in death.

What are you doing, you mighty men of valor? What are you doing, you servants of the cross? Will you thus cast holy things to dogs, pearls before swine?[10] How great a number of sinners have here confessed with tears and obtained pardon for their sins since the time when these holy precincts were cleansed of pagan filth by the swords of our fathers! The evil one sees this and is enraged, he gnashes his teeth and withers away in fury. He stirs up his vessels of wrath[11] so that if they do but once lay hands upon these holy places there shall be no sign or trace of piety left. Such a catastrophe would be a source of appalling grief for all time, but it would also be a source of confusion and endless shame for our generation. . . . Do not hesitate. God is good, and were he intent on your punishment he would not have asked of you this present service or indeed have accepted it even had you offered it. Again I say, consider the Almighty's goodness and pay heed to his plans of mercy. He puts himself under obligation to you, or rather feigns to do so, that he can help you to satisfy your obligations toward himself. . . . I call blessed the generation that can seize an opportunity of such rich indulgence as this, blessed to be alive in this year of jubilee, this year of God's choice. The blessing is spread throughout the whole world, and all the world is flocking to receive this badge of immortality.

Your land is well known to be rich in young and vigorous men. The world is full of their praises, and the renown of their courage is on the lips of all. Gird yourselves therefore like men and take up arms with joy and with zeal for your Christian name, in order to "take vengeance on the heathen and curb the nations." For how long will your men continue to shed Christian blood; for how long will they continue to fight amongst themselves? You attack each other, you slay each other and by each other you are slain. What is this savage craving of yours? Put a stop to it now, for it is not fighting but foolery. Thus to risk both soul and body is not brave but shocking, is not strength but folly. But now, O mighty soldiers, O men of war, you have a cause for which you can fight without danger to your souls; a cause in which to conquer is glorious and for which to die is gain.

But to those of you who are merchants, men quick to seek a bargain, let me point out the advantages of this great opportunity. Do not miss them. Take up the sign of the cross and you will find indulgence for all the sins which you humbly confess. The cost is small, the reward is great. . . .

For the rest, not I but the Apostle warns you, brethren, not to believe every spirit.[12] I have heard with great joy of the zeal for God's glory which burns in your midst, but your zeal needs the timely restraint of knowledge. The Jews are not to be persecuted, killed, or even put to flight. Ask anyone who knows the Sacred Scriptures what he finds foretold of the Jews in the psalm. "Not for their destruction do I pray," it says.[13] The Jews are for us the living words of Scripture, for they remind us always of what our Lord suffered. They are dispersed all over the world so that by expiating their crime they may be everywhere the living witnesses of our redemption. . . . Under Christian princes they endure a hard captivity, but "they only wait for the time of their deliverance. . . ." I will not mention those Christian money lenders, if they can be called Christian, who, where there are no Jews, act, I grieve to say, in a manner worse than any Jew. If the Jews are completely wiped out, what will become of our hope for their promised salvation, their eventual conversion? If the pagans were similarly subjugated to us then, in my opinion, we should wait for them rather than seek them out with swords. But as they have now begun to attack us, it is necessary for those of us who do not carry a sword in vain to repel them with force. It is an act of Christian piety both "to vanquish the proud" and also "to spare the subjected,"[14] especially those for whom we have a law and a promise, and whose flesh was shared by Christ, whose name be for ever blessed. *[Trans. Dom Bruno Scott James]*

As the Crusade was preached by Bernard and the bishops of the West, not only were more recruits enlisted for the expedition, but, in addition, the objectives of the Crusade itself were enlarged. Soon, Pope Eugene was moved to extend the privileges which he had granted to the Crusaders in his bull of 1145[15] to those Christian knights and soldiers who would undertake to fight the Moslems in Spain. Then, in the spring of 1147, the Pope authorized the opening of another Crusading front when he proclaimed a Crusade against the heathen Slavs in eastern Germany. St. Bernard of Clairvaux also undertook to gather recruits for this expedition as well as for the Crusade in the East.

ST. BERNARD APPEALS FOR CRUSADERS
TO FIGHT THE SLAVS[16]

To his lords and reverend fathers, the archbishops, bishops, and princes, and to all the faithful of God, the spirit of strength and deliverance, from Bernard, styled Abbot of Clairvaux.

Without doubt it has been heard in your land, without doubt the news has gone forth in oft repeated words that God has stirred up the spirit of kings and princes to take vengeance on the pagans. . . . How good and great is the bounty of God's mercy! But the evil one sees this and resents it, he gnashes his teeth and withers away in fury, for he is losing many of those whom he held bound by various crimes and enormities. Abandoned men are now being converted, turning aside from evil, and making ready to do good. But the evil one feared far more the damage he would incur from the conversion of the pagans, when he heard that their tale was to be completed, and that the whole of Israel was to find salvation. This is what he believes to be threatening him now and with all his evil cunning he is endeavoring to see how he can best oppose such a great good. He has raised up evil seed, wicked pagan sons,° whom, if I may say so, the might of Christendom has endured too long, shutting its eyes to those who with evil intent lie in wait, without crushing their poisoned heads under its heel. . . . Because the Lord has committed to our insignificance the preaching of this Crusade, we make known to you that at the council of the king, bishops, and princes who had come together at Frankfort, the might of Christians was armed against the Slavs, and that for the complete wiping out or, at any rate, the conversion of these peoples, they have put on the cross, the sign of our salvation; and we, by virtue of our authority, promised them the same spiritual privileges as those enjoy who set out toward Jerusalem. Many took the cross on the spot, the rest we encouraged to do so, so that all Christians who have not yet taken the cross for Jerusalem may know that they will obtain the same spiritual privileges by undertaking this expedition, if they do so according to the advice of the bishops and princes. We utterly forbid that for any

° The Slavs.

reason whatsoever a truce should be made with these peoples, either for the sake of money or for the sake of tribute, until such a time as, by God's help, they shall be either converted or wiped out. We speak to you, archbishops and bishops, and urge you to oppose any such plan for a truce with all your strength, and to watch with the greatest care this matter, and to apply all the zeal of which you are capable to seeing that it is carried through manfully. . . . The uniform of this army, in clothes, in arms, and in all else, will be the same as the uniform of the other, for it is fortified with the same privileges. It has pleased all those who were gathered together at Frankfort to decree that a copy of this letter should be carried everywhere and that the bishops and priests should proclaim it to the people of God, and arm them with the holy cross against the enemies of the cross of Christ, and that they should all meet at Magdeburg on the feast of the Apostles Peter and Paul. *[Trans. Dom Bruno Scott James]*

By the late spring of 1147, the armies were ready to set out and to fight Christendom's enemies on three fronts: against the Moslems in the East and in Spain and against the Slavs in eastern Germany. Papal legates were appointed to accompany the principal armies, and the Crusade was ready to commence its formidable task.

CHAPTER VI

1 The modern literature on the Second Crusade is comparatively scanty. The best treatments of this Crusade in English are those by Runciman, *Crusades*, II, 247-88, and Virginia G. Berry, in Setton, *Crusades*, I, 463-512. There is a valuable article by Giles Constable, "The Second Crusade as Seen by Contemporaries," in *Traditio*, IX (1953), 213-79. The most exhaustive treatment of the Second Crusade is that of Bernhard Kugler, *Studien zur Geschichte des zweiten Kreuzzuges* (Stuttgart: Ebner and Seubert, 1866). On St. Bernard's part in the Crusade, the literature is much more extensive. See especially André Séguin's article, "Bernard et la seconde Croisade," in *Bernard de Clairvaux* (Paris: Editions d'Alsatia, 1953) and also E. Willems, "Cîteaux et la seconde Croisade," in *Revue d'histoire ecclésiastique*, XLIX (1954), 116-51. In addition, see the general biographies of St. Bernard: Watkin Wynn Williams, *Saint Bernard of Clairvaux* (Manchester: Manchester University Press, 1935); Elphege Vacandard, *La Vie de Saint Bernard, abbe de Clairvaux* (3d ed.; Paris: V. LeCoffre, 1902); Alibe J.

Luddy, *Life and Teaching of St. Bernard* (Dublin: M. H. Gill and Son, 1927).

2 The bull *Quantum Praedecessores*, text taken from Bishop Otto of Freising, *Gesta Friderici Imperatoris*, G. H. Pertz, (ed.), *MGH*, *SSRG* (Hanover: Hahn, 1867), I, 35 (pp. 55-58).

3 Odo of Deuil, *La Croisade de Louis VII roi de France*, I, Henri Waquet (ed.), ("Documents relatifs à l'histoire des croisades," Vol. 3, [Paris: Paul Guethner, 1949]), pp. 20-23.

4 March 31, 1146.

5 Geoffrey of Rochetaille, former prior of Clairvaux and disciple of St. Bernard.

6 Cf. Ps. 19:10.

7 Cf. Matt. 11:30.

8 See above, p. 86.

9 *The Letters of St. Bernard*, Bruno Scott James (trans.), (London: Burns Oates, 1953), pp. 460-63.

10 Matt. 7:6.

11 Rom. 9:22.

12 I John 4:1.

13 Ps. 58:12.

14 *Aeneid*, VI, 853.

15 See above, pp. 86-88.

16 *The Letters of St. Bernard*, pp. 466-68.

Chapter VII

THE SECONO CRUSAOE IN ACTION

I

The first groups to depart on the Second Crusade were companies of Anglo-Norman and Flemish sailors and troops who sailed from Dartmouth on May 19, 1147, bound for Spain to take part in the Spanish phase of the Crusade. The principal objective of these Crusaders was the conquest of a number of strong positions on the western coast of the Iberian peninsula, among them the important city of Lisbon, in what is now Portugal.[1] Affonso I of Portugal with his army was already in the field there when the Anglo-Norman contingents landed on the beaches close by, late in June, 1147.

THE IBERIAN FRONT: THE CAPTURE OF LISBON[2]

The city of Lisbon at the time of our arrival consisted of sixty thousand families paying taxes—this figure includes the suburbs round about, except the free ones, which pay taxes to no one. A circular wall there surrounds the top of the hill and, at the left and right, the city walls descend to the banks of the Tagus River. The suburbs, down below the city wall, are cut into the banks of the river in such a way that each of them has a superbly fortified citadel. The place is girded with pitfalls. The city was populous beyond belief, for, as we learned from its alcayde, or governor, after the capture of the city, it had one hundred fifty-four thousand men, not counting women and children, but including the citizens of Scantarem[3] who had been expelled during this year from their stronghold and who were living in Lisbon as guests and immigrants. This number also included the leading citizens of Cintra, Almada, and Palmela, and many merchants from all parts of Spain and Africa. Although there were many citizens, the city had only fifteen thousand lances and shields with which to arm its men. They therefore came out in shifts, exchanging their weapons with one another, as their prince decreed.

The city's buildings were jammed so closely together that it was scarcely possible, save in the merchants' quarters, to find a street more than eight feet wide. The reason for such a dense population was that there was no established religion there.* Each man was a law unto himself. As a result the basest element from every part of the world had gathered there, like the bilge water of a ship, a breeding ground for every kind of lust and impurity. . . .

On the vigil of St. Peter the Apostle[4] we arrived there at the dinner hour. After the meal some of our men landed from the ships on the shore next to the city. The Moors opposed their landing, but they were unable to withstand our forces and were driven back, not without losses, to the gate of the suburb. Saher of Archelle, however, angered at the enemy's scheme, called our men back from the attack and thanked God that, unlike those who had previously attempted this task, we had had a different experience at the outset. He convoked those who were there and ordered that the tents be pitched atop the hills which overlooked the town, barely a stick's throw away. He held that it would be a shame to give ground after the first brush with the enemy, lest we seem to be yielding to them. All those present favored his stand. When the first watch of the night came, however, only two tents—those of Hervey of Glanville and Saher of Archelle—had been pitched, for all the others had gone back to the ships. Although there were but a few of us—a mere thirty-nine—we kept watch, not without fear, through the night and so celebrated the solemn vigil of St. Peter with our hauberks on. In the morning everyone pitched his tent as quickly as he could, as if they had not known before about our situation. As had previously been arranged, the bishops who were with us went to the King to make

* Presumably the connection between the lack of an established faith and the density of the city's population lay in the fact that Lisbon had become a refuge for persons who were persecuted for religious reasons elsewhere.

him come out to meet us. They returned with him in a short time, since he had been in the vicinity for more than eight days awaiting our arrival. He had heard of our coming from those of our men who had separated from our expedition and had come in five ships after a five-day sail from Dartmouth. This group had arrived eight days earlier than we did. When the King arrived, therefore, almost all of us, rich and poor, went out to meet him as usually happens in such a mob. When the King inquired who were the chief men among us, or whose advice carried most weight with us, or if we had entrusted the charge of replying for the whole army to anyone, he was told in short order that we had so-and-so as our chief men, that their advice and actions carried the most weight, but that they had not yet decided to whom they would entrust the office of spokesman. . . .

Representatives were elected from among our leaders, together with those of the men from Cologne and Flanders, so that they could act on our behalf with the King and reach a definite agreement between us and him. Later, the representatives together with the King, the Archbishop and the bishops, the clergy, and the laity caused the protocol of the confirmation of the agreements to be published before everyone in these words:

"Let the terms of the agreement reached between me and the Franks be known to all sons of the Church, both present and to come. Namely that I, Affonso, King of the Portuguese, with the consent of all my people, so that it may be remembered by future generations, do provide by this protocol of confirmation that the Franks who shall remain with me in the siege of the city of Lisbon shall have and take into their power and possession the goods of whatever kind belonging to the enemy and that I and my men shall have no part whatever of them. The Franks shall freely have the ransom money from the enemy prisoners who are taken alive and who wish to be ransomed. The prisoners, moreover, they shall release to me. If they should, perchance, take the city, they shall have it and hold it until it has been searched and despoiled, both of prisoners for ransom and of everything else. Then, when it has been as thoroughly searched as they wish, they shall turn it over to me. Afterwards, the city and the conquered territory shall, under my direction, be divided among the Franks according to ranks, as these are best known to me, to be held in accordance with the most honorable customs and liberties of the Franks.

Over them there shall be reserved for me only the power of an *advocatus*.[5] I release firmly and in good faith, moreover, the ships and goods of the men who shall have been together with me at the siege of Lisbon and their heirs from all of the commercial tax which is commonly known as the *pedatica* from this time onward in perpetuity throughout my whole land. . . ."

Twenty sure hostages, bishops and laymen, were given on oath and warranty, on behalf of the King for the observance of this agreement. The King swore, moreover, that he would observe the treaty and agreement aforesaid. He further agreed that he would not desert us unless he were stricken with a mortal sickness or unless his lands were occupied by the enemy. . . . We also bound ourselves likewise to uphold the agreement, took an oath, and gave twenty hostages. . . .

When morning[6] came the constables and leaders of our side went again to the King's court at about the ninth hour of the day in order to turn over the hostages and to attend to the many things necessary for the siege. Those of our boys who were carrying slings, meanwhile, provoked the enemy into advancing onto the field with the result that, being the more provoked by the slinging of stones from a distance, the enemy ventured a major attack. As our men, little by little, armed themselves, the enemy shut themselves within the suburb. They threw stones from the roofs of the houses which were enclosed by parapets, and thus they made it difficult for our men to enter. Our men, who were looking for an opening whereby they might get in, if there were such a thing, drove them back into the middle of the suburb. There they put up a strong resistance to us. Our men, little by little, increased in numbers and made a fiercer attack. Many, meanwhile, were struck by arrows and the missiles of the balistas and fell, for the volley of stones made it impossible to approach closer. Thus a great part of the day was spent. Finally, at sunset, our men got through some twisting passages which were scarcely passable even for unarmed men and, after a major encounter, occupied part of a hill. . . .

The Moors, meanwhile, made frequent sorties against our men by day because they held three gates against us. With two of these gates on the side of the city and one on the sea, they had an easy way to get in and out. On the other hand, it was difficult for our men to organize themselves. The sorties caused casualties on both sides, but theirs were always greater than ours. While we kept watch, meanwhile, under their walls through the days and nights, they heaped derision and many insults upon us. They considered us worthy of a thousand deaths, especially since they thought that we spurned our own things as vile and lusted after others' goods as precious. Nor did they recall doing us any injury, save that if they had anything of the best quality in their possession we might consider them unworthy of having it and judge it worthy of our possession. They taunted us with the many children who were going to be born at home while we were gone and said that our wives would not be anxious about our deaths, since home was well supplied with little bastards. They promised that any of us who survived would go home miserable and poverty-stricken and they mocked us and gnashed their teeth at us. They also continuously attacked Blessed Mary, the mother of God, with insults and with vile and abusive words, which infuriated us. They said that we venerated the son of a poor woman with a worship equal to that due to God, for we held that he was a God and the Son of God, when it is apparent that there is only one God who began all things that have begun and that he has no one coeval with him and no partaker in his divinity. . . . They attacked us with these and similar calumnies. They showed to us, moreover, with much derision the symbol of the cross. They spat upon it and wiped the feces from their posteriors with it. At last they urinated on it, as on some despicable thing, and threw our cross at us. . . .

[Finally, after the siege had lasted for nearly seventeen weeks, on October 23 we] decided, when all had returned to the camp, to enter the town at sword's point. The men of Cologne and the Flemings, meanwhile, were indignant because the King seemed to be favoring the hostages. They rushed armed out of their camp to sieze the hostages violently from the King's camp and to take vengeance on them. All around there was tumult and clashing of arms. We were midway between the King's camp and theirs, still talking and waiting, and we reported to the King what was being prepared. The Flemings' leaders, Christian and the Count of Aerschot, although they were barely armed, put a stop to the tumult among their men as soon as they learned of it. When the tumult had been quieted they went to pacify the King, assuring him that they were not involved in this action. After he had taken surety from them and had finally quieted the Flemings down, the King ordered them to put down their arms, asserting roundly that he would put off the siege until the next day. It was decided, therefore, on the following day that all the followers of each of our leaders would swear fealty to the King on behalf of themselves and their people, to be kept so long as they remained in his land.

When these matters had been agreed upon by both sides, the arrangements which the Moors had proposed on the previous day for the delivery of the city, were accepted. It was decided among us that one hundred and forty of our armed men and one hundred and sixty of the Flemish and the Cologne contingents should enter the city before everyone else and peacefully take over the fortifications of the upper fortress so that the enemy might bring all of their money and possessions there and give a guarantee by swearing before our men. When all these things had been collected, the city was then to be searched by our men. If any further possessions were found, the man in whose house they were discovered was to pay for it with his head. When everyone had thus been despoiled, they were to be let go in peace outside of the city. When the gates had been opened and those who were chosen were allowed to enter, the men of Cologne and the Flemings thought up a sly method of deceiving us: they requested our men to allow them to enter first for the sake of their honor. When they had received permission and got a chance to enter first, they slipped in more than two hundred of their men, in addition to those who had been selected. These were also in addition to others who had already slipped through the ruined places in the walls which lay open to them, while none of our men, except those selected, had presumed to enter.

The Archbishop and the other bishops went in front of us with the Lord's cross and then our leaders entered together with the King and those who had been selected. How everyone rejoiced! What special glory for all! What great joy and what a great abundance there was of pious tears when, to the praise and honor of God and of the most Holy Virgin Mary the saving cross was placed atop the highest tower to be seen by all as a symbol of the city's subjection, while the Archbishop and bishops, together with the clergy and everyone, intoned with wonderful rejoicing the *Te Deum Laudamus* and the *Asperges Me*, together with devout prayers.

The King, meanwhile, went around the strong walls of the fortress on foot. The men of Cologne and the Flemings, when they saw in the city so many spurs to their greed, did not observe their oaths or their religious guarantees. They ran hither and yon. They plundered. They broke down doors. They rummaged through the interior of every house. They drove the citizens away and harassed them improperly and unjustly. They destroyed clothes and utensils. They treated virgins shamefully. They acted as if right and wrong were the same. They secretly took away everything which should have been common property. They even cut the throat of the elderly Bishop of the city, slaying him against all right and justice. . . . The Normans and the English, however, for whom faith and religion were of the greatest importance, contemplating what such actions might lead to, remained quietly in their assigned position, preferring to stay their hands from looting rather than to violate the obligations of their faith and their oathbound association. This affair covered the Count of Aerschot, Christian, and their leaders with very great shame, for while their men had patently disregarded their oath, ours, by staying out of it, made the greed of the others plain. Finally they came to themselves and besought our men with earnest prayers that we should occupy the remaining sections of the city together with them so that, after the loot had been divided, all the injuries and thefts might be discussed peacefully and they would be prepared to make amends for the evils they had presumed to commit. The enemy, when they had been despoiled in the city, left the town through three gates continuously from Saturday morning until the following Wednesday.[7] There was such a multitude of people that it seemed as if all of Spain were mingled in the crowd.

Thereafter a miracle worthy of great admiration was reported: for fifteen days before the capture of the city, the enemy's food supplies had become inedible because of an intolerable stench. Afterward we tasted them and found them pleasing and acceptable, both to us and to the enemy. When the city was despoiled, there was found in the cellars some eight thousand seams[8] of wheat and barley and some twelve thousand pints[9] of oil. . . . There was discovered in their temple, which rises on seven ranks of columns with arches atop them, nearly two hundred corpses as well as more than eight hundred other persons who were sick and who had remained there in all their squalor and filth.

[*Trans. James A. Brundage*]

II

When the Anglo-Norman forces began their attacks on Lisbon, the German forces who were to take part in the expeditions against the Slavs were still attempting, rather hectically, to assemble and to organize. The Crusade against the Slavs was the outgrowth of some two hundred years of warfare in which German soldiers and colonists had gradually pushed their way eastward in central and northeastern Germany. Conquest and colonization in this territory had gone hand-in-hand for generations and the Crusade against the Slavs in 1147 was complicated by the fact that several of the leaders of the Crusade were far more interested in preserving Slavic territory in suitable condition for agricultural exploitation than they were either in exterminating or in converting the Slavs themselves.[10] The situation was further complicated by the fact that in the neighborhood of Bremen the Slavs were well aware of the campaign planned against them and took advantage of their foreknowledge to strike at the Crusaders before the Crusading armies were ready to commence their campaign.

The Saxon and Danish forces which participated in this expedition were dilatory in their preparations, divided as to their exact objectives, and feeble in the prosecution of their campaign. The result was, as might have been expected under these circumstances, unimpressive. The siege of the Wendish stronghold of Dobin was fitfully and unenthusiastically prosecuted until, at last, a peace treaty was concluded which called for the Slavs to renounce their pagan religion, to return the Crusaders whom they had captured, and to ally themselves with the Count of Holstein. The first two of these conditions were, in fact, never carried out.

The siege of Demmin, the stronghold of the Slavic Liutizi, was also a fiasco and resulted only in the ravaging of the countryside roundabout the town. Another group of Crusaders attacked the Christian city of Stettin, for reasons which seem to have had no close connection with the ostensible purposes of the Crusade. This group, too, returned home without having gained its objective.

This phase of the Crusade, then, must be pronounced a complete failure: its only result was to create further tension between German and Slav and to add more fuel to the smoldering fire of mutual distrust between pagans and Christians in Germany.[11]

III

Meanwhile, the armies bent upon relieving the situation of the Latin states in the East had also been assembled and had started on their way. Two main armies were engaged in this phase of the Second Crusade: a German army, led by the German king and emperor, Conrad III, and a French army, led by King Louis VII. Both of these groups took the same general route to the East, the one which had been followed by Peter the Hermit and the Popular Crusade fifty years earlier. The German army assembled at Nuremberg in May 1147, marched without serious incident through Hungary, and reached the Byzantine frontier at Branits about July 20. There the Germans were met with the now familiar Byzantine demand for an oath to guarantee that the Crusaders would do no injury to Byzantine territory or interests. The oath was taken and the Germans marched peacefully into the Bulgarian province of Byzantium. Some friction developed between the German troops and the Byzantines as the Germans headed for Constantinople. At one point, indeed, Conrad is said to have threatened to attack Constantinople itself. Nothing came of this threat, however, and in mid-September the German forces crossed the straits into Asia Minor. From Chalcedon, where the Germans landed, they decided to push on into the hinterland of Anatolia without waiting to join forces with the French. The folly of this decision became clear toward the end of October, for as the Germans passed near Dorylaeum, they were ambushed by an enormous Seljuk army. The German army was nearly annihilated and the Emperor himself only barely managed to escape the general slaughter. Conrad and his few remaining German troops made their way as best they could back to Nicaea, where they were only too willing now to join the French forces.

While the Germans were marching heedlessly toward defeat, the French army, led by King Louis VII, was following in their tracks, about a month behind. The story of their journey is related by the French King's chaplain, Odo of Deuil:

THE FRENCH ARMY IN CENTRAL EUROPE[12]

In what we have written the description of outstanding actions is given as a good example; the names of the cities are given to show the route of the journey; the description of the character of the localities is given as a guide to show what types of provisions are needed. Since there will always be pilgrims to the Holy Sepulcher, it is hoped that they will be more cautious in view of our experiences.

The rich cities of Metz, Worms, Würzburg, Ratisbon, and Passau, then, lie a three-day journey from one another. From the last named city it is a five-day journey to Wiener-Neustadt and from there it takes one day to reach the Hungarian border. The country in between these towns is forested and provisions must be brought from the towns, since the countryside cannot provide enough for an army. There are plenty of rivers there and also springs and meadows. When I passed through that area the mountains seemed rugged to me. Now, however, compared to Romania,[13] I would call it a plain. This side of Hungary is bordered by muddy water. On the other side it is separated from Bulgaria by a clear stream. The Drave River is in the middle of Hungary. One bank of the river is steep and the other has a gentle slope, so that it is shaped like a ball. The result of this is that when even a little rain falls and is added to the water of the nearby swamps, even rather distant places are flooded. We heard that many of the Germans who preceded us were suddenly flooded out there. When we came to the place where their camp had been, we could scarcely ford it. We had only a few small boats and it was therefore necessary to make the horses swim. They found it easy to get in but hard to get out; however, with some work and God's protection they came across without losses.

All the rest of this country is covered with lakes, swamps, and springs—if springs can be made by travellers, even in the summer, by scraping the earth a little bit—except for the Danube, which follows a straight enough course and carries the wealth of many areas by ship to the noble city of Gran. This country is such a great food-producing area that Julius Caesar's commissariat is said to have been located there. The marketing and exchange facilities there were sufficient for our needs. We crossed Hungary in fifteen days.

From there, at the entrance to Bulgaria, the fortress called the Bulgarian Belgrade presented itself; it is so called to distinguish it from the Hungarian town of the same name. One day from Belgrade, with a river between them, lies the poor little town of Branicevo. Beyond these towns the country is, so to speak, forested meadow or crop-producing woods. It is bountiful in good things which grow by themselves and it would be good for other things if it had any farmers. It is not flat, nor is it rugged with mountains; rather it is watered by streams and very clear springs which flow between the hills, vines, and usable fields. It lacks any rivers, and between there and Constantinople we had no use for our boats. Five days from this place lies Nish, which, though small, is the first city of this section of Greece. The cities of Nish, Sofia, Philippopolis, and Adrianople are four days apart from each other and from the last of these it is five days to Constantinople. The countryside in between is flat. It is full of villages and forts and abounds in all kinds of good things. On the right and left there are mountains close enough to be seen. These are so long that they enclose a wide, rich, and pleasant plain. . . .

Thus far we had been at play, for we had neither suffered any damages from men's malice nor had we feared any dangers from the plots of cunning men. From the time when we entered Bulgaria and the land of the Greeks, however, both the strength and morale of the army were put to the test. In the impoverished town of Branicevo, as we were about to enter an uninhabited area, we loaded up with supplies, most of which came via the Danube from Hungary. There was such a number of boats there, brought by the Germans, that the populace's supplies of firewood and timber for building were assured for a long time. Our men took the smaller boats across the river and bought supplies from a certain Hungarian fortress which was not far away. Here we first encountered the *stamina,* a copper coin. We unhappily gave —or rather, lost—five *denarii* for one of them and a mark[14] for twelve *solidi.* Thus the Greeks were tainted with perjury at the very entrance to their country. You may remember that, as has been said, their representatives had sworn, on the Emperor's behalf, that they would furnish us with a proper market and exchange. We crossed the rest of this desolate country and entered a most beautiful and wealthy land which stretches without interruption to Constantinople. Here we first began to receive injuries and to take notice of them. The other areas had sold us supplies properly and had found us peaceful. The Greeks, however, shut up their cities and fortresses and sent their merchandise down to us on ropes suspended from the walls. The supplies purveyed in this manner, however, were insufficient for our multitude. The pilgrims, therefore, secured the necessary supplies by plundering and looting, since they could not bear to suffer want in the midst of plenty.

It seemed to some that the Germans who had preceded us were at fault in this respect, since they had looted everything and we discovered that they had burned several settlements outside the walls of towns. The story must be told, although reluctantly. Outside of the walls of Philippopolis was a noble town inhabited by Latin peoples who sold a great many supplies to travellers for profit. When the Germans settled down in the taverns there, a joker was present, as bad luck would have it. Although he did not know their language, he sat down, made a sign, and got a drink. After guzzling for a long time, he took a charmed snake out of his pocket and placed it in his schooner, which he had deposited on the ground. He went on to play other joker's tricks among people of whose language and customs he was ignorant. The Germans rose up in horror, as if they had seen a monster, seized the entertainer, and tore him to pieces. They blamed everyone for the misdeeds of one man and declared that the Greeks had tried to murder them with poison. The town was aroused by the tumult in the suburb and the Duke came out beyond the walls with a group of his men to settle the disturbance. The Germans, whose eyes were bleary with wine and anger, saw, not unarmed men, but a posse. The angry Germans, therefore, rushed upon the men who had come to preserve peace in the belief that they were going to take revenge for the murder. The Germans snatched up their bows—for these are their weapons—and went out once more to turn to flight those from whom they had fled. They killed and wounded the Greeks and when all the Greeks had been expelled from the suburb, the Germans stopped. Many of the Germans were killed there, especially those who had gone into the inns, for, in order to get their money, the Greeks threw them into caves. When the Germans had plucked up their spirits and had taken up their weapons again, they returned and, in order to redress their shame and the slaughter of their men, they burned nearly everything outside of the walls.

The Germans were also unbearable to us. On one occasion some of our men wished to get away from the crowding of the multitude around the King. They therefore went on ahead and stayed near the Germans. Both they and the Germans went to market, but the Germans would not allow the Franks to buy anything until they got enough for themselves. From this arose a brawl, or rather a squabble, for when one man denounces another whom he does not understand in a loud voice, that is a squabble. The Franks struck them and the Germans struck back. The Franks then returned from the market with their supplies. The Germans, who were numerous, were scornful of the pride of a few Franks and took up arms against them. The Germans attacked them fiercely and the Franks, who were armed in a similar fashion, resisted spiritedly. God put an end to this wickedness, for night soon fell. . . .

Thus, as the Germans went forward they disturbed everything and for this reason the Greeks fled from our peaceful Prince who followed the Germans. Nonetheless, the congregation of the churches and all the clergy came out from the cities with their icons and other Greek paraphernalia and they always received our King with due honor and with fear. . . .

[*Trans. James A. Brundage*]

The French forces arrived at Constantinople on October 4, 1147. There they were both impressed by the splendor of the city and alarmed by the suspicious actions of the Greeks:

THE FRENCH ARMY AT CONSTANTINOPLE[15]

Constantinople is the glory of the Greeks. Rich in fame, richer yet in wealth, the city is triangular in shape, like a ship's sail. In its inner angle lies Santa Sophia and the Palace of Constantine, in which there is a chapel honored for its sacred relics. The city is hemmed in on two sides by the sea: approaching the city, we had on the right the Arm of St. George and on the left a certain estuary[16] which branches off from it and flows on for almost four miles. There is set what is called the Palace of Blachernae, which,

The Second Crusade in Action

although it is rather low, yet, rises to eminence because of its elegance and its skillful construction. On its three sides the palace offers to its inhabitants the triple pleasure of gazing alternately on the sea, the countryside, and the town. The exterior of the palace is of almost incomparable loveliness and its interior surpasses anything that I can say about it. It is decorated throughout with gold and various colors and the floor is paved with cleverly arranged marble. Indeed, I do not know whether the subtlety of the art or the preciousness of the materials gives it the greater beauty or value. On the third side of the city's triangle there are fields. This side is fortified by towers and a double wall which extends for nearly two miles, from the sea to the palace. This wall is not especially strong, and the towers are not very high, but the city trusts, I think, in its large population and in its ancient peace. Within the walls there is vacant land which is cultivated with hoes and plows. Here there are all kinds of gardens which furnish vegetables for the citizens. Subterranean conduits flow into the city under the walls to furnish the citizens with an abundance of fresh water. The city is rather squalid and smelly and many places are afflicted with perpetual darkness. The rich build their houses so as to overhang the streets and leave these dark and dirty places for travellers and for the poor. There murder and robberies occur, as well as other sordid crimes which love the dark. Life in this city is lawless, since it has as many lords as it has rich men and almost as many thieves as poor men. Here the criminal feels neither fear nor shame, since crime is not punished by law nor does it ever fully come to light. Constantinople exceeds the average in everything—it surpasses other cities in wealth and also in vice. It has many churches which are unequal to Santa Sophia in size, though not in elegance. The churches are admirable for their beauty and equally so for their numerous venerable relics of the saints. Those who could enter them did so, some out of curiosity in order to see them, and some out of faithful devotion.

The King also was guided on a visit to the holy places by the Emperor. As they returned, the King dined with the Emperor at the latter's insistence. The banquet was as glorious as the banqueters; the handsome service, the delicious food, and the witty conversation satisfied eyes, tongue, and ears alike. Many of the King's men feared for him there, but he had placed his trust in

God and with faith and courage he feared nothing. Since he harbored no wicked designs himself, he was not quick to believe that others harbored wicked designs on him. Even though the Greeks gave no evidence of their treachery, however, I believe that they would not have shown such vigilant helpfulness if their intentions were honest. They were concealing the grievances for which they were going to take revenge after we crossed the Arm of St. George. It should not be held against them, however, that they kept the city gates closed against the commoners, since they had burned many of the Greeks' houses and olive trees, either because of a lack of wood or else because of the insolence and drunkenness of fools. The King frequently had the ears, hands, and feet of some of them cut off, but he was unable to restrain their madness in this way.

[Trans. James A. Brundage]

The French forces crossed the straits into Asia Minor about October 16, 1147, and then headed straightway into the hinterland of Anatolia or, as Odo calls it, Romania:

THE FRENCH ARMY IN ASIA MINOR[17]

Romania, furthermore, is a very wide land with rugged, stony mountains. It extends south to Antioch and is bounded by Turkey on the east. All of it was formerly under Greek rule, but the Turks now possess a great part of it and, after expelling the Greeks, have destroyed another part of it. In the places where the Greeks still hold fortresses, they do not pay taxes. Such are the servile conditions in which the Greeks hold the land which French strength liberated when the Franks conquered Jerusalem.[18] This indolent people would have lost it all, save for the fact that they have brought in soldiers of other nations to defend themselves. They are always losing, but since they possess a great deal, they do not lose everything at once. The strength of other peoples, however, is not sufficient for a people which totally lacks strength of its own. Nicomedia first made this clear to us: located among briars and brambles, its towering ruins demonstrated its ancient glory and the slackness of its present masters. In vain does a certain estuary of the sea flow from the Arm and terminate after a three-day journey at Nicomedia to better the city's facilities.

From Nicomedia three routes of various lengths and quality lead to Antioch. The road which turns to the left is the shorter of them and, if there were no obstacles along it, it could be traversed in three weeks. After twelve days, however, it reaches Konya, the Sultan's capital, which is a very noble city. Five days beyond the Turkish territory this road reaches the land of the Franks. A strong army fortified by faith and numbers would make light of this obstacle if it were not frightened by the snow-covered mountains in the winter. The road running to the right is more peaceful and better supplied than the other, but the winding seacoast which it follows delays the traveller three times over and its rivers and torrents in the winter are as frightful as the snow and the Turks on the other road. On the middle road the conveniences and difficulties of the other routes are tempered. It is longer but safer than the shorter road, shorter and safer than the long road, but poorer. The Germans who preceded us, therefore, had a disagreement. Many of them set out with the Emperor through Konya on the left hand road under sinister omens. The rest turned to the right under the Emperor's brother, a course which was unfortunate in every way. The middle road fell to our lot and so the misfortunes of the other two sides were tempered.

[Trans. James A. Brundage]

Though they were more fortunate than the other forces which had preceded them into Anatolia, the French expedition's journey through the peninsula was difficult, slow, and painful. The rugged countryside, the continual harassment of the troops by the Turks, the persistent difficulties with supplies and communications, all combined to discourage the leaders and to make inroads upon the army's strength. As the French forces pushed further during the winter of 1147-1148, their despair deepened. Turkish raids took a mounting toll, while the weather impeded progress and did its own share in weakening the morale of the men. By the time the Crusaders reached Adalia, King Louis and his advisors had had their fill. Despairing of the prospect of continuing to fight their way toward Jerusalem, the King and his advisors decided to continue the rest of the way by sea. Unfortunately for these plans, however, the available Byzantine shipping was insufficient to transport the whole army and they could not wait indefinitely in Adalia for the arrival of further ships. As a result, King Louis with his household and a scattering of knights from the army were taken aboard the available ships and sailed to St. Simeon, the port city of Antioch, leaving the rest of the Crusading army to continue the journey as best it could. Many of the troops thus left behind at Adalia were killed in combat with the Turks in the vicinity of the town when they attempted to continue their journey by land. Those who managed to break through the Turkish cordon around the city were decimated by further Turkish and Arab attacks and only a handful remained alive to complete their journey to Jerusalem.[19]

CHAPTER VII

1 Runciman, *Crusades, II*, 558-59.

2 Osbernus, *De expugnatione Lyxbonensi*, W. Stubbs (ed.), in *Chronicles and Memorials of the Reign of Richard I* ("Rolls Series" [London: Longmans, 1864]) I, clv-clvi, clx-clxi, clxiv, clxvi, clxxviii-clxxx.

3 An ancient town located on the Tagus, some forty-six miles from Lisbon. It was captured from the Moslems by Affonso Henriques on March 15, 1147.

4 Saturday, June 28, 1147.

5 An *advocatus* was a secular official who acted as the overseer and protector of the property of an ecclesiastical establishment and who received, in return for his services, certain rights and prerogatives in the internal affairs of the institution.

6 June 30, 1147.

7 From October 25 to October 29, 1147.

8 A measure containing about eight bushels.

9 *Sextarii*: measures containing between a pint and a quart.

10 Cf. the objectives of the Slavic Crusade as outlined by St. Bernard, above pp. 94-95.

11 Setton, *Crusades*, I, 479, 492-95; James Westfall Thompson, *Feudal Germany* (Chicago: University of Chicago Press, 1928), pp. 560-61.

12 Odo of Deuil, *La Croisade de Louis VII*, II-III, pp. 30-32, 35-37.

13 Asia Minor, i.e. the land of the Romans. See Robert Lee Wolff's discussion of this term in his article "Romania: The Latin Empire of Constantinople", *Speculum*, XXIII (1948), 1-34.

14 As a monetary unit, the mark was theoretically worth thirteen *solidi* and four *denarii*.

15 Odo of Deuil, *La Croisade de Louis VII*, IV, pp. 44-46.

16 This is the Golden Horn.

17 Odo of Deuil, *La Croisade de Louis VII*, V, pp. 54-55.

18 A reference to the recovery of Byzantine territory in Asia Minor as a result of the First Crusade.

19 Setton, *Crusades*, I, 495-503; Runciman, *Crusades*, II, 268-77; Grousset, *Croisades*, II, 240-45.

The Second Crusade in Action

Chapter VIII

FAILURE OF THE SECOND CRUSADE

King Louis and his entourage arrived in the harbor of St. Simeon, near Antioch, on March 19, 1148. Welcomed by Prince Raymond of Antioch, the King and his retainers settled down to enjoy the friendly reception accorded them by their friends, who saw in King Louis' army the potential saviors of the Principality of Antioch and of all the Latin states. And, indeed, the presence of Louis' cavalry forces greatly strengthened the position of the Latins in the East. Although Louis had lost or been separated from the great majority of the troops and pilgrims who had set out with him originally, the Crusading forces which finally landed at Antioch were far from negligible.

Almost at once, Louis was besieged with urgent requests from various Latin princes and noblemen to lend his army to the favorite military schemes of the individual leaders. To all the plans presented to him, Louis demurred. As a Crusader he had sworn when he took the cross to visit the shrines of Jerusalem, and he quickly made it clear that the fulfillment of this vow was to be his first consideration in the East. King Louis' decision was also influenced, no doubt, by the dubious relationship which had sprung up between his wife, Eleanor of Aquitaine, and Prince Raymond of Antioch, Eleanor's cousin. Accordingly, King Louis and his army were soon on the march again. They stopped for a short time at Tripoli and then continued on their way to Jerusalem. On their arrival there, they found Conrad of Germany, together with a small contingent of the survivors from his army, awaiting them.

After King Louis had fulfilled his vows by worshipping at the holy shrines of Jerusalem, he was ready to consider proposals to put his military forces to use in the defense of the Latin states. On June 24, 1148, a general council of the princes and military leaders then in the Holy Land was held at Acre. After vigorous discussion of various plans of action, the assembly finally decided to concentrate all the available forces on a supreme effort to conquer the ancient, venerable, and wealthy city of Damascus, a vital center of commerce and communications. Accordingly, the forces of the various sovereigns were mustered.[1] The King of Jerusalem, Baldwin III, the Templars and Hospitallers, the various lords of the other Latin states, and the French and German kings joined together to justify by military conquest the enormous effort which had brought the Second Crusade to the East.

THE FIASCO AT DAMASCUS[2]

Damascus is the largest city of lesser Syria and is its metropolis, for as it is said, "Damascus is the head of Syria."[3] The city is also known as the Phoenicia of Lebanon and is named after a certain servant of Abraham who is believed to have founded it. The name means "bloody" or "dripping with gore." The city is located on a plain in a land which is barren and arid, save where it is irrigated by waters brought down for its benefit through ancient canals. A stream descends from a nearby mountain ridge in the highlands of that area and is channeled through the various lower sections of the region so as to fertilize the barren fields. Since there is an abundance of water, the surplus is used to nourish the orchards of fruit trees which are located on either side of the stream. The stream flows along the eastern wall of the city.

When the kings came to the place which had been agreed upon, namely Daria, which was close to Damascus, they organized their lines for battle and settled the order of battle for their legions lest, if they went ahead in disorderly fashion, quarrels should break out among them and hinder their common task.

By the common decision of the princes it was agreed that the King of Jerusalem and his men were to go first, principally because they were supposed to be familiar with the lay of the land.

Failure of the Second Crusade

They were supposed to open the way for the rest who were following them. The French King and the men of his expedition were ordered to take the second, or center, place, so that, if necessary, they could assist those ahead of them. The Emperor, by the same token, was ordered to keep in the third and last place, so that he would be ready to resist the enemy if perchance they should attack from the rear. He was thus to make the forces ahead secure from behind. When the three armies had been placed in proper order, they moved the camp forward and attempted to approach the city.

On the western side of Damascus from which our troops approached, and on the northern side, too, the city enclosed far and wide by orchards which are like a dense woods or a shady forest, extending five miles or more toward Lebanon. These orchards are enclosed by mud walls—rock is not plentiful in that region—so that their ownership will not be in doubt and also to keep out trespassers. The orchards are, therefore, enclosed by defensive walls in such a way that each man's possessions are identified. Paths and public roads, though they are narrow, are left open so that the gardeners and those who have charge of the orchards can make their way to the city with the animals which carry the fruit. These orchards are the city's greatest protection. Because of their density, because of the number of the trees, and because of the narrowness of the roads, it seemed difficult—indeed, almost impossible—for those who wished to approach Damascus to do so from that side. From the beginning, however, our princes had decided to bring the army in through this area to gain access to the city. There was a double reason for this: on the one hand, it was done so that after the most securely guarded areas in which the Damascenes had the greatest faith had been occupied, what remained would seem easy and would be more readily accomplished. On the other hand, the approach was made in this way so that the army would not be deprived of the benefits of food and water.

The King of Jerusalem, therefore, sent his fighting formations in first through those narrow orchard paths. The army could scarcely make headway and did so with great difficulty, both because it was hemmed in by the narrow roads and also because it was hindered by the ambushes of the men who were hidden in the thickets. Also, the army had sometimes to engage the enemies who appeared and seized the circuitous paths.

All the people of Damascus came out together and descended upon the aforesaid orchards in order to block the army's passage both by stealth and by open attack. There were, furthermore, walls and large, tall houses among the orchards. These were defended by soldiers whose possessions lay nearby. They defended the orchard walls by shooting arrows and other missiles and allowed no one to approach them, while the arrows shot from on high made the public roads exceedingly dangerous for those who wished to pass through them. Nor were our men beset with formidable obstacles only on one side. Rather, on every side there was equal peril for the unwary and danger of sudden and unforeseen death. There were, moreover, men with lances hiding inside of the walls. When these men saw our men passing by, they would stab them as they passed, through little peepholes in the walls which were cleverly designed for this purpose, so that those hiding inside could scarcely be seen. Many are said to have perished miserably that day in this way. Countless other kinds of danger, too, faced those who wished to pass through those narrow paths.

As our men became aware of this, they pushed on more fiercely. When they had broken down the barricades in the orchards, they occupied them eagerly. Those whom they discovered within the walls or in the houses, they pierced with their swords or threw into chains as captives. When the townsmen who had come out to defend the orchards heard this, they feared that they would perish as the others had. They left the orchards and returned to the city in droves. Thus, when the defenders either had been slaughtered or had been turned to flight, a free path forward lay open to our men.

The cavalry forces of the townsmen and of those who had come to their assistance realized that our army was coming through the orchards in order to besiege the city and they accordingly approached the stream which flowed by the town. This they did with their bows and ballistas so that they could fight off the Latin army, which was fatigued by its journey and also so that they could prevent the thirsty men from reaching the river and the water which was so necessary for them. Our men hurried to the river, which they had heard was nearby, in order to relieve their thirst, which had grown intense from the difficulties of their labors and the dense clouds of dust which were raised by the feet of horses and men. There they saw such a multitude of the enemy that they halted for a time. After a while they collected their men. They were given strength and hardiness by necessity. Once and then again they strove to get to the water, but in vain. While the king of Jerusalem and his men struggled vainly, the Emperor, who commanded the formations in the rear, demanded to know why the army was not moving forward. He was told that the enemy had seized the river and that they were blocking the progress of our men. When he learned of this, the Emperor was angered and, together with his lieutenants, he speedily made his way through the French King's ranks to the place where the fight for the river was going on. They dismounted from their horses and became infantrymen—as the Germans are accustomed to do in the crisis of battle. With shields in hand they fought the enemy hand-to-hand with swords. The enemy, who had earlier resisted valiantly, were unable to withstand the attack. They relinquished the river bank and fled at full speed to the city.

In this combat the Lord Emperor is said to have performed a feat which will be remembered through the ages. It is related that one of the enemy was resisting manfully and vigorously and that the Emperor with one blow cut off this enemy soldier's head and neck with the left shoulder and arm attached, together with part of his side—despite the fact that the foe was wearing a cuirass. At this deed the citizens, both those who witnessed it and those who learned of it from others, were thrown into such a fright that they despaired of resisting and even of life itself.

When the river had been won and its banks had been freely yielded, the Crusaders camped far and wide around the city, with the advantage of using freely the orchards, for which they had so strenuously fought, as well as the river. The townsmen were astonished both at the amazing number of our troops and at their courage. They began to be troubled about their own men and whether they could withstand us. They feared a sudden attack by us and counted nothing safe when they considered what kind of men they had discovered us to be in the previous day's battles. They conferred, therefore, and with the ingenuity which is characteristic of those suffering misery and adversity, they had recourse to desperate devices. In all the sections of the city which faced our camps they heaped up huge, tall beams, for they could only hope that while our men were working to tear down these barriers they might be able to flee in the opposite direction with their wives and children. It seemed evident to our men that if the divine favor was with us the city would soon be taken by the Christians. But it seemed otherwise to Him Who is "terrible in his judgments of the sons of men."[4] The city, as we have said, was in despair and its citizens held no hope of resisting or of being saved, but rather they were packing their bags and preparing to leave. At this point, for our sins, they began to work on the greed of our men. Using money, they attempted to conquer the hearts of those whose bodies they could not overcome. With consummate skill they proposed a variety of arguments to some of our princes and they promised and delivered a stupendous sum of money to them so that the princes would strive and labor to lift the siege. They persuaded these princes to assume the role of the traitor Judas. Corrupted by gifts and promises, led on by greed, the root of all evil, these princes fell in with the crime. By impious suggestions they persuaded the kings and the leaders of the pilgrims, who trusted their good faith and industry, to leave the orchards and to lead the army to the opposite side of the city. To camouflage their plot they alleged that on the opposite side of Damascus, which faced south and west, there were neither orchards to strengthen the city nor any moat or river to hinder their approach to the walls. The wall, they said, was low and was made of sunbaked bricks and it would scarcely withstand the first attack. There, they asserted, neither engines nor any great force would be needed. In the first attack the wall could immediately be torn down by hand and it would not be difficult to break into the city. . . .

The kings and all the leaders of the army believed them and they deserted the places which they had earlier won with so much sweat and at the cost of the lives of so many of their men. They transferred all of their formations and, under the leadership of the traitors, they camped on the opposite side of the city.

There they found themselves located far from access to water, deprived of the abundance of fruit, and lacking almost all supplies. They were saddened and they discovered, all too late, that they had maliciously been led to move from a region of abundance.

Failure of the Second Crusade

119

The food supply in the camp began to run out. Before the men had set out on the expedition, they had been persuaded to believe that the city would be quickly taken and they had brought along provisions for only a few days. This was especially true for the pilgrims, nor could they be blamed for it, since they were unfamiliar with the country. They had been persuaded, too, that the city would be taken at once in the initial attacks and they were assured that in the meantime a large army could be fed on the fruit supply which they could get for nothing, even if all other food were lacking.

The doubtful men deliberated publicly and privately as to what they were to do. To return to the places they had left seemed hard, even impossible, for, when our men had left, the enemy saw that what they desired had been accomplished. They had entered those places more strongly than before and had barricaded the roads by which our men had earlier entered: they had blocked them by piling up beams and large rocks and had sent in an immense company of archers who made access impossible. To attack the city from the area where the camps were now located would, on the other hand, involve delay; but the lack of food supplies would not allow a long respite.

The pilgrim princes consulted one another. Seeing the manifest discomfort of the men whose spiritual care and whose Crusade had been confided to them and knowing that they could make no headway, they decided to return, despising the false pretenses of the men who had betrayed them.

Thus a company of kings and princes such as we have not read of through all the ages had gathered and, for our sins, had been forced to return, covered with shame and disgrace, with their mission unfulfilled. They returned to the kingdom by the same route over which they had come. Henceforth, so long as they remained in the East, they regarded the ways of our princes with suspicion. With good reason they turned down all their wicked plans and henceforth the leaders of the Crusade were lukewarm in the service of the Kingdom. Even after they had returned to their own lands they constantly remembered the injuries they had suffered and detested our princes as wicked men. Nor were they alone affected. For they also caused others who had not been there to neglect the care of the kingdom, so that henceforth those who undertook the pilgrimages were fewer and less fervent. Even today those who come are careful lest they fall into a trap and they strive to return home as soon as possible.

[*Trans. James A. Brundage*]

The fiasco at Damascus gave rise to great bitterness, as William of Tyre noted, both among the Crusaders themselves, who suspected that treachery was involved, and also in the West. After the withdrawal from Damascus, the grand alliance was irrevocably shattered. Conrad of Germany at once set out for home by way of Constantinople. King Louis of France lingered longer in Palestine, but finally left the Holy Land in the summer of 1149 without having attempted any further military action.

The attitude of the West toward the Crusade and toward those who had played a prominent part in it was hostile and suspicious. The anonymous annalist of Würzburg reflects the current Western attitude in his account of the Crusade:

A HOSTILE VIEW OF THE SECOND CRUSADE[5]

God allowed the Western church, on account of its sins, to be cast down. There arose, indeed, certain pseudo prophets, sons of Belial, and witnesses of anti-Christ, who seduced the Christians with empty words. They constrained all sorts of men, by vain preaching, to set out against the Saracens in order to liberate Jerusalem. The preaching of these men was so enormously influential that the inhabitants of nearly every region, by common vows, offered themselves freely for common destruction. Not only the ordinary people, but kings, dukes, marquises, and other powerful men of this world as well, believed that they thus showed their allegiance to God. The bishops, archbishops, abbots, and other ministers and prelates of the church joined in this error, throwing themselves headlong into it to the great peril of bodies and souls. . . . The intentions of the various men were different. Some, indeed, lusted after novelties and went in order to learn about new lands. Others there were who were driven by poverty, who were in hard straits at home; these men went to fight, not only against the enemies of Christ's cross, but even against the friends of the Christian name, wherever opportunity appeared, in order to relieve their poverty. There were others who were oppressed by debts to other men or who sought to escape the service due to their lords, or who were even awaiting the punish-

Failure of the Second Crusade

121

ment merited by their shameful deeds. Such men simulated a zeal for God and hastened chiefly in order to escape from such troubles and anxieties. A few could, with difficulty, be found who had not bowed their knees to Baal, who were directed by a holy and wholesome purpose, and who were kindled by love of the divine majesty to fight earnestly and even to shed their blood for the holy of holies. *[Trans. James A. Brundage]*

One of the few leaders of Western Europe who refused to be daunted by the failure of the Crusade was St. Bernard of Clairvaux, against whom was vented so much of the bitterness over the failure of the Crusade. Shortly after the outcome of the Crusade became known in the West, St. Bernard wrote a defiant *apologia,* defending the role he had played in preaching and organizing the recent expedition:

ST. BERNARD'S APOLOGIA FOR THE SECOND CRUSADE[6]

I remember, most Holy Father Eugene, my promises,* made to you long ago, and at long last I shall acquit myself. The delay, were I aware that it proceeded from carelessness or contempt, should cause me shame. It is not thus, however. As you know, we have fallen upon grave times, which seemed about to bring to an end not only my studies but my very life, for the Lord, provoked by our sins, gave the appearance of having judged the world prematurely,[7] with justice, indeed, but forgetful of his mercy.[8] He spared neither his people nor his name. Do not the heathen say: "Where is their God?"[9] Nor do I wonder, for the sons of the Church, those who bear the label, "Christian," have been laid low in the desert and have either been slain by the sword or consumed by famine. . . .

We said "Peace, and there is no peace";[10] we promised good things, "and behold, trouble."[11] It might seem, in fact, that we acted rashly in this affair† or had "used lightness."[12] But, "I did not run my course like a man in doubt of his goal,"[13] for I acted on your orders, or rather on God's orders given through you. . . . The judgments of the Lord are true[14] indeed. Who does not know that? This judgment, however, "is a great deep,"[15]

* To complete the treatise, *De Consideratione,* which was addressed to Pope Eugene III and of which the first book was already in the Pope's hands.
† The Second Crusade.

so much so, that it seems to me not unwarranted to call him blessed who is not scandalized thereat."[16]

How, then, does human rashness dare reprove what it can scarcely understand? Let us put down some judgments from on high, which are "from everlasting,"[17] for there may, perhaps, be consolation in them. . . . I speak of a matter which is unknown to no one, but of which no one now seems to be aware. Such is the human heart, indeed, that what we know when we need it not, is lost to us when it is required.

When Moses was going to lead the people out of the land of Egypt, he promised them a better land.[18] Otherwise, would that people, who knew only earthly things, ever have followed him? He led them away—but he did not lead them into the land which he had promised them. The sad and unexpected outcome, however, cannot be laid to the rashness of the leader, for he did everything at the Lord's command, with "the Lord aiding them and attesting his word by the miracles that went with them."[19] But, you may say, they were a stiff-necked race,[20] forever contending against the Lord and Moses his servant. Very well, they were rebellious and unbelieving; but what about these other people?* Ask them. Why should it be my task to speak of what they have done? One thing I shall say: How could they make progress when they were always looking backward as they walked? Was there a time in the whole journey when they were not in their hearts returning to Egypt? But if the Jews were vanquished and "perished because their iniquity,"[21] is it any wonder that those who did likewise suffered a similar fate? Would anyone say that the fate of the former was contrary to God's promise? Neither, therefore, was the fate of the latter. . . .

These few things have been said by way of apology, so that your conscience may have something from me, whereby you can hold yourself and me excused, if not in the eyes of those who judge causes from their results, then at least in your own eyes. The perfect and final apology for any man is the testimony of his own conscience. As for myself, I take it to be a small matter to be judged[22] by those "who call evil good, and good evil, whose darkness is light, whose light darkness."[23]

* The Crusaders.

If one or the other must be done, I would rather that men murmur against us than against God. It would be well for me if he deigns to use me for his shield. . . . I shall not refuse to be made ignominious, so long as God's glory is not attacked.

[Trans. James A. Brundage]

Despite St. Bernard's courageous resignation, the results of the Crusade were indeed ominous. The Second Crusade had embittered large numbers of Western Europeans against the whole notion of Crusading, and thereby both the Papacy and the West as a whole suffered a setback. The Second Crusade, in fact, was destined to be the last Crusade in which the armies were accompanied by large groups of pilgrims and other noncombatants. Henceforth, the Crusades were to become more strictly military expeditions, whose objectives were limited, military ones.

Even more important, perhaps, was the deterioration of relationships between Byzantium and the Crusaders and between the princes of the West and the rulers of the Latin states in the East. Most important of all, in the final analysis, was the effect of the Second Crusade upon the Moslems. The failure of the Crusade to achieve any victories whatever in the East emboldened Moslem military leaders, destroyed the myth of Western prowess in arms, and was to be responsible, at least in part, for causing the Moslem states of the East to draw closer together, to unite for further attacks upon the Latin states.[24]

The First Crusade had succeeded in achieving its objectives and it had been possible to found Latin states in the East largely because the Moslems had been divided against one another and had thus been almost completely unable to cooperate effectively to stave off their Western foes. The end of the Second Crusade saw the Moslems preparing to unite, for the first time, against the Latin intruders in their midst, while the Latins, for their part, were divided sharply against one another.

The portents for the future of the Latin East were dark in 1148, but no one then could have foreseen the manner in which these portents were to be fulfilled.

CHAPTER VIII

1 Setton, *Crusades*, I, 503-07; Runciman, *Crusades*, II, 278-81; Grousset, *Croisades*, II, 245-55.

2 William of Tyre, *Historia*, XVII, 3-6 (*P.L.*, CII, 675-79).

3 Isa. 7:8.

4 Ps. 65:5.

5 *Annales Herbipolenses, s. a.* 1147, *MGH, SS, XVI*, 3.

6 St. Bernard of Clairvaux, *De Consideratione Libri Quinque*, II, 1 (*P.L.*, CLXXXII, 741-45).

7 I Cor. 4:5.

8 Ps. 9:4.

9 Ps. 113 (B):2.

10 Jer. 6:14.

11 Jer. 14:19.

12 II Cor. 1:17.

13 I Cor. 9:26.

14 Ps. 18:10.

15 Ps. 32:7.

16 Cf. Matt. 11:16.

17 Ps. 24:6.

18 Exod. 32:9.

19 Mark 16:20.

20 Exod. 32:9.

21 Ps. 72:19.

22 I Cor. 4:3.

23 Isa. 5:20.

24 See the important article of Giles Constable, "The Second Crusade as Seen by Contemporaries," pp. 212-79, as well as Runciman, *Crusades*, II, 274-77; Grousset, *Croisades*, II, 267-72; Setton, *Crusades*, I, 510-12.

Chapter IX

MOSLEM UNITY AND LATIN RIVALRY

The Second Crusade had done nothing to halt the advance of Islam against the Latin states, and in the years immediately following the fiasco at Damascus the Moslem advance continued apace. The County of Edessa was no longer tenable by the Latins. The Countess Beatrice in 1158 finally recognized the futility of trying to maintain a hold upon the county and accepted the offer of the Byzantine Emperor, Manuel Comnenus, to buy up her rights there.[1] The Principality of Antioch was also in trouble, for its prince, Raymond, had been killed in an ambush in 1149 and King Baldwin III of Jerusalem had taken charge of the Principality as regent for Raymond's widow, Constance.[2] The boundaries of the Principality were, moreover, now painfully constricted, due to the military successes of Nur ad-Din in the upper and middle Orontes Valley.

A further blow to the Latin states came in 1152, with the murder by a group of assassins of Count Raymond II of Tripoli.[3] Baldwin of Jerusalem, accordingly, became regent of Raymond's state, too.

After defeating an attempt by his mother, the dowager Queen Melisende, to partition the Latin Kingdom itself,[4] Baldwin took the offensive against his Moslem enemies by launching a large-scale attack upon Ascalon.

THE CAPTURE OF ASCALON (AUGUST 22, 1153)[5]

Ascalon is one of the five cities of the Philistines. It is situated on the seashore and is shaped like a semicircle whose chord or diameter lies along the shore, while its circumference or arc lies on the land facing east.

The whole city lies in a kind of basin which is tilted down toward the sea. It is girded round with artificial mounds on which are walls, studded with towers. It is solidly fashioned and its stones are held together by cement which is as hard as stone. The walls are of a proper thickness and as high as is proportionally fitting. Even the outer fortifications which circle around the city are constructed with the same solidity and are diligently fortified. There are no springs within the circuit of the walls nor are there any nearby, but wells both outside and within the city supply an abundance of delicious drinking water. As a further precaution the citizens have built within the city several cisterns to collect rain water.

There are four gates in the circuit of the walls. These are most carefully fortified with high, solid towers. The first gate, which opens to the east, is called the Great Gate and is commonly known as the Jerusalem Gate, since it faces toward the Holy City. It is flanked by two very high towers which dominate the city and are its strength and protection. In front of this gate there are three or four lesser gates in the barbican by which one may come to the Great Gate through some winding passages.

The second gate faces westward and is called the Sea Gate because the citizens can pass through it to the sea. The third faces the south, toward the city of Gaza . . . from which it takes its name. The fourth faces north and is called the Jaffa Gate, after the neighboring city which is located on the same coast.

Ascalon derives no advantage from being situated on the sea-coast, for it offers no port or safe harbor for ships. It has a mere sandy beach and the violent winds make the sea around the city exceedingly choppy so that, unless the sea be calm, those who come there are very suspicious of it. The soil around the city is covered with sand and is unfit for cultivation, although it is suited for vines and fruit-bearing trees. There are, however, a few little valleys to the north of the city which, when fertilized and irrigated with well water, furnish some vegetables and fruits to the citizens.

The city has a large population and it is commonly said that even the smallest of its inhabitants, including the children, receive salaries from the Egyptian Caliph's treasury. The aforesaid lord and his princes take the very greatest care of Ascalon, for it is their opinion that if it were lost and were to come under our control there would be nothing to prevent our princes from invading Egypt freely and without difficulty and from occupying the Kingdom. . . .

For fifty years and more after the Lord had delivered the other areas of the promised land to the Christian people Ascalon still resisted all of our attempts until at last they attempted the difficult and virtually impossible task of besieging it. For, in addition to its walls and barbicans, its towers and ramparts, the city was supplied with arms and provisions beyond all expectation and it had an experienced population accustomed to the use of arms. There were so many of them that from the beginning of the siege to its end the numbers of the besieged were double those of the besiegers.

The lord King and also the lord Patriarch, our predecessor the lord Peter, Archbishop of Tyre, and the other magnates of the realm, both princes and ecclesiastical prelates, together with citizens from each of the towns pitched their tents separately and besieged Ascalon by land. The lord Gerard of Sidon, one of the leading barons of the kingdom, commanded the fleet of fifteen beaked ships which were ready to sail, so that they could blockade the city by sea and both prevent those who wished to enter from getting in and also stop those who wished to leave from getting out.

Our men—first the knights, and then the infantry—made attacks on the town almost every day. The townsmen met them boldly and resisted them vigorously, fighting for their wives and children and, what was most important, for their freedom. Sometimes they came out ahead in these engagements, sometimes we did, as usually happens in this kind of affair, but our men more often got the better of the fight.

It is said that there was such security in the camps and such an abundance of all kinds of supplies that the people lived in their tents and pavillions just as they were accustomed to live in their houses in the walled cities.

The townsmen took particular care of the city at night and took the watches in turn. Even their magnates took turns keeping watch and marched around the walls through many sleepless nights. Along the circuit of the walls and towers there were glass lamps in the battlements. The lamps were made with glass windows to protect the flame which was fed with oil. Those who made the circuit of the walls used these lamps to provide themselves with a light as bright as day.

Our men in the camps were also given the watches at various times. In addition, the task of keeping guard never ceased, for we feared that the townsmen might make nocturnal attacks upon the camps or that the Egyptians who were hurrying to aid Ascalon might harm the army in a sudden and unforeseen attack. This fear was lessened, however, by the presence of scouts in many areas around Gaza who could warn our men swiftly of the enemy's arrival.

Thus the siege continued in the same fashion for two months. About Easter time the usual passage arrived, which brought in a crowd of pilgrims. A council was held and men were sent from the army to forbid the sailors and pilgrims, on royal authority, to return. They promised them pay and invited them all to participate in the siege and in the work which was so acceptable to God. They also brought ships, both large and small. Thus it happened that quickly, within a few days, because of a good wind, all the ships which had come over on the passage appeared before the city and a tremendous host of pilgrims, both knights and sergeants, joined our expedition. The army increased in size daily. In the camps, therefore, there was joy and the hope of winning a victory. Among the enemy, however, sorrow and worry grew greater and although they were frequently harassed, they lost confidence in their men and rarely emerged to fight. They sent couriers frequently to the Egyptian Caliph and begged him to send them reinforcements in time, for they intimated that otherwise they would soon give up. Through those of his princes who were charged with this work, the Caliph speedily had a fleet prepared and an army mustered. Large ships were loaded with weapons, provisions, and machines. The Caliph appointed commanders and supplied money, called for speed and censured delay.

Our men, meanwhile, had bought ships at a great price. When the masts had been removed, workmen were summoned to construct with all haste a very tall wooden tower. The tower was carefully protected against fire inside and out with wickerwork and hides, so that the men who were to attack the city in it might be kept safe. From the remaining wood from the ships, they built portable sheds, which they set in place for breaking down the walls. From this material, too, they constructed "swine"* to level the fortifications.

When all these matters had been properly arranged and when it had been decided which sector of the wall could most easily be attacked by our wooden tower, the ramparts of the chosen area were leveled by the aforementioned machines and the tower was brought up to the wall with much shouting. From the top of the tower the whole city could be seen and a hand-to-hand fight was carried on with the men in the nearby towers.

The citizens struggled and pressed us fiercely, shooting with their bows and balistas both from the walls and from the ramparts, but their labor was in vain, for they could not harm the men who were hidden in the tower and who were moving the machine. A group of the townsmen gathered on the section of the wall just opposite the tower. The bolder men of this group were ordered to try our strength by waging a continuous and long drawn out battle with the men in the tower. In addition, there were skirmishes and serious struggles at various other places along the wall, so that scarcely a day passed without some mortalities, not to mention the wounded, of whom there were great crowds on both sides. . . .

After our men had persisted in the siege for five months on end, it became apparent that the enemy's strength was failing slightly and that our chances of taking the city had improved. Suddenly, however, an Egyptian fleet, sped on by favoring winds, appeared on the scene. When the people of Ascalon saw this they raised their hands skyward and lifted up their voices in a great shout, saying that we would now have to retreat or else we would shortly be overwhelmed. . . .

The enemy fleet approached the city boldly, bringing the townsmen the consolation they had hoped for. There were said to be seventy galleys in the fleet, as well as other ships loaded to the gunwales with men, weapons, and provisions. The fleet was huge and it had all been sent by the aforesaid Egyptian prince for the relief of the city. The townsmen revived and with help in sight they began anew to do battle with our forces, and

* These are movable sheds similar to those just described.

they sought combat more frequently and more boldly with our men. Although the townspeople were rather cautious, as a result of their earlier experience with us, the new arrivals were fresh and greedy for glory and so desired to display their strength and boldness. Since they labored without caution, they suffered casualties frequently until they also had had a taste of our firmness and learned to attack more sparingly and to resist the force of our attacks more modestly. . . .

Meanwhile the men in our expedition pursued the campaign they had begun and continued their constant attacks on the besieged city and on what is called the Great Gate. They renewed their assaults, which constituted a grave menace to the townsmen. Volleys of projectiles sapped the towers and walls and, within the city, the huge rocks weakened the foundations of the houses and also caused much bloodshed. The men who were in the tower and who were in charge of it harassed with their bows and arrows not only the citizens who were putting up resistance in the towers and on the walls, but also those who tried to move about through the city on urgent business. The citizens easily concluded that whatever they had to suffer from other quarters, even though it be difficult, was tolerable when compared to what they suffered from these attacks. The townsmen, therefore, took counsel together and their most experienced men advised that, whatever the danger might be and whatever the risk, they must place some dry wood and other suitable kindling which would increase the heat between the tower and the wall so that, when they stealthily set it afire, the tower would be incinerated. Otherwise there seemed to be no hope that they would be saved nor any faith that they could continue their resistance, so oppressed and mightily afflicted were they. Certain strong men, outstanding for their strength and spirit, were aroused by their admonitions. These men prepared to save the citizenry rather than themselves and they exposed themselves to the danger. They gathered wood at that part of the wall which was closest to the tower and pitched it out into the space between the tower and the wall. When they had piled up a very large stack of wood, one which seemed to be large enough to burn up the tower, they poured over it pitch, oil, and other liquids which would feed flames and increase the heat of a fire. Then they set it ablaze. It was obvious that the Divine Mercy was with us, for, as the fire blazed up, strong winds immediately arose in the east and, with violent gusts, blew the whole force of the fire against the walls. The force of the wind directed the flames and the fire against the wall throughout the night and reduced it to ashes. In the morning, just about daybreak, the whole foundation of the wall between two of the towers gave way so that the sound of the crash aroused the whole army. All of the men in the army, excited by the sound of the wall's destruction, picked up their weapons and rushed to the place where God's will had been made manifest. They were ready to enter the city, but Bernard de Tremelay, the Master of the Knights Templars, and his brethren got there before many of the others and took over the breach in the walls. They allowed no one save their own men to enter. It was said that he barred others from entering so that his men, as the first to enter, would get the greater part of the spoils and the choicer booty, for up to the present time* the custom among us—a custom which has the force of law—was that when cities were taken by storm, whatever a man seized for himself was possessed by him and his heirs in perpetuity. Everyone could have entered without distinction and taken the city, and there would have been sufficient loot for the victors, but when an evil stems from an evil root and wicked intentions it rarely produces a good result, for "Property gained in devious ways produces no good result."[6] Overcome by greed, then, they would not have any partners in the spoils and it was only just that they alone were exposed to mortal danger. About forty of them entered the city, but the others who were following them were not able to get in. The townspeople were seeking to preserve their own lives and were prepared without qualms, to go to any lengths to do so. Thus, when they saw the Templars they drew their swords and butchered them.

The townsmen reformed their lines and, like men reborn, they again picked up their weapons which they had previously dropped like vanquished men. Now they all rushed together to the place where the wall had been breached. They filled in the gap in the wall by piling up beams of great size and huge quantities of timber, of which they had a large supply from their ships.

* That is, in the last quarter of the twelfth century.

They closed up the entrance to the city and speedily made that area impenetrable. After buttressing the towers which stood on either side of the area which had been burned out and which they had deserted when it became impossible to withstand the force of the flames, the townsmen again took up the battle. Once more they assembled their men and, just as if they had met with no reverses, they challenged our men to battle. Our men in the tower, however, were aware that its substructure had been weakened and that the lower parts of its solid framework had been damaged and they therefore fought with less vigor, since they could not depend upon the tower's strength. The enemy shamed us by dangling the bodies of our dead from ropes thrown over the battlements of the walls. They expressed the joy which had arisen in their minds by jeering at our men with words and gestures. . . . Our men, on the other hand, were confused in mind and spirit. They were thrown into sadness and bitterness of heart, they despaired of victory and became half-hearted.

The lord King, meanwhile, assembled the princes . . . [but discovered that] there were differences of opinion among them and they gave varying estimates of the situation. . . . [Finally, after much bickering, agreement was reached and] all of our men took up their weapons. The horns sounded. The sound of the trumpets and the voices of the heralds roused the whole force to battle. They yearned to redress the injuries visited upon our dead; they gathered before the city with unusual eagerness and most heatedly challenged the enemy to battle. Our formations looked as if they had never suffered harm or lost men. They rushed upon the enemy as if they were determined to be wiped out and they attacked with such great vigor that the enemy companies were astounded. The increased force of our men was unbeatable. Their perseverance could not be overcome. The enemy attempted to resist and to overcome the onslaught, but they could not withstand the force of our attack or beat down our swords. That day's battle was fought by most unequal forces, but both our cavalry and infantry forces triumphed everywhere over the enemy and won the victor's palm on every front. There was a very great slaughter of the foe and our reverses three days earlier were more than paid back. There was not a family in the city which did not suffer some do-

Moslem Unity and Latin Rivalry

mestic sorrow and which was not troubled by worry over its members. The city was covered with distress and earlier perils seemed light when compared with the present dangers. . . .

It happened that, by public demand, certain of the leading citizens were sent as intermediaries to the king to ask for a truce for a time so that when we had exchanged the bodies of their dead in return for the corpses of our own dead, each side might hold suitable funeral rites and pay its highest honors to the dead according to their respective customs. The conditions which were proposed pleased our men and, when they had received the bodies of our dead, they buried them with solemn funeral rites.

After the people of Ascalon had witnessed the slaughter of their men and had felt the heavy hand which the Lord had laid upon them, their sorrow and anxiety of spirit was renewed and their spirits were flooded with a vast grief. So that there would be nothing lacking to complete their sadness, it happened on that same day that, as forty of their strong men were carrying a beam of immense size to the place where it was needed, a huge rock was catapulted from our throwing machine and landed by chance on the beam. The men who were bearing the weight of the beam sank to the ground beneath it and were crushed.

The city fathers who were still alive, bowed down by the weight of their misfortunes, assembled the people, who gathered amid weeping and lamentation. All were there, including mothers who held their nursing babes at the breast and old men breathing their last gasp. With the common consent of all, some prudent and eloquent men addressed the whole population in this fashion: "Men of Ascalon, you who live within these gates! You know—none better—what perils and difficulties we have experienced with these cruel and determined Christians during the past four years. . . . The city fathers have, therefore, decided that, if you approve, we shall try to escape at this time from our sufferings. We shall send envoys in the name of the whole people to the powerful King who is besieging us and we shall try to secure definite peace terms to enable us to leave freely with our wives and children, servants and handmaids, and all our household goods in return for the surrender to the King— we say it with groans—of our city, so that we may put an end to such misfortunes."

The speech found favor in the eyes of all and all together they let out a great shout that matters should be thus arranged. Prudent and discreet men of venerable age were elected by all the people to carry the proposals they had decided upon to the King and his princes. The envoys passed through the gate, after arranging for a truce and a safe conduct, and they approached the lord King.

After all the princes had assembled, as the envoys asked, they stated their proposal and explained systematically its details. The King ordered the envoys to leave for a while and took counsel with the princes. He diligently sought each man's opinion. The princes wept for joy and lifted up their eyes and hands to the sky, giving abundant thanks to the Creator because he had deigned to grant such abundant treasure to unworthy men. They recalled the envoys and made their common answer: the conditions would be accepted if the whole city were evacuated within the next three days. The envoys agreed, but demanded that oaths be sworn to them to make the agreement more firm. An oath was solemnly sworn. . . .

After the envoys had first given the hostages who the King named, the envoys joyfully returned to their people. They took back with them certain of our knights who, as a sign of victory, placed the King's banner upon the city's tallest towers. Our army waited with great anticipation. When the royal banner was spotted on the highest towers the people broke into shouts of exaltation. . . .

Although the people of Ascalon, according to the conditions of the treaty, had three full days, they were so terrified by the presence of our men that within two days they had packed their baggage and had left the city with their wives and children, servants and handmaids, and with all their household goods loaded for the journey. The lord King gave them guides, according to the provisions of the treaty, as far as al-Arish, an ancient city in the desert. There they sent them away in peace.

The lord King and the lord Patriarch, together with the princes of the Kingdom, the prelates of the church, and all of the clergy and people, with the Lord's cross leading the way, entered the city singing hymns and spiritual songs. . . . The aforesaid city was taken in the year of the Lord's incarnation 1154.[7]   [Trans. James A. Brundage]

The acquisition of Ascalon brought the monarchs of Jerusalem into more direct contact than hitherto with Egypt. The following decade, during the last years of Baldwin III's life, was too hectic within the Kingdom for any further expansion to be possible. Baldwin III was preoccupied with dynastic quarrels among the members of the royal family and with the pretensions of the Byzantine Emperor, Manuel, to suzerainty over Antioch.

Baldwin's death, early in 1162, and the accession of his brother Amalric, signaled a revival of Frankish interest in Egypt and the beginning of a competition for power there between the Latin king and his Moslem competitor, Nur ad-Din. Egypt, fertile and prosperous, was a prize worth striving for. Archbishop William of Tyre, a close friend of King Amalric, describes it thus:

EGYPT IN THE TWELFTH CENTURY[8]

The whole territory of Egypt, from its furthermost frontiers, which are said to border on Ethiopia, lies between two sandy deserts which are doomed to perpetual sterility. Egypt would neither know nor produce fruitful harvests of any kind if it were not fertilized at certain times by the overflowing bounty of the Nile. The river, however, makes the adjoining areas fit for crops only if the lay of the land is suitable, for, where it finds a level surface near it, the river spreads out more freely and where it has spread out, it renders a wider stretch of land fertile.

From Cairo downstream to the sea, the river finds a wide plain where it has free range. Here the fertile areas are thus spread out very freely and quite broadly. This both enriches the kingdom and also enlarges it. From the fortress called Phacusa, which neighbors Syria, to Alexandria, the last city of the Kingdom, which borders on the Lybian sands, the blessings of cultivation and fertility spread out for a hundred miles and more. From above Cairo down to Chus, the most distant of Egypt's cities, which is said to border on the Ethiopian Kingdom, the country is narrowly confined between sand dunes, so that the river's inundations rarely extend for seven or eight miles and frequently spread out for only four or five miles, sometimes on both sides of the stream and sometimes only on one side. The river thus expands or contracts the extent of the Kingdom, for the places which are not irrigated by the river are doomed, as we have said, to the burning sun and to perpetual sterility. This upper territory is called *Seith* in their language. We have not yet been able to discover the meaning of this name, except that it is said that in very early times there was a very ancient city called Sais in upper Egypt. Our Plato makes mention of it in the *Timaeus* through the mouth of his disciple Critias, when he introduces Solon, a man of pre-eminent authority. We have decided to give his words in order to lend greater weight to the evidence, lest any authority be lacking: "There is," he says, "a region of Egypt called the Delta. At the head of this region, the Nile's stream is divided. Nearby there was a great city named Sais, which was ruled by an ancient custom called the Satyrian Law. The Emperor Amasis was from this city." . . .[9]

There is also another region which belongs to Egypt. This region lies one day's journey from Cairo through an uninhabitable country. This region also benefits by being visited by some branches of the river and accordingly it has an especially good and fertile soil and rejoices in a wealth of fields and vineyards. The Egyptians call this area *Phium*[10] in their language. According to an old tradition this area was originally quite useless: it had never known the plow and had lain uncultivated and uncared for from the beginning of the world, like the other parts of the desert in which it is situated. Joseph, that most prudent procurator of Egypt and that splendid provider of good things, saw that this region was lower than the surrounding areas and that if some mounds which lay between the habitable land and this desert were cut through, this area could readily get the benefits of the river. He threw up some dykes and leveled off the intervening land and then conducted the Nile's overflow into the channels which had been prepared. Thus that land achieved a fertility unknown there throughout the ages.

Although we do not know its ancient name, we believe that in early times it was called the Thebiad. The legion of the Holy Thebians, which was crowned with martyrdom under the Emperors Diocletian and Maximian and whose leading martyr, we read, was Mauritius, came from there. Another argument may be added: the best opium ever discovered originated there and it is called "Theban" by physicians.

The land of Goshen, which we read that Joseph gave to his brothers, is in that section of Egypt which borders on Syria, as the diligent reader may easily discover by reading the book of Genesis.[11] The Thebiad, however, is on the opposite side of Egypt, beyond the river's banks, in the region which faces Lybia. It is not a small area: it is said to include within its boundaries 366 towns and villages.   *[Trans. James A. Brundage]*

Amalric of Jerusalem had set his eye upon Egypt and in September 1163 he led an expedition there. The campaign was badly timed, however, for the Nile was in flood and the Egyptians were able to channel the flood waters so as to force the Latins to give up the siege of Pelusium which they had begun.[12]

Nur ad-Din, too, was well aware of the advantages which control of Egypt would bring to the Latin states. The Moslem leader determined to secure Egypt for himself before any Latin campaigns there could succeed. In the spring of 1164, therefore, he sent his trusted general, Shirkuh, who was accompanied by his twenty-year-old nephew, Saladin, to intervene in Egypt. Shirkuh's invasion was successful and by late May 1164 Shirkuh was entrenched in Egypt.

The Egyptian vizier, Shawar, was as anxious to retain his independence of Nur ad-Din as he was to keep out of the clutches of the *farangi*. Accordingly, the vizier now invited King Amalric to come to his aid against Shirkuh. Amalric quickly accepted the invitation, joined forces with Shawar, and besieged Shirkuh's army at Bilbeis. After a three-month siege an agreement was reached whereby both of the invaders were to withdraw and Amalric was to be reimbursed by Shawar for his trouble. The Latin King, accordingly, withdrew from Egypt once again, the more quickly because his own Kingdom had during his absence been attacked by Nur ad-Din.[13]

Egypt was not thus easily delivered from her enemies. Early in 1167 Nur ad-Din once again sent Shirkuh and his forces into Egypt, while Amalric came to the assistance of Shawar, the vizier. After heavy fighting and a striking defeat of the Latin forces near Minya, the earlier course of events repeated itself. On this occasion, however, Amalric's reward included a promise by the vizier to pay the Latin King an annual tribute of 100,000 gold pieces.[14]

The vizier's promise to pay tribute and the collection of the agreed sum, however, were two different matters. In 1168, Amalric once more invaded Egypt, this time to collect the money due to him from Shawar. Now the vizier appealed to Shirkuh for help against the Latins, an appeal to which Shirkuh readily responded. The intervention of Shirkuh produced the desired withdrawal of the Latin troops early in 1169.[15] But Shirkuh had no intention of withdrawing his men this time. In January 1169 there was a palace revolution.

REVOLUTION IN EGYPT: SALADIN COMES TO POWER[16]
Shirkuh saw that now was the opportune time to fulfill his vows, for, with the king gone, there would be no one to block his wishes. He ordered what he had previously planned to be carried out.

He placed his camp before Cairo and, as if his entry were to be peaceful, he remained there patiently for a few days. Like a prudent man, he breathed no harsh words and manifested no hatred. He concealed his designs with the shrewdness of which he was a master. The Sultan Shawar came out to him daily in the camps, accompanied by a very large retinue and with much pomp, and after his dutiful visit, with an affectionate greeting and the giving of gifts, the Sultan returned to the city.

The complete safety of the successive visits and returns seemed to promise well and the fact that one time after another he was honorably received built up the Sultan's confidence. He felt secure and trusted far too much in the good faith of the Turks, which gave the murderer his chance. Secretly Shirkuh gave orders to his men that on the following day when he went out at dawn as if to walk by the water, they should do away with the Sultan when he came on his customary visit. Shawar, at the usual time, went to the camp to make his customary visit and pay his usual respects. The ministers of death ran up to him and carried out the execution which had been ordered: they threw him to the ground, stabbed him with their swords, and cut off his head. When Shawar's sons saw what was happening, they mounted their horses and fled to Cairo. Terrified, they went

Moslem Unity and Latin Rivalry

down on their knees to beg the Caliph for their lives. The Caliph is said to have replied that they might hope for their lives on condition that they make no secret agreements with the Turks. They violated this agreement at once, however, by sending representatives secretly to arrange a truce with Shirkuh. When the Caliph heard of this, he ordered them both to be slain by the sword.

Thus, while the King was absent, Shawar was removed from the scene and Shirkuh carried out his designs. He occupied the Kingdom and went to the Caliph to pay his respects. He was received with many honors and granted the dignity and office of sultan. Thus he acquired power by the sword and seized all of Egypt for himself. . . . But the joy of his succession did not last long. He had scarcely held the reins for a year when he was removed from human affairs.[17]

Shirkuh was succeeded by Saladin, the son of his brother, Najm ad-Din. Saladin was a man of keen intelligence. He was vigorous in war and unusually generous. The first sign of the character of his rule came when he visited his lord, the Caliph, to pay him the customary homage. It is said that when he entered he knocked the Caliph to the ground with a stick that he held in his hand and killed him.* He then put all of the Caliph's children to the sword, so that he might be subject to no superior but might rule as both caliph and sultan. He was afraid, since the Turks were hated by the people, that sometime when he went to visit the Caliph, the Caliph might order his throat to be slit. He therefore anticipated the Caliph's design and inflicted upon the unsuspecting Caliph the death which, it was said, the latter intended for him.

When the Caliph was dead, Saladin took possession of the royal wealth, the treasury, and all the assets of the Caliph's house. With his excessive generosity, Saladin gave everything away to his soldiers, so that within a few days all the closets had been emptied and he was forced to borrow money. He thus placed himself heavily in debt to others.

[Trans. James A. Brundage]

* William's account of the Caliph's death is not supported by other sources and it would appear that the Caliph Adid died a natural death on September 13, 1171, bringing the Fatimid caliphate to an end in Egypt.

The union of Egypt under Saladin with Nur ad-Din's empire presented an obvious and immediate peril to the Latin states of the East. Attempts to convince the magnates of Western Europe of the urgency of the threat were unsuccessful and, although an attempt was also made to bind the Latin states closer to Byzantium, the final outcome of these negotiations is unknown. The power of Saladin as ruler of Egypt produced tensions, too, within Nur ad-Din's empire. Relations between Saladin and his nominal overlord worsened steadily during the first five years after Saladin's rise to power in Egypt. It seemed, almost, as if Saladin and Nur ad-Din would be at one another's throats, thus saving the Latin states from the peril of imminent attack. Before an open break between the two Moslem leaders occurred, however, Nur ad-Din died in 1174.[18]

This event changed the whole situation. Furthermore it seemed as if the empire which Nur ad-Din had created would soon disintegrate into a number of warring, bickering, rival states. Before King Amalric could intervene to take advantage of this situation, however, he died, leaving his son, Baldwin IV, to inherit the Latin Kingdom.

BALDWIN IV BECOMES KING OF JERUSALEM[19]

The sixth[20] of the Latin kings of Jerusalem was the lord Baldwin IV, son of the lord King Amalric of illustrious memory and of the Countess Agnes, daughter of the younger Count Jocelin of Edessa. . . . While Baldwin was still a boy, about nine years old, and while I was still Archdeacon of Tyre, King Amalric put him in my care, after asking me many times and with a promise of his favor, to teach him and to instruct him in the liberal arts.[21] While he was in my hands, I took constant care of him, as is fitting with a king's son, and I both carefully instructed him in literary studies and also watched over the formation of his character.

It so happened that once when he was playing with some other noble boys who were with him, they began pinching one another with their fingernails on the hands and arms, as playful boys will do. The others evinced their pain with yells, but, although his playmates did not spare him, Baldwin bore the pain altogether too patiently, as if he did not feel it. When this had

Moslem Unity and Latin Rivalry

happened several times, it was reported to me. At first I thought that this happened because of his endurance, not because of insensitivity. Then I called him and began to ask what was happening. At last I discovered that about half of his right hand and arm were numb, so that he did not feel pinches or even bites there. I began to have doubts, as I recalled the words of the wise man: "It is certain that an insensate member is far from healthy and that he who does not feel sick is in danger."[22]

I reported all this to his father. Physicians were consulted and prescribed repeated fomentations, anointings, and even poisonous drugs to improve his condition, but in vain. For, as we later understood more fully as time passed, and as we made more comprehensive observations, this was the beginning of an incurable disease. I cannot keep my eyes dry while speaking of it. For as he began to reach the age of puberty it became apparent that he was suffering from that most terrible disease, leprosy.[23] Each day he grew more ill. The extremities and the face were most affected, so that the hearts of his faithful men were touched by compassion when they looked at him.

Baldwin was adept at literary studies. Daily he grew more promising and developed a more loving disposition. He was handsome for his age and he was quick to learn to ride and handle horses—more so than his ancestors. He had a tenacious memory and loved to talk. He was economical, but he well remembered both favors and injuries. He resembled his father, not only in his face, but in his whole appearance. He was also like his father in his walk and in the timbre of his voice. He had a quick mind, but his speech was slow. He was, like his father, an avid listener to history and he was very willing to follow good advice.

Baldwin was scarcely thirteen years old when his father died. He had an elder sister named Sibylla, born of the same mother. She was raised in the convent of St. Lazarus at Bethany by Lady Ivetta, the abbess of the convent, who was her father's maternal aunt.

When Baldwin's father died, all the princes of the Kingdom, both ecclesiastical and secular, assembled. All were in agreement as to what they wanted and Baldwin was anointed and crowned solemnly and in the usual fashion in the Church of the Lord's Sepulcher on the fifteenth of July, four days after his father's death, by the Lord Amalric of good memory, the Patriarch of Jerusalem, in the presence of the archbishops, bishops, and other prelates of the church.

[*Trans. James A. Brundage*]

The accession of the young leper king to the Latin throne came at a time when Saladin was making his successful bid to take over the lands formerly controlled by Nur ad-Din. As Saladin tightened his hold upon a large, powerful Moslem empire, the Latin states showed signs of an increasingly serious internal cleavage.

Differences between two kinds of Western knights and settlers in the East had frequently been noted by contemporary observers. "Everyone who is a fresh emigrant from the Frankish lands," wrote a shrewd Syrian memoirist, "is ruder in character than those who have become acclimatized and have held long association with the Moslems."[24] This distinction between the Latins who had long been settled in the East and their newly arrived compatriots permeated the internal policies, the foreign policy, and the whole atmosphere of the Latin states. These two divergent groups—called, for convenience, the natives and the newcomers—were at odds with one another on a host of important issues. The newcomer faction wanted land, titles, and positions within the Kingdom for themselves. They felt thwarted by the vested interests of the other party, whose forefathers had come to the East with the armies of the First Crusade or shortly thereafter and who had acquired a hold upon the most desirable posts and lands of the Latin states. The newcomers, too, frequently professed alarm at the degree to which the members of the other faction had adopted the native dress, customs, food, and languages of the East—to say nothing of the scandalous (so they seemed to new arrivals) dealings between the barons of the Holy Land and the infidel Moslem rulers who were their neighbors.

Dissension between the native and newcomer factions was heightened during the reign of Baldwin IV. As the young King was both a leper and a minor, he must of necessity rule with the aid of a regent. Furthermore, the powers of the regent must necessarily become more important as the king's disease ran its inevitable course, as Baldwin became pro-

Moslem Unity and Latin Rivalry

gressively feebler, increasingly disabled by the effects of his affliction. In this situation the newcomer element saw a chance to advance its cause. Let one of their number be named to the regency and the power of the native barons might be crippled, perhaps broken completely.

During the opening years of the reign of Baldwin IV, however, the regency was claimed by Count Raymond III of Tripoli, Baldwin's closest male relative. Raymond was distinctly unacceptable to the newcomers. To achieve their purposes, some means must be found to dislodge him.

When Baldwin came officially of age in 1177, Raymond's influence and that of the party he represented waned perceptibly, for Baldwin IV was at first determined to rule in his own right. Then in 1180 Baldwin's widowed young sister, Sibylla, at the urging of her mother, married Guy de Lusignan, a younger son of a prominent French noble family.[25] Guy was himself new to the East and he rapidly became the accepted spokesman of the newcomer group in the politics of the Holy Land.[26] Members of the prominent newcomer families flocked to the court of the Latin Kingdom and persuaded the King in 1180 to break openly with Raymond of Tripoli.

ESTRANGEMENT BETWEEN RAYMOND OF TRIPOLI AND BALDWIN IV[27]

Now while the Kingdom, as we have said, was enjoying a certain tranquillity during the temporary peace which had been agreed upon between Saladin and the King, there were some sons of Belial and foster sons of iniquity who had restless spirits. These men caused disturbances in the Kingdom and plotted internal strife.

The Count of Tripoli had, for two years in a row, been kept in Tripoli by various kinds of business and, delayed by this, he had been unable to visit the Kingdom. It happened, however, that because he was anxious about the city of Tiberias, which his wife had inherited, he now planned to return to the Kingdom. When he had arranged everything for the journey and had come as far as Jubail, the aforesaid troublemakers got around the King's simplicity with an evil suggestion: they persuaded him that the count wished to enter the Kingdom for a sinister purpose—to arrange secretly to overthrow the King. The too credulous King listened to their persuasive words and sent a royal envoy to the count and, without warning, flatly forbade him to enter the Kingdom.

When this happened, the Count, who had done nothing to deserve such a reproof, was confused and filled with just indignation. Unwillingly, he abandoned his plans and returned to Tripoli after making many useless expenditures.

The aforesaid troublemakers intended that while the Count, who was a vigilant man and circumspect in all things, was absent, they would be able to deal with the royal business as they pleased and they hoped to turn the King's infirmities to their own profit. Among them was the King's mother—a woman hateful to God, a thoroughly grasping woman—and also her brother, the King's seneschal, and a few of their followers: impious men who shamelessly forced the King to make this move.

When what had happened was later made known to the princes, the more sensible ones were upset and were alarmed at heart, for they feared that the Kingdom might later regret the loss of the patronage of such a prince and that, according to the Lord's word, "being divided against itself, it might not stand."[28] They were fearful especially because the King, whose illness daily grew worse, was becoming weaker and was less and less fit to handle the affairs of the Kingdom. Indeed he was scarcely able to stand up and he might collapse altogether.

The great men of the Kingdom saw the danger which was certain to follow from the aforesaid incident. They set to work to try to recall the Count and to appease his indignation. At length, after many meetings and various proposals, the King unwillingly allowed them to bring the Count into the Kingdom. That illustrious man prudently overlooked the injuries which had been done to him and peace was renewed between him and the King.   [Trans. James A. Brundage]

Internal quarrels such as this within the Latin states made it imperative for the Latin settlements in the East to remain at peace with their Moslem neighbors. At the same time the anarchy of the internal politics of the Latin states and the lack of an effective organization for the implementation of policy within the states made it most unlikely that peace could be long preserved. The newcomer group for the most

Moslem Unity and Latin Rivalry

part favored war with the Moslems. War against the infidel was necessary to achieve the goals of the group.

The terms of a treaty concluded in 1180 between Saladin and the Latins guaranteed free commercial communication between Christian and Moslem territory. The passage of caravans of Moslem merchants through Latin held country was a constant invitation to lawless and irresponsible men, whom the government of the Latin states could not easily check. Rich caravans owned by infidel merchants passed constantly before the eyes of such men in the Latin states and they well knew that the King and the barons of the realm were unlikely to take serious reprisals against a man who yielded to temptation and plundered a caravan. Although such an action might bring with it the threat of war, still war itself would bring opportunity as well as peril to those clever enough to seize the main chance.

In the summer of 1181, Reginald of Chatillon, a handsome, reckless member of the newcomer group, gave in to the lure of easy gain and attacked a caravan en route from Damascus to Mecca. Saladin complained to the Latin authorities of the violation of the treaty. The prostrate Latin King could do nothing to secure redress. After jailing fifteen hundred pilgrims at Damietta as hostages, Saladin took to war.[29] Saladin and his Egyptian forces eluded the army of the Latin Kingdom by crossing the Sinai Desert to Damascus. From there the Moslems invaded the Latin states in July 1182. The campaign, however, was inconclusive. Both sides claimed victory and retired to prepare for further combat.

By 1182 Baldwin IV had fallen so grievously ill that to continue his personal direction of affairs was impossible. A regency once more was necessary.

GUY DE LUSIGNAN BECOMES REGENT
FOR BALDWIN IV[30]

While the army was waiting in this state of suspense at the spring of Saffuriyah the King was at Nazareth suffering from a high fever. His leprosy, which he had had from the beginning of his reign and, indeed, from early adolescence, had grown worse than usual. He had lost his sight and his extremities were covered with ulcerations so that he was unable to use either his hands or his feet. Although some persons suggested to him that he resign and provide a decent and tranquil life for himself from his royal possessions, nevertheless up to this time he had refused to lay aside the royal dignity and the administration. Although his body was feeble and impotent, his mind was still strong and vigorous. In order to hide his illness and to carry on the royal duties he had labored beyond his strength.

He was laid low, as I have said, by the fever and now he despaired of his life. Now he summoned his princes to him and in the presence of his mother and the lord patriarch he made Guy de Lusignan, the Count of Jaffa and Ascalon, who was his sister's husband . . . regent of the Kingdom. He reserved the royal title for himself and kept only the city of Jerusalem and an annual income of ten thousand gold pieces. He transferred to Guy the free and general administration of the rest of the Kingdom and commanded his faithful men and all of his princes at large to become Guy's vassals and to swear fealty to him. This was done. It is said that, at the King's command, Guy first swore that while the King lived he would not transfer to another any of the castles possessed at present by the King and that he would alienate nothing from the treasury. It is believed that this was carefully and very diligently enjoined on him and that he was obliged to take a solemn oath to observe these stipulations faithfully in the presence of all the princes. This was done because Guy had promised nearly every one of the great princes no small part of the Kingdom in order to gain their support and their votes for the position he sought. It is also said that he had taken a similar oath to the princes that he would fulfill his promises. I cannot positively affirm this because I do not have definite evidence. Frequent rumors to this effect, however, were current among the people.

There were some, indeed, who were not much pleased by this change. Some of these people were inclind to oppose it because of their personal affairs and out of secret reasons. Others opposed it on the grounds of public policy and because they were anxious and disturbed over the state of the Kingdom. The latter group asserted publicly that the aforesaid Count was not equal to the burden of administration and that he was not qualified to conduct the affairs of the Kingdom. There were others, however, who were hopeful that his ascendancy would improve their own lot. These asserted that it was well done. There were murmurs and many dissenting voices among the people and, as it is proverbially said, "many men have many minds."[31]

The Count, however, did not rejoice very long in the post which he had long desired and which had now been conferred upon him, as will appear later. At first, indeed, he gloried in it rather rashly.

I have said that the Count took this burden upon himself rashly, for this reason: that he did not carefully appraise his own strength in comparison to the obligation that he assumed. His strength and his prudence were not equal to the intolerable burden which he placed upon his shoulders. He was not familiar enough with the gospel saying in which it is suggested that the man who wishes to build a tower should first sit down and count the cost to see if he has sufficient strength to complete it, lest he fail and hear it said, "Here is a man who began to build and could not finish his building."[32]

[Trans. James A. Brundage]

Under Guy's regency, the internal structure of the Latin states deteriorated still further. This deterioration was hastened and accentuated by further attacks upon the Kingdom by Saladin in 1183. Under the pressure of the Moslem attacks and the evident incompetence of Guy de Lusignan, the King and the regent quarreled. The government again tottered on the brink of the abyss and Raymond III was called in to replace Guy as regent.

RAYMOND III OF TRIPOLI REPLACES GUY DE LUSIGNAN AS REGENT[33]

Meanwhile the hatred which had arisen between the King and the Count of Jaffa* was increased for secret reasons and grew stronger every day. The enmity which up to now† had been suppressed burst out and the King was openly trying to collect reasons to procure a separation of his sister from her husband and to break up their marriage. He publicly approached the Patriarch for this purpose and asked that, since he was going to impugn the marriage, the Patriarch set a day on which the annulment might be solemnly proclaimed in his presence.

* Guy de Lusignan, the husband of Baldwin IV's sister, Sibylla.
† Late in 1183 or early in 1184.

The Count was informed of these matters as he returned from campaign. He left the rest of the army and journied by the shortest route to Ascalon. Meanwhile he sent a warning to his wife, who was then staying in Jerusalem, that she should leave the city immediately and journey to Ascalon before the King's return. The Count feared that if the King got her in his power he would not allow her to return again to her husband.

The King therefore sent an emissary to the Count to summon him and to disclose to him the reasons for the summons. The Count, however, refused the summons, gave reasons for his noncompliance, and pretended that he was sick. When he had been summoned many times and had failed to appear, the King himself determined to go to Ascalon to call the Count to justice by word of mouth. When the King arrived there in company with some of his princes he found that the gates of the city were barred against him. He knocked on them with his hand three times and ordered that they be opened. When he discovered that no one would obey his command, he returned, properly indignant. All the people of the city were looking on, for when they heard of the King's arrival they had stationed themselves on the walls and towers to see how the affair would end.

The King proceeded from Ascalon directly to Jaffa. A great many of the leading citizens of both classes* came out to meet him before he arrived at the city. They opened the town to him and the King entered without any difficulty. There he named a provost to take charge of the place and went on to Acre. In that city he decided to call a general council. When the princes of the Kingdom assembled there on the appointed day, the Patriarch and both masters—that is, of the Templars and the Hospitallers—having agreed on the matter, approached the King and on bended knee began to intercede for the Count. They asked that the disagreement be laid aside and that the King restore him to favor. When they were not attended to at once, they retired in a dudgeon, not only from the court, but even from the city.

A proposal was made in the presence of the assembled princes that emissaries be sent to the ultramontaine kings and other princes to invite them to come to the aid of the Kingdom and of Christianity. This should have been dealt with first but,

* The nobility and the bourgeoisie.

as we have said, the Patriarch got the first word and made his speech first. Then, as we have said before, he lost his temper and left Acre.

The count of Jaffa, when he learned that the King was not inclined to make peace, acted worse than before. He took the forces which he had with him and set out for a fortress named Daron. He made a surprise attack on the camp of some Arabs who had put up their tents in that area in order to pasture their flocks. The Arabs had done so with the King's permission and they were staying there on his promise of security. The Count's attack took them unawares and he drove off their flocks and slaves. After this he returned to Ascalon.

When the King heard of this he once again summoned the princes and delegated the care and general administration of the Kingdom to the Count of Tripoli, since he had faith in his prudence and generosity. When this was done it seemed to satisfy the wishes of all the people and princes. It seemed to everyone that the only way to safety was to place the affairs of the Kingdom in the hands of the Count of Tripoli.

[Trans. James A. Brundage]

Baldwin IV was fast failing and in March 1185 the twenty-four year old monarch died. In accordance with the leper King's wishes, the barons of the Latin Kingdom passed the crown to his nephew, Baldwin V, an eight-year-old child. Raymond of Tripoli remained in power as regent and quickly sought to negotiate a truce with Saladin. The latter, immersed in his own quarrels within Egypt, assented to the proposal.

Momentary equilibrium had been reached. The situation was quickly unbalanced, however, by further developments within the Latin states. In August 1186 Baldwin V died at Acre. While the regent, Raymond, was absent, Baldwin IV's sister, Sibylla, the wife of Guy de Lusignan, was proclaimed queen and, in short order, she crowned her husband as king. This left the newcomer party in control of the Kingdom and caused an irreparable rift within the Latin ranks.

Raymond of Tripoli refused to recognize the new monarchs and he was joined in his opposition by Bohemund III, the Prince of Antioch, and a minority of the other long-standing members of the Latin nobility. At this most unpropitious moment, the irresponsible Reginald of Chatillon chose once again to break the truce between the Latins and Saladin. As he had done five years earlier, he now attacked another Moslem caravan on the road to Cairo. Saladin demanded redress; Reginald refused; Guy, the Latin King, could or would do nothing; and Saladin prepared again to attack.

CHAPTER IX

[1] Franz Dölger, (ed.), *Register der Kaiserurkunden des oströmischen Reiches* (3 vols.: Munich and Berlin: R. Oldenbourg 1924-32), #1379, II, 68; William of Tyre, *Historia,* XVII, 16 (*RHC, Occ,* I, 784-86).

[2] William of Tyre, *Historia,* XVII, 18 (*RHC, Occ,* I, 771-73, 789-91).

[3] William of Tyre, *Historia,* XVII, 19 (*RHC, Occ,* I, 791-92).

[4] William of Tyre, *Historia,* XVII, 13-14 (*RHC, Occ,* I, 779-83).

[5] William of Tyre, *Historia,* XVII, 22-25, 27-30 (*PL, CCI,* 696-708).

[6] Ovid, *Amores,* I, x, 48.

[7] This date is erroneous: the year was 1153 and the day of the month was probably August 22.

[8] William of Tyre, *Historia,* XIX, 23 (*PL.,* 201, 770-71).

[9] William quotes here from the Latin version of the *Timaeus* which was then current in the West.

[10] Fayum.

[11] Gen. 46:28; 46:1-6.

[12] William of Tyre, *Historia,* XIX, 5 (*RHC, Occ.* I, 890-92).

[13] William of Tyre, *Historia,* XIX, 7 (*RHC, Occ,* I, 893-94).

[14] William of Tyre, *Historia,* XIX, 21-31 (*RHC, Occ,* I, 915-38).

[15] William of Tyre, *Historia,* XX, 5-10 (*RHC, Occ,* I, 948-58).

[16] William of Tyre, *Historia,* XX, 11-12 (*PL., CCI,* 788-79).

[17] Shirkuh died on March 23, 1169, just two months after becoming Vizier of Egypt.

[18] Runciman, *Crusades,* II, 383-400.

[19] William of Tyre, *Historia,* XXI, 1-2 (*PL., CCI,* 813-15).

[20] Or the seventh, if Godfrey of Bouillon is included among the Latin kings, as William later decided he should be.

[21] William probably became Baldwin's tutor in 1170.

[22] Cf. Hippocrates, *Aphorisms,* II, 6.

[23] The symptoms which William describes are those of neural leprosy with its initial lesions probably affecting the ulnar nerve to produce the areas of paresthesia in the hand and forearm, which William noted as the first sign of the disease. This is a common clinical pattern.

[24] Usamah ibn Munqidh, *Memoirs,* trans. Philip K. Hitti (New York: Columbia University Press, 1929), p. 163.

[25] On the Lusignan family, see Sidney Painter, "The Houses of Lusignan and Chatellerault,

1150-1250," *Speculum,* XXX (1955), 374-84.

26 Setton, *Crusades,* I, 590-98; Runciman, *Crusades,* II, 403-26; Grousset, *Croisades,* II, 609-17, 686-99.

27 William of Tyre, *Historia,* XXII, 9 *(P.L., CCI,* 856-57).

28 Matt. 12:25.

29 William of Tyre, *Historia,* XXII, 14 *(RHC, Occ,* I, 1087-1089); Setton, *Crusades,* I, 580-81; Runciman, *Crusades,* II, 431.

30 William of Tyre, *Historia,* XXII, 25 *(P.L., CCI,* 879-80).

31 A quotation from Terence *(Phormio,* II, 4, 14), much used in the legal literature of the Middle Ages.

32 Cf. Luke 14:28-30.

33 William of Tyre, *Historia,* XXIII, 1 *(P.L., CCI,* 890-92).

Chapter X

ATTACK AND COUNTERATTACK

Amid mutual hatred and distrust within their own ranks, the Latin barons faced the renewed Moslem attack. Raymond III of Tripoli and his friends stood opposed to the Latin King and his coterie. Raymond had, in fact, made an alliance with Saladin in order to protect the county of Tripoli against the possibility of Moslem invasion. Yet in this extremity, under grave pressure from the other Latin princes, Raymond and his party yielded and prepared to join the Christian army in defense of the Holy Land. Such a belated reunion, however, could not erase the distrust and bitterness engendered by recent events within the Latin states.

By late June, 1187 the armies of the Latin King had assembled to face Saladin's onslaught.

THE BATTLE OF HATTIN[1]

In the year of the Lord's incarnation 1187, the King of Syria* gathered together an army as numerous as the sands of the seashore in order to wage war on the land of Juda. He came up to the Jaulan,† across the [Jordan] River, and there made camp.

The King of Jerusalem‡ also gathered his army from all of Judea and Samaria. They assembled and pitched camp near the springs at Saffuriyah. The Templars and Hospitallers also assembled many people from all their castles and came to the

---

* Saladin.
† The region northeast of Tiberias.
‡ Guy de Lusignan.

camp. The Count of Tripoli* likewise rose up with all his people, whom he collected from Tripoli and Galilee and came into the encampment. Prince Reginald of Montreal† also came with his people, as did Balian of Naples‡ with his, Reginald of Sidon§ with his, and the lord of Caesarea in Palestine‖ with his. Not a man fit for war remained in the cities, towns, or castles without being urged to leave by the King's order. Nor was this host sufficient. Indeed, the King of England's treasure# was opened up and they gave a fee to everyone who could bear a lance or bow into battle. The army was quite large: 1,200 knights, innumerable Turcopoles, and 18,000 or more infantry. They gloried in their multitude of men, the trappings of their horses, in their breastplates, helmets, lances, and golden shields, but they did not believe in God, nor did they hope in the salvation of him who is the protector and savior of Israel. Rather, they were taken up with their own thoughts and became vain.

They sent to Jerusalem to ask the Patriarch to bring the Holy Cross with him to the camp . . . so that they might become bearers and keepers of the Lord's cross. . . .

Meanwhile, the Syrians crossed the Jordan. They overran and laid waste the area around the springs of Cresson, from Tiberias to Bethany . . . up to Nazareth and around Mount Tabor. Since they found the region deserted by men, who had fled out of fear of them, they set fire to the threshing floors and put everything they found into the flames. The whole region flamed in front of them like a ball of fire. Not satisfied even with this, they ascended the holy mount to the sacred spot on which our Savior, after the appearance of Moses and Elias, showed his disciples Peter, James, and John the glory of the future resurrection in his transfiguration.[2] The Saracens defiled this place. . . .

* Raymond III of Tripoli.
† Reginald of Chatillon.
‡ Balian d'Ibelin.
§ Reginald Garnier.
‖ Walter Garnier.
King Henry II of England had a few years earlier donated a considerable sum of money for the defense of the Holy Land. His treasury, which had been placed at the disposal of the military order, was now broken open and used to hire mercenaries to help throw back Saladin's attack.

After these advance parties had wrought their destruction, Saladin and his whole army crossed the river. Saladin ordered his forces to push on to Tiberias and besiege it. On Thursday, July 2, the city was surrounded by archers and the battle was joined. The Countess* and the Galileans, since the city was not fortified, sent messengers to the Count and King with the news: "The Turks have surrounded the city. In the fighting, they have pierced the walls and are just now entering against us. Send help at once or we shall be taken and made captive."

The Syrians fought and won. When the Galileans saw they could not hold out, they yielded the ramparts and the city. They fled before the pagans into the castle, though the city was taken and burned. But since the King of Egypt† heard that the Christian army was approaching against him, he was unable to besiege the castle. He said: "So be it! They are my prisoners."

Toward evening on Thursday, July 2, the King of Jerusalem, after he had heard the Galileans' letter, called together all the leaders of the army so that they might give council concerning the action to be taken. They all advised that at dawn they should march out, accompanied by the Lord's cross, ready to fight the enemy, with all the men armed and arrayed in battle formation. Thus arrayed they would relieve the city of Tiberias. The Count of Tripoli, when he heard this, spoke: "Tiberias is my city and my wife is there. None of you is so fiercely attached, save to Christianity, as I am to the city. None of you is so desirous as I am to succor or aid Tiberias. We and the King, however, should not move away from water, food, and other necessities to lead such a multitude of men to death from solitude, hunger, thirst, and scorching heat. You are well aware that since the heat is searing and the number of people is large, they could not survive half a day without an abundance of water. Furthermore, they could not reach the enemy without suffering a great shortage of water, accompanied by the destruction of men and of beasts. Stay, therefore, at this midway point, close to food and water, for certainly the Saracens have risen to such heights of pride that when they have taken the city, they will not turn aside to left or right, but will head straight through the vast solitude

* The Countess Eschiva, wife of Raymond III of Tripoli, was in charge of the garrison at Tiberias.
† Saladin.

to us and challenge us to battle. Then our men, refreshed and filled with bread and water, will cheerfully set out from camp for the fray. We and our horses will be fresh; we will be aided and protected by the Lord's cross. Thus we will fight mightily against an unbelieving people who will be wearied by thirst and who will have no place to refresh themselves. Thus you see that if, in truth, the grace of Jesus Christ remains with us, the enemies of Christ's cross, before they can get to the sea or return to the river, will be taken captive or else killed by sword, by lance, or by thirst. But if, which God forbid, things were perchance to go against us, we have our ramparts here to which we could flee. . . ."

But the saying of wisdom: "Woe to the land whose King is a child and whose citizens dine in the morning,"[3] was fulfilled in them.For our young King followed youthful counsel, while our citizens, in hatred and jealousy, ate their neighbors' meat. They departed from the advice which would have saved them and others. Because of their foolishness and simple-mindedness they lost land, people, and selves.

On Friday, July 3, therefore, they marched out by troops, leaving behind the necessities of life. The Count of Tripoli was in the first rank, as befitted his dignity. The others followed on his left or right, according to the custom of the realm. The royal battalion and the battalion of the Holy Cross followed and, because of the lay of the land, the Templars came last, for they were the army's rear guard.

They marched to Saffuriyah so that, as was said before, they could go on to Tiberias. Three miles from the city they came to a hamlet called Marescallia. At this place they were so constrained by enemy attacks and by thirst that they wished to go no further.

They were going to pass through a confined, rocky area in order to reach the Sea of Galilee, which was a mile away. For this reason the Count sent word to the King: "We must hurry and pass through this area, so that we and our men may be safe near the water. Otherwise we will be in danger of making camp at a waterless spot." The King replied: "We will pass through at once."

The Turks were meanwhile attacking the army's rear, so that the Templars and the others in the rear were barely able to struggle on. Suddenly the King (a punishment for sin) ordered the tents to be pitched. Thus were we betrayed to our death. The Count, when he looked back and saw the tents pitched, exclaimed: "Alas, Lord God, the battle is over! We have been betrayed unto death. The Kingdom is finished!"

And so, in sorrow and anguish, they camped on a dry site where, during the night, there flowed more blood than water. . . .

The sons of Esau[4] surrounded the people of God[5] and set fire to the desert [brush] round about them. Throughout the night the hungry and thirsty men were harassed further by arrows and by the fire's heat and flames. . . . That night God indeed gave them the bread of tears to eat and the wine of compunction[6] to drink. . . .

At length . . . after the clouds of death had opened, light dawned on a day of sorrow and tribulation, of grief and destruction. When day had dawned, the King of Syria forsook the city of Tiberias and with his whole army came up to the camping ground to give battle to the Christians. He now prepared to attack our men.

Our men formed their battle lines and hurried to pass through this region in the hope that when they had regained a watering place and had refreshed themselves, they could attack and fight the foe more vigorously. The Count moved out to take the spot which the Turks had already begun to approach.

When our men were arrayed and grouped in battle formation the infantry were ordered to take positions facing the enemy's arrows, so that the infantry would be protected from an enemy charge by the knights' lances. Thus, with each providing protection for the other, they would both be safe.

By this time the Saracens had already arrived. The infantry, banded together in a single wedged-shaped formation, clambered at full speed to the very summit of a high mountain, leaving the army to its fate. The King, the Bishop, and others sent word, begging them to return to defend the Lord's cross, the heritage of the Crucified, the Lord's army, and themselves. They replied: "We are not coming because we are dying of thirst and we will not fight." Again the command was given, and again they persisted in their refusal.

The Templars, Hospitallers, and Turcopoles, meanwhile, were engaged in a fierce rear guard action. They could not win, however, because enemies sprang up on every side, shooting arrows and wounding Christians. When they had gone on for a little bit, they shouted to the King, asking for some help. The King and the others saw that the infantry were not going to return and that they themselves could not hold out against the Turkish arrows without the sergeants. Accordingly, by the grace of the Lord's cross, they ordered the tents to be put up, in order to block the Saracen charges and so that they could hold out more easily. The battle formations were, therefore, broken up. The units gathered around the Holy Cross, where they were confused and intermixed here and there. The men who were with the Count of Tripoli in the first group saw that the King, the Hospitallers, the Templars, and everyone else were jumbled together and mingled with the Turks. They also saw that there was a multitude of the barbarians between themselves and the King, so that they could not get through to return to the Lord's cross. They cried out: "Those who can get through may go, since the battle is not going in our favor. We have now lost even the chance to flee." Meanwhile, thousands and thousands of Syrians were charging at the Christians, shooting arrows and killing them.

In the meantime, the Bishop of Acre, the bearer of the Lord's cross, was mortally wounded. He passed on the task of bearing the cross to the Bishop of Lydda. A large group of pagans charged on the infantry and pitched them from the top of the steep mountain to whose summit they had previously fled. They destroyed the rest, taking some captive and killing others. . . .

Upon seeing this the Count and his men, who had been riding onward, together with Balian of Naples, Reginald of Sidon, and the other half-castes,[7] turned back. The speed of their horses in this confined space trampled down the Christians and made a kind of bridge, giving the riders a level path. In this manner they got out of that narrow place by fleeing over their own men, over the Turks, and over the cross. Thus it was that they escaped with only their lives.

The Saracens gathered around the Lord's wooden cross, the King, and the rest, and destroyed the church. What more can be said? The Saracens triumphed over the Christians and did with them as they pleased. . . . What can I say? It would be more fitting to weep and wail than to say anything. Alas! Should I describe with impure lips how the precious wood of the Lord, our redeemer, was seized by the damnable hands of the damned? Woe to me that in the days of my miserable life I should be forced to see such things. . . .

The next day Prince Reginald of Montreal was killed. The Templars and Hospitallers were ransomed from the other Turks and were killed. Saladin gave orders that the Countess and the men who were in the citadel of Tiberias might leave the fort and that, having accepted the security of life, they might go in peace where they wished. Thus it was done. The city was relinquished. Saladin moved in. After the citadel had been fortified, he went to Saffuriyah. On the site where the Christian army had formerly camped, the King of Syria ordered his tents to be pitched. . . . He remained there for several days, gleefully celebrating the victory. He divided the heritage of the Crucified, not among the heirs, but rather among his execrable emirs and leaders, giving to each his proper portion.   *[Trans. James A. Brundage]*

The Battle of Hattin decimated the knights and soldiers of the Latin states. The remnants of the fighting forces of the Kingdom sought refuge in the fortified coastal cities and especially at Tyre. Through the months of July and August, Saladin successively occupied the remaining towns, cities, and castles of the Holy Land. His initial attack upon Tyre failed, however, and the city was by-passed. Late in September Saladin's armies camped before the Holy City itself.

SALADIN CAPTURES JERUSALEM[8]

The Holy City of Jerusalem was besieged on September 20. It was surrounded on every side by unbelievers, who shot arrows everywhere into the air. They were accompanied by frightening armaments and, with a great clamor of trumpets, they shrieked and wailed, "Hai, hai." The city was aroused by the noise and tumult of the barbarians and, for a time, they all cried out: "True and Holy Cross! Sepulchre of Jesus Christ's resurrection! Save the city of Jerusalem and its dwellers!"

The battle was then joined and both sides began courageously to fight. But since so much unhappiness was produced through sorrow and sadness, we shall not enumerate all the Turkish attacks and assemblies, by which, for two weeks, the Christians were worn down. . . . During this time it seemed that

Attack and Counterattack

159

God had charge over the city, for who can say why one man who was hit died, while another wounded man escaped? Arrows fell like raindrops, so that one could not show a finger above the ramparts without being hit. There were so many wounded that all the hospitals and physicians in the city were hard put to it just to extract the missiles from their bodies. I myself was wounded in the face by an arrow which struck the bridge of my nose. The wooden shaft has been taken out, but the metal tip has remained there to this day. The inhabitants of Jerusalem fought courageously enough for a week, while the enemy settled down opposite the tower of David.[9]

Saladin saw that he was making no progress and that as things were going he could do no damage to the city. Accordingly, he and his aides began to circle around the city and to examine the city's weak points, in search of a place where he could set up his engines without fear of the Christians and where he could more easily attack the town. . . . At dawn on a certain day[10] the King of Egypt (that is, Saladin) ordered the camp to be moved without any tumult or commotion. He ordered the tents to be pitched in the Vale of Jehosephat, on the Mount of Olives, and on Mount Joy,[11] and throughout the hills in that region. When morning had come the men of Jerusalem lifted up their eyes and, when the darkness of the clouds had gone, they saw that the Saracens were pulling up their tents as if they were going to leave. The inhabitants of Jerusalem rejoiced greatly and said: "The King of Syria has fled, because he could not destroy the city as he had planned." When the turn of the matter was known, however, this rejoicing was quickly turned into grief and lamentation.

The tyrant[12] at once ordered the engines to be constructed and balistas to be put up. He likewise ordered olive branches and branches of other trees to be collected and piled between the city and the engines. That evening he ordered the army to take up arms and the engineers[13] to proceed with their iron tools, so that before the Christians could do anything about it, they would all be prepared at the foot of the walls. The cruelest of tyrants also arrayed up to ten thousand armed knights with bows and lances on horseback, so that if the men of the city attempted a foray they would be blocked. He stationed another ten thousand or more men armed to the teeth with bows for shooting arrows, under cover of shields and targets. He kept the rest with himself and his lieutenants around the engines.

When everything was arranged in this fashion, at daybreak they began to break down the corner of the tower and to attack all around the walls. The archers began shooting arrows and those who were at the engines began to fire rocks in earnest.

The men of the city expected nothing of the sort and left the city walls without guard. Tired and worn out, they slept until morning, for unless the Lord watch the city, he labors in vain who guards it.[14] When the sun had risen, those who were sleeping in the towers were startled by the noise of the barbarians. When they saw these things they were terrified and overcome with fear. Like madmen they yelled out through the city: "Hurry, men of Jerusalem! Hasten! Help! The walls have already been breached! The foreigners are entering!" Aroused, they hastened through the city as bravely as they could, but they were powerless to repulse the Damascenes from the walls, either with spears, lances, arrows, stones, or with molten lead and bronze.

The Turks unceasingly hurled rocks forcefully against the ramparts. Between the walls and the outer defenses they threw rocks and the so-called Greek fire, which burns wood, stone, and whatever it touches. Everywhere the archers shot arrows without measure and without ceasing, while the others were boldly smashing the walls.

The men of Jerusalem, meanwhile, were taking counsel. They decided that everyone, with such horses and arms as could be mustered, should leave the city and march steadily through the gate which leads to Jehosephat. Thus, if God allowed it, they would push the enemy back a bit from the walls. They were foiled, however, by the Turkish horsemen and were woefully defeated. . . .

The Chaldeans* fought the battle fiercely for a few days and triumphed. The Christians were failing so by this time that scarcely twenty or thirty men appeared to defend the city walls. No man could be found in the whole city who was brave enough to dare keep watch at the defences for a night, even for a fee of a hundred besants.[15] With my own ears I heard the voice of a public crier between the great wall and the outer works pro-

* Saladin and his Saracen army.

claiming (on behalf of the lord Patriarch and the other great men of the city) that if fifty strong and brave sergeants could be found who would take up arms voluntarily and keep guard during the night over the corner which had already been destoyed, they would receive five thousand besants. They were not found. . . .

Meanwhile, they sent legates to the King of Syria, begging him to temper his anger toward them and accept them as allies, as he had done for others. He refused and is reported to have given this reply: "I have frequently heard from our wise men, the *fakih*,[16] that Jerusalem cannot be cleansed, save by Christian blood, and I wish to take counsel with them on this point."[17] Thus, uncertain, they returned. They sent others, Balian and Ranier of Naples[18] and Thomas Patrick, offering a hundred thousand besants. Saladin would not receive them and, their hopes shattered, they returned. They sent them back again with others, demanding that Saladin himself say what kind of agreement he wanted. If possible they would comply; if not, they would hold out to the death.

Saladin had taken counsel and laid down these ransom terms for the inhabitants of Jerusalem: each male, ten years old and over, was to pay ten besants for his ransom; females, five besants; boys, seven years old and under, one. Those who wished would be freed on these terms and could leave securely with their possessions. The inhabitants of Jerusalem who would not accept these terms, or those who did not have ten besants, were to become booty, to be slain by the army's swords. This agreement pleased the lord Patriarch and the others who had money . . . .

On Friday, October 2, this agreement was read out through the streets of Jerusalem, so that everyone might within forty days provide for himself and pay to Saladin the tribute as aforesaid for his freedom. When they heard these arrangements, the crowds throughout the city wailed in sorrowful tones: "Woe, woe to us miserable people! We have no gold! What are we to do? . . ." Who would ever have thought that such wickedness would be perpetrated by Christians? . . .

But, alas, by the hands of wicked Christians Jerusalem was turned over to the wicked. The gates were closed and guards were posted. The *fakihs* and *kadis*,[19] the ministers of the wicked error, who are considered bishops and priests by the Saracens,[20] came for prayer and religious purposes first to the Temple of the Lord, which they call Beithhalla[21] and in which they have great faith for salvation. They believed they were cleansing it and with unclean and horrible bellows they defiled the Temple by shouting with polluted lips the Moslim precept: "*Allahu akbar! Allahu akbar! . . .*"[22]

Our people held the city of Jerusalem for some eighty-nine years. . . . Within a short time, Saladin had conquered almost the whole Kingdom of Jerusalem. He exalted the grandeur of Muhammed's law and showed that, in the event, its might exceeded that of the Christian religion.

[Trans. James A. Brundage]

With Jerusalem in his hands Saladin and his army retired from the field, leaving the remaining defenders of the Holy Land concentrated in Tyre, the only major Latin stronghold left in the East.[23] The conqueror's army could not, in any case, have been kept together much longer and there must have seemed little likelihood that Tyre or its garrison could cause any great difficulty for the new master of the Holy Land. Saladin could afford to postpone an attack upon Tyre until some more convenient time.[24]

News of the disaster in the Holy Land was carried quickly to the West. The collapse of Western Christendom's design to hold the shrines of the Holy Land was apparent and only heroic measures would suffice to retrieve the situation. On October 29, 1187, Pope Gregory VIII appealed for another Crusade, even before the news of Saladin's capture of Jerusalem had reached him.[25] The Pope also ordained for all the faithful a general abstinence from meat on Fridays for a five-year period in atonement for the sins which had brought on the recent disasters in the East.[26]

Even before the full measure of the disaster was known in the West, efforts were made to enlist the services of the three greatest European monarchs in a grand expedition to Palestine. Contact was made with the German Emperor, Frederick Barbarossa, with the King of France, Philip Augustus, and with the King of England, Henry II. The obstacles to a joint expedition by these monarchs were formidable. Barbarossa was elderly and had spent the greater part of his career at odds with the Papacy. Philip Augustus was not enthusiastic for the venture and, furthermore, he had been almost constantly at war with Henry II of England. To expect either the French King or the English King to depart for the East and to leave his rival behind in Europe was simply unrealistic. Either both must go or neither would go, and cooperation between the two men would not be easy to arrange.

In January 1188 the French and English Kings met at Gisors to discuss the situation. After much talking an agreement was reached which obliged the monarchs with their respective armies to proceed to the Holy Land together. Peace between the kingdoms was not so quickly arranged, however. Before the year was out, war between them had begun again; then, in July 1189, while the war was still in progress, Henry II of England died. The accession of his son, Richard, greatly improved the prospects for the expedition. Another meeting between the English and French monarchs took place and new agreements about the Crusade were made.[27]

Barbarossa, meanwhile, had already set his part of the expedition in order and in May 1189 a German army departed on Crusade. Barbarossa's force was large, well-equipped, admirably controlled. The German army set out to follow the land route through the Balkans and Asia Minor to the Holy Land. Aside from some incidents near Constantinople, the German army passed through the Balkans with a minimum of difficulty. In Asia Minor the Germans were harried from time to time by Turkish soldiers, but only one pitched battle took place there, near Konya on May 17, 1190. Barbarossa's men were victorious and his army passed from Konya through the Taurus Mountains and on to the plains of Seleucea.[28]

THE DEATH OF FREDERICK BARBAROSSA[29]

One June 10 [1190] the advance unit of the army camped on the plains of Seleucea. Up to this point the whole army of the Holy Cross—the rich and the poor, the sick and those who seemed healthy—had journeyed through the glare of the sun and the burning heat of summer along a torturous road which led them across rocky cliffs accessible only to birds and mountain goats. The Emperor,[30] who had shared in all the dangers, wished both to moderate the inordinate heat and to avoid climbing the mountain peak. Accordingly, he attempted to swim across the very swift Calycadmus River. As the wise man says, however, "Thou shalt not swim against the river's current."[31] Wise though he was in other ways, the Emperor foolishly tried his strength against the current and power of the river. Although everyone tried to stop him, he entered the water and plunged into a whirlpool. He, who had often escaped great dangers, perished miserably. Let us comment the secret judgment of God, "to Whom no man dares say: Why have you acted thus,"[32] when he takes such or so many men in death. The Emperor was, indeed, a knight of Christ and a member of his army. He was taken up while on a laudable mission to recover the Lord's land and his cross and thus, even though he was taken unexpectedly, we may believe that, without doubt, he was saved. When, therefore, the other nobles around him hastened, although too late, to help him, they took him from the water and dragged him to the bank.

Everyone was afflicted with great sorrow over his death; so much so, indeed, that some, caught between hope and dread, would have ended their lives with him. Others, however, despaired and, as it seemed that God did not care for them, they renounced the Christian faith to become pagans among the heathen.

Mourning and unrestrained sorrow—not unmerited by the death of such a prince—occupied the hearts of all, so that they could rightly lament, saying with the prophet: "Alas, we are sinners, the wreath has faded from our brows; there are sad hearts everywhere."[33] The Duke of Swabia, a most illustrious prince and his father's right noble heir, was duly chosen and acclaimed as leader of Christ's army. The Duke took up his father's body and bore it with him to the city of Tarsus in Cilicia, where his father's intestines were devotedly laid to rest.

The army divided there. Some made their way toward Tripoli, which was in Christian hands. The others, who followed the Duke of Swabia, marched toward Antioch. On June 17 they came to Port Saint Simeon and on June 19 they came to Antioch, where the messengers of the Lord Leo of the Mountain had come to meet the lord Emperor. The messengers had as yet heard nothing of the Emperor's death; learning of it there, they were affected more than the others. In Antioch the Emperor was given a royal burial, as was fitting. To the accompaniment of disconsolate mourning, they laid the remains of his body to rest in the cathedral church of Peter, Prince of the Apostles.

[Trans. James A. Brundage]

The death of the Emperor crippled the Crusade. Of the army which had accompanied Barbarossa on the expedition, only a minority was to give any effective service to the Latin cause. Many of the men returned to Europe directly after the Emperor's death, while many of the rest were lost to the enemy on the remainder of the journey to the Holy Land.

The French and English monarchs, meanwhile, were still readying themselves and their armies for the expedition. The two Kings did not complete their preparations until July 1190, when they met at Vézelay to set out jointly on the Crusade. Their principal armies went by sea to the East, but only after many delays. The Kings had agreed much earlier that they and their armies would meet again at Messina in Sicily before starting on the principal part of their sea journey. In Sicily the Crusaders became embroiled in a series of quarrels with Tancred of Lecce, the pretender to the Sicilian throne.[34] Peace between Tancred and the Crusading Kings was patched up only in November 1190 and the Kings with their armies settled down to spend the remainder of the winter in Sicily. They sailed from Sicily in the spring of 1191; Philip Augustus left in March, Richard in April.

Philip Augustus and his fleet made straight for Tyre, where they arrived without incident. Richard and his fleet had a more arduous voyage. Richard's fleet stopped first at Crete, then at Rhodes, and, on what was supposed to be the last lap of the journey to Palestine, the fleet ran into a storm off the Island of Cyprus.[35]

RICHARD THE LION-HEARTED CONQUERS CYPRUS[36]

Shortly before sundown on the vigil of St. Mark the Evangelist[37] a black cloud darkened the sky. All at once a blowing storm and high winds buffeted the turbulent waves of the sea and turned back the sailors. Even before the coming of the storm,

King Richard's ships had been dispersed by the uneven winds and were making for Cyprus. These ships were thrown about by the waves during the storm, were blown back by the wind, and were dashed against some rocky crags. So many men were being thrown violently about by the wind that, although the sailors tried to prevent it, three of the King's ships were shattered by the rushing waves and some of the men in them were drowned. . . . Among the others who drowned there was Roger, known as Malchiel, the Keeper of the King's seal. The seal was also lost. Later, Roger's body was thrown ashore by the waves and one of the common people found the seal and brought it to the army in order to sell it. The seal was thus recovered and was restored to the King.

The natives of the place pretended that their intentions were peaceful. They joyfully received those who escaped to land from the shipwreck. They comforted the shipwrecked men in their misfortune and brought them to a nearby castle to refresh themselves. When the survivors got there, however, they were deprived of all their weapons and were placed in custody. This was done, it was said, lest, if they were to go out armed, they might spy on the country or even get into a fight. The Cypriot Greeks claimed that they could not do otherwise until they had ascertained the Emperor's* wishes. Our chiefs pitied our shipwrecked men who were kept in confinement and sent them clothes and other necessary things. Stephen of Turneham, the King's Marshal and Treasurer sent them a great quantity of necessities, but, in fact, everything sent to the prisoners was confiscated by the Cypriots and the keepers at the entrance of the castle where our men were confined. . . .

When he heard the pilgrims' complaints about the stealing of their money and the injuries done to them, the Emperor promised full redress: he would return the shipwrecked men's money. He even delivered four hostages in token of his good faith. Under these conditions, the pilgrims further obtained the right of free entrance and exit from the city of Limassol. Meanwhile the Emperor ordered all the warriors of his kingdom to assemble and he gathered together a very strong army. On the day after

* Isaac Dukas Comnenus, who claimed the title of Emperor in Cyprus as a result of his successful revolt against Byzantium.

his arrival,[38] the Emperor (disguising his scheme with peaceful words) called upon the Queens* to come in safety.

He alleged that they might count on him, that they would be at liberty in every particular, that there would be no molestation of their people, and that there would be no danger to fear. They declined to come, but again, the next day, the Emperor, on the pretext of doing them honor, sent welcoming gifts to them: bread, goat meat, and the best wine of the Cypriot grapes, said to be unlike that of any other nation. On the third day, a Sunday,[39] he tried to get around the Queens with blandishments and to lead them astray with his wiles. They were now in a difficult position and shifted from one alternative to the other. They were worried lest, if they yielded to the Emperor's persuasions, they might be made captive, while, if they steadfastly refused to accede to him, they feared that he might do them violence. . . .

While they were conferring and speaking sadly with one another that Sunday, the lookouts all at once spied two ships bearing directly toward them, looking like waving spikes among the frothy tips of the curling waves. While the Queens and those with them were still arguing about this unverified news, they caught sight of still more ships following the first ones. There was no delay. The naval force was followed by a multitude of ships and they were heading directly for the port. Discussing this royal fleet they were jubilant with great glee, in proportion as they had previously been desperate and despairing. Now, indeed, after many unwelcome labors, by God's providence, King Richard was brought to the Island of Cyprus. On the feast of St. John before the Latin Gate,[40] King Richard and his whole army arrived in the port of Limassol. The King, however, remained on board ship.

When the King learned of the hardships of the shipwrecked men, of the stealing from them, and about the other things which had meanwhile befallen them, he was deeply grieved. The next day, a Monday,[41] he sent two knights as emissaries to the Emperor and peacefully asked him and his men to make voluntary satisfaction for the injuries which had been done and also to restore in full the goods stolen from the shipwrecked men.

* Richard's younger sister, Queen Joanna of Sicily, and his fiancée, Joanna of Navarre.

The Emperor was quite indignant at this command, as if the greatest injury had been done to him. He heaped harsh words upon the King's emissaries and said scornfully to them: "Tut, tut, my lords."[42] He claimed that the English King was as nothing to him and, glorying mightily in his usurped imperial excellence, he believed that whatever he wished to do was quite all right.

When the ambassadors reported his reply to the King, he was displeased with the Emperor's arrogance and with his rude reply, as well as with the treatment of his men. The King at once cried out and ordered all his men: "Arm yourselves!" They obeyed immediately. The King armed himself and set off with all his men in the skiffs of the transport ships to land in the port.

The Emperor with many forces resisted the landing parties. All sorts of obstacles and bars and every sort of impediment that could be found in the town were placed at each of the entrances to the port to ward off the attackers. They collected the very doors and windows, which they ripped from houses, together with jars and posts, stools and stairsteps, and long timbers which they laid down, along with bucklers and shields, old galleys as well as boats which had been deserted and left to rot, and all kinds of utensils. What else? Every kind of portable wood or stone that could be found in Limassol was gathered by the Cypriots on the shore to keep off the landing crews.

The Emperor, moreover, armed himself and with his people patrolled the shore. The Emperor's men were ever so nicely decked out! They were carefully armed and clad in expensive, multicolored costumes, with warlike steeds which frothed and chewed at their bridles and with very beautiful mules. They came out with innumerable streamers and precious golden banners waving. They were prepared for the fight, either to hold off the attackers for a long while or else to draw out the fight courageously. They sought to frighten away our men, who were hurrying to the attack, with terrible sounding shouts, like dogs baying. The shouting affected us like dogs and the enemy hastened to attempt the impossible. They had on shore some ballistas and archers; also five galleys, sufficiently well armed and full of young men experienced in naval fighting. It seemed an unequal combat to many of our men, for they were setting out, rowing themselves, in a very few fragile skiffs to occupy a port full of men. Furthermore, they were deprived of many men who were exceedingly fatigued from the continual tossing of the sea. Also, the infantry were fully weighed down with their own weapons. The natives, on the other hand, were in their own homeland and were acting entirely of their own free will.

When our men advanced one by one into the skiffs, the nearer ones at first stood up to fight the balistarii and archers who were attacking them in the boats. Our balistarii turned on them and during an attack in which the two sides pelted one another with rocks many of the Cypriots were killed. The rest retreated, since they could not bear up under the weight of the fighting. The arrows were flying thick and fast and three or four of the men who were retreating flung themselves to death in the waves in order to escape from the arrows. As they fled eagerly to the fort, their men were running into each other.

When our men had taken their galleys and had landed their own boats, balistarii and the archers, emboldened by their first success, hurled torrents of javelins at those whom they saw trying to escape from the beach. Without delay, the Cypriots, who could not bear up under the brunt of our attack, gave up the site and retreated to firmer ground. Both our balistarii and theirs were using arrows and javelins continuously. The sky seemed clouded over by them and the serenity of the day was darkened by the showers of javelins. The city boiled with a throng of men and the whole area was occupied by a multitude of balistarii who were working persistently. Victory hung in the balance and wavered as to which party it would favor. All of our men gave the foe tit for tat, but they were making no progress, while the King deliberated for a bit over sending our brave men out of the skiffs and on to the shore.

Then, he leaped first from his barge into the sea and bravely set upon the Cypriots. Our other men imitated his steadfast attitude. Henceforth they accompanied the King and shot arrows at those who were resisting, in order to make the Cypriots take flight. As soon as our people rushed in, their mangled battle lines gave up. There could be seen the flying rain of spears, the Greeks, who had been overcome, fleeing. You could hear the sounds of the advancing men, the groans of the fallen, the cries of those who were retreating.

When the Greeks had retreated, our men drove them back first to the town and then from the town to the nearby camp on the plains. While the King was pursuing the fleeing Emperor, he acquired a mount, or horse, with a little bag fixed behind his saddle. He mounted at once into the saddle, which had ropes instead of straps. He rushed immediately to the Emperor and said: "My Lord Emperor, come and begin a single combat with me!" The Emperor made as if to obey and then immediately fled. The King then occupied the town of Limassol. He had the Queens brought from Buza and lodged them in a villa. There, after many adventures and discomforts at sea, they refreshed themselves quietly and securely.

The King spent that night[43] in his tents and had his horses brought out from the transport ships. The Emperor, however, surmised that the King had no horses with him. At nightfall, when he was two leagues away from the King, the Emperor put up for the night in his tent. The next day, about the ninth hour, the King advanced with his horses. He found some Greeks not far away, standing with their splendid banners in an olive grove. The King at once pursued the fugitives. Since our horses, in fact, had been tossed about at sea for a month and had been standing all the while, many of them were upset. Our men, therefore, spared the horses and pursued the enemy rather modestly until, from a vantage point, they spied the Emperor's army, which had spent the night in the next valley. Then, when the Greeks had seen them, our men ceased the pursuit and halted. The Greeks began to make noises. With clamor and tumult they flung horrid sounding insults at our men. The Emperor was roused from his sleep by this. He mounted his horse and with his army he slowly advanced toward us, up to the adjoining hill, to see what he might do about engaging the armies. . . .

The King had with him, at this point, only about fifty knights. He, indeed, was emboldened by their fear. Letting his horse go, he charged swiftly at the enemy. He broke up the enemy's crowded battleline by charging through it. He dealt now with this group, now with that one, and in short order, he dispersed them all. . . .

The Emperor reflected upon the courage of our men and the flight of his people. Then, when he saw that he remained alone, he spurred his horse and speedily fled to the mountains. The

King struck at the banner which the Emperor bore and ordered the noble and remarkable banner to be reserved for himself. Our knights followed the fleeing Greeks as closely as they could for two miles. Then they returned peacefully to our lines, moderating their speed as they withdrew. The people returned to the loot and they made off with much booty: arms, valuable silk garments, and even the Emperor's tents, together with all that was in them, including gold and silver vessels, the Emperor's bed with its choice appointments, and all his furnishings, his special helmets, breastplates, and swords. They also took a great deal of booty in flocks and heards of oxen and cattle, goats and sheep, noble mares and colts, fat hogs, and hens. They found both choice wines and a great quantity of food and they took captive the army, which consisted of an infinite multitude of men. They took so many, indeed, that the looters were disdainful because of the great multitude of men.

What more can be said? Because of the great abundance of loot, desire was satiated and one gave no regard to any gift, no matter how valuable, which might be added to one's own full load.

When all these things had been done, the King proclaimed a decree, in a voice like a town crier. He decreed that all poor peace-loving men might come and go without hindrance from his men and that they might rejoice, since their liberty was preserved. Anyone who considered the King an enemy should beware, lest he fall into the hands of him or his men. He professed that he would show himself an enemy to those who were said to be his enemies and that he would be to each of them as they were to him.

A great many men afterwards flocked to the King or to his army and the Emperor thereafter took refuge in a very strong castle called Nicosia, where he was confused and sorrowful because he could not make the progress he wished for. . . .

[After the rest of Richard's fleet arrived in Cyprus, the Emperor and Richard met and agreed upon peace terms. However,] the following night, the Emperor fled swiftly, trusting in the darkness of night and riding on his best tawny horse. He fled from that place at the prompting of one of his mendacious knights, a man named Pagan of Haifa. This knight declared that King Richard proposed to set upon the Emperor and to throw him into chains that night. The Emperor was much distressed by this and, leaving his tents, his very good war horses, and all his clothing, he fled early in the night to the city of Famagusta.

The King, when he heard this, began to follow him in his galleys, declaring that the Emperor had broken his word and was a perjuror. The King left in the hands of Guido the task of leading the army by the land route to Famagusta. The King himself arrived there on the third day and found it deserted by men.

The Emperor was aware that it would not be safe for him to be besieged, since if he were shut up he would be unable to escape. He therefore hid in out-of-the-way, wooded spots so that he could fall upon our men as they passed by. King Richard, when he had come to Famagusta in his galleys, ordered the seaport to be watched very closely so that if the Emperor were to try to flee he could be caught.

While they waited there for three days, the Bishop of Beauvais and Drogo of Merlo (a famous and noble man from the domains of the King of France) came as messengers to King Richard. They urged him to sail quickly to Acre for, they declared, the King of France was not going to attack the city before Richard's arrival. . . .

The King paid no heed to the messengers and moved his army to Nicosia. Each man brought his own necessary food, for the area was deserted. They proceeded in their spread-out battle formations, for they had learned that the Emperor was going to ambush them as they passed by. The King himself went in the last formation to repel any chance sudden attack.

All at once the Emperor and about seventy Greeks leaped suddenly out of a hiding place. Their balistarii hurled spears at our men in the rear ranks, but they could not break up our formations, which stayed together in a disciplined way. The Emperor emerged from hiding slowly, like a scout. He proceeded on an irregular course so that either our formation, when it saw him, would spontaneously break up or in order that he might shoot arrows at the King when he found him. After he spied the King in the last formation, he shot two poisoned arrows at him. The King was violently outraged at this. He spurred his horse toward the Emperor in order to strike him with his lance. The Emperor saw him coming and slipped away. He fled at the

Attack
and
Counterattack

173

speediest pace to his stronghold called Kantara. There he was extremely sorrowful and confused because he could not do as he wished. . . .

The Emperor meditated that the fates were against him. His only daughter had been captured, a fact that weighed upon his mind, while his castles had been occupied or had surrendered, and for a long time now he had been supported rather than loved by his alienated men. Seeing that no hope of resistance remained, he decided out of necessity, though with reluctance, to seek peace and mercy. He sent messengers to lay his case before King Richard and the King's spirit was eminently inclined to compassion.

The Emperor came down from Kantara with doleful mien and dejected countenance. He came up to the King and humbled himself at the King's feet. Kneeling, he declared that he would submit to the King's mercy in all things, that he would keep neither land nor castle for himself, but that, for the rest, the King should be his lord, so long as he did not cast him into iron chains.

The King was moved by pity. He made the Emperor arise and sit beside him. When the King caused the Emperor's daughter to be brought to see him, the Emperor was unspeakably overjoyed. He embraced her affectionately and insatiably kissed her many times, while tears flowed freely.

This took place on the Friday after the feast of St. Augustine and before Pentecost.[44]

Richard cast the Emperor into chains, not of iron, but of silver.   [Trans. James A. Brundage]

The capture of Cyprus was an unexpected by-product of Richard's Crusade and the island was later to prove of great value to the Latin states in the East. At the moment, however, there was urgent need of Richard's presence with his army and his fleet in the Holy Land itself.

Since 1189 the city of Acre had been under siege by the knights and soldiers remaining in the Latin Kingdom. The capture of Acre was to mark, it was hoped, the first stage in a Latin reconquest of the Holy Land. The siege, however, had not gone well and after a year and a half of fighting the city still held out. The explanation of the prolonged resistance of Acre and its garrison lay, in part, in the physical situation of the town. Lying on the coast below Tyre, possessed of an excellent harbor and strong fortifications, Acre was virtually impregnable so long as its defenders had control of the sea, over which food, materials, and reinforcements could be brought to the town. Furthermore, Saladin had moved his field army to the vicinity of the city shortly after the siege of Acre had begun, so that the besiegers had both to deal with the garrison of the town and with a field army which continually harassed them and hampered their communications and their supply routes. The arrival of the French fleet and army in April 1191 had somewhat relieved the situation. The speedy arrival of the English forces was now urgently desired.

Accordingly, after pacifying Cyprus, Richard hurried to Acre.

THE SIEGE AND CAPTURE OF ACRE[45]

At dawn the anchors were raised and the sails were hoisted. King Richard had not gone far when . . . Scandelion appeared. Then, after he had passed by Casal Imbert, the highest towers of the city of Acre appeared in the distance. Little by little the other defensive works of the town came into view.

Acre was hemmed in on all sides, besieged by an infinite multitude of people, people from every Christian nation under heaven,[46] people chosen from all the Christians, people well fitted for war and unremitting labor. The people had now besieged Acre for a very long time and they had been troubled by many afflictions, by constant labors, by shortages of food, and by many adversities, as has in part been pointed out above.

There appeared beyond them, furthermore, an innumerable army of Turks, who covered the mountains and valleys, hills, and plains. Here and there they fixed their tents, made of various patterns of flowing colors.

They also saw the pavillions of Saladin and the tents of his brother, Saif ad-Din, and of Taki ad-Din, the steward of paganism. The latter superintended the sea and the fort, and he frequently set up assaults and serious attacks against the Christians.

King Richard seemed to be sizing up all their armies. When he put into port, the King of France and the magnates, commanders, and great men of the armies there marched out to

Attack
and
Counterattack

175

him. They received him with joy and exultation, for they had very much desired his arrival. . . .

The King of France, loathing so much delay in making an attack, signified to King Richard that the time was now opportune for making an assault and for having the criers order the army to move forward to attack. King Richard informed him, however, that he was not yet able to undertake this project, both because he was grievously sick and because of the absence (due to adverse winds) of some of his men. They hoped that the latter would arrive with the next fleet of ships and would bring material for building siege machinery.

The King of France, however, was unwilling to give up his project. He ordered the criers to announce throughout the army that an assault was to be made. On the Monday next after the feast of St. John the Baptist,[47] the French King had his engines set up and ordered his men to be armed. You could see there an incomprehensible multitude of armed men, outfitted respectably with weapons. There were so many shining coats-of-mail, so many glittering helmets, so many noble horses neighing, so many white-colored mantles, so many select knights, so many assistants of great probity and daring, so many banners of various kinds that never had so many appeared to be reckoned up. When the men stationed at the barricades had organized their defenses, because of the threat of an attack by Saladin and the outer Turkish army, the armed men approached the city walls and delivered a terrific assault, firing stones and missiles without interruption from their balistas and engines. But, when they perceived that they were surrounded, the Turks made such a tumult with their shouting and the sounding of their trumpets that their yells must have reached the stars, for the air resounded with a clamor such as follows a lightning flash. Some of them were appointed by the officers to strike upon the timbrels and pots, to beat the drums, and in other diverse ways to make noise and send up smoke from the fires to let Saladin and the outer army know that, as arranged, they were supposed to come to the help of the town.

When they had seen and heard all this, the outer Turks attacked in groups. The Turks assembled all kinds of material in order to cover the barricades so that they could more easily cross over to attack our men, but they were unable to carry this scheme into effect. Geoffrey of Lusignan, an exceptionally worthy knight, resisted them and very quickly drove them out of the barricades which they had occupied above us. Wielding a two-edged sword with his hand he killed more than ten of them and none whom he struck escaped alive. He captured many alive. He bore himself with such agility and perseverance that everyone said that no one, since the time of those famous knights Roland and Oliver, had been so deserving of praise. He recovered one of the barricades, though with great labor and travail, because of the great multitude of Turks who were fighting doggedly against him. They fought a dual contest for a long time. The violent battle was joined and an insufferable conflict ensued. The contending parties clashed horribly and with great clamor. Those who were fighting against the city, after leveling the barricades, made a hot assault outside the city walls, but they were forced to retreat and to give up the attack altogether. They were unable both to attack the city and, at the same time, to keep up their defense in the face of an attack by the Turks outside the town. Many of the Franks were killed there by the spears, by the missiles and stones of the balistas, and by the spreading of Greek fire. There was great mourning among the people, with wailing and lamentation. . . . After the French had laid down their arms, the Turks vilely reproached our men, taunting them with the fact that the Franks were unable to finish what they had begun. They furthermore shot Greek fire and, little by little, destroyed the engines as well as the other implements of war which the French king had had made with such tender care.

On this account the French king was so overcome with wrath and rage that, so it is said, he fell into a fit of melancholy and, in his confusion and desolation he would not even mount a horse. . . .

King Richard had not yet fully recovered from his illness. He was anxious to be doing things and he was free especially to attend to the capture of the city. He saw to it therefore that the city was attacked by his men so that, perchance, by divine grace the deed might be accomplished in accord with his vow. He had a latticework shed (commonly called a "cercleia") made. It was made solid with many joints, and when it had painstakingly been put together, he ordered it to be taken to the trench outside the city walls. When his most experienced balistarii were in position, he had himself carried out on a silken litter, so that the Saracens might be awed by his presence and also so that he could encourage his men for the fight. His balista, with which he was experienced, was then put into action and many were killed by the missiles and spears which he fired. His miners also made an underground passage to the tower at which his siege engines were firing. The miners sought out the foundations of the tower and hacked out part of it. They filled up the hole with timbers which they set afire. Then the repeated hits of the stone missiles suddenly knocked the tower to bits.

The King pondered the difficulties of proceeding in this enterprise and the great bellicosity of his opponents. He decided that, since in the business world work makes progress through excellence, he might more readily attract the spirits of the young by posting a reward than by giving orders through the commanders. Who, indeed, is not attracted by the scent of money?

The King ordered the criers to proclaim that anyone who removed a stone from the wall next to the aforesaid tower would receive two pieces of gold from the King. Later he promised three gold pieces and then four, so that however many stones anyone removed, he received a payment of four gold pieces for each. Then you could see the young men rush forward and the courageous followers swarm to the wall. When the stones were taken out they would go on eagerly, greedy for praise as well as for payment. Even in the midst of the enemy's missiles they worked on bravely at tearing down the wall. Many of them were wounded, however, and were put out of action. Others, in fear of death, stayed away from danger. But some of them manfully pushed the Turks back from the wall and some of these men were protected neither by shields nor weapons. The wall was extremely high and immoderately thick. The men, however, inspired with courage, overcame danger and removed a great many stones from the massive wall. . . .

Saladin concluded that further delay would be dangerous. He therefore agreed to the requests of the besieged men [to allow them to surrender]. He was persuaded to take this course especially by his emirs, satraps, and powerful friends, some of whom were parents, relatives, and friends of the besieged. . . . He also recalled the wives of the besieged men and the sorrows of their families whom they had not seen now for the three years during which the siege had continued. They said, further, that he would only be losing a city, rather than such upright people.

Saladin's princes persuaded him on these and similar scores and, lest their last state be worse than the first,[48] he agreed that they should make peace on the best terms they could get. It was therefore provided and declared that they would agree to the better peace terms. When the messengers [from the garrison of the town] announced the decision of Saladin and his counsellors, the besieged men were overjoyed. The principal men among them came out to our Kings. Through an interpreter they offered to give up the city of Acre, free and clear, and to give up the Holy Cross and two hundred of the Christians whom they held captive and to surrender fifty men.

When our people found these terms unacceptable, the Moslims offered two thousand noble Christians and five hundred lesser captives, whom Saladin would seek out throughout his domains. The Turks were to leave the city, each man taking with him nothing except his clothing. They were to leave behind their weapons, food, and everything else. As ransom for their captives, moreover, they were to give two hundred thousand Saracen talents to the two Kings. To assure faithful performance of these terms they were to give as hostages the more noble and important Turks who were to be found in the city.

Our Kings conferred with their wiser men and with each other over whether they should allow these terms to be granted. The universal decision on the matter was that the offer was to be received and the conditions accepted. Oaths were taken and the agreement was put into writing as security. Then, when the hostages had been handed over, the Turks left the city empty-handed.

On the Friday next after the feast of the translation of St. Benedict,[49] the hostages, that is, the wealthier and more noble emirs, were delivered and accepted. It was arranged that the Holy Cross was to be delivered at the end of the month; also, the captives who were being sought out were to be delivered at the same time. When these arrangements for the city's surrender were made known by rumor (since they affected everyone) the ignorant mob was inflamed with anger. The wiser men, however, were filled with a not unmerited joy, because they had obtained expeditiously and without danger the aim which they had previously been unable to obtain for such a long time.

It was then announced by the criers that it was forbidden for anyone, by word or deed, to revile the Turks with insults or to injure the conquered men. Nor was anyone to hurl missiles at the wrecked walls or at the Turks whom they might happen to see atop the fortifications. On this critical day the probity of these Turks was admirable, as was their great bravery, for they were most vigorous in military enterprises, distinguished in their magnificence. Now, as they crossed over their high walls on their way out of the city, they were regarded by the deeply curious eyes of the Christians, who admired them especially as soldiers and who recalled their memories. Their appearance, as they emerged almost empty-handed from the city was, nonetheless, amazing in its gracefulness and dignity. They were unconquered by their adversities. Although extreme necessity had just vanquished them, reducing them almost to beggary, the defeated men who emerged were not broken up by gnawing worry nor dejected by the loss of their possessions. Their constancy had not disappeared; rather, in their spirited appearance they seemed victorious. Their lying, superstitious cult, however, had perverted their powers as men. Their miserable error was corrupted into idolatry.

When all the Turks had left the city, the Christians, on the orders of the two Kings, opened the gates and freely entered the city, joyfully dancing and exulting at the top of their voices. They glorified the Lord and gave thanks, for God had showed his great mercy to them[50] and he had visited and worked redemption for his people.[51] The banners and manifold flags of the Kings were run up atop the walls and towers. The city was equally divided by the two Kings. They also made a proportionally equal distribution of the supplies of arms and of food. The captives of the highest degree of nobility were divided between them by lot. . . . The King of France, moreover, for his part had the noble palace of the Templars with all its appurtenances. King Richard got the royal palace, to which he sent his queens with the children and their servants. Thus each of the Kings peacefully secured his position. The army was housed throughout the city. After the prolonged day-by-day agonies of the siege, they now quietly refreshed themselves in much desired peace. On the night following our entry, Saladin and his army, out of fear of our people, left the place where they had camped and occupied a mountain further away.

[Trans. James A. Brundage]

Philip Augustus regarded the capture of Acre as a personal liberation from the Crusade. Philip had never been as enthusiastic a Crusader as Richard and he had, moreover, been in bad health since his arrival in Palestine. With Acre once more in Christian hands Philip considered that his part in the Crusade had been accomplished and he began immediately preparing to return to the West.

PHILIP AUGUSTUS RETURNS TO FRANCE[52]

When things had thus been arranged after the surrender of the city, toward the end of the month of July [during which the Turks had promised to give back the Holy Cross in return for the freeing of those who were besieged] a rumor circulated all at once through the army that the King of France, upon whom the people's hopes rested, wished to go home and earnestly desired to prepare for his journey. How shameful, how disgraceful it was for him to wish to leave while the task was still pending, unfinished. How shameful, too, for him whose job it was to rule such a multitude of people, to arouse Christian men to this pious and necessary venture, and to see to the continuation of this difficult business. . . .

But what could be done about it? The French King professed that illness had been the cause of his pilgrimage and that he had now fulfilled his vow insofar as he could. But, especially since he was well and healthy when he took the Cross with King Henry* between Trier and Gisors, this assertion of his does not agree with the witnesses.

He was not, in fact, leaving the work wholly undone. The King of France had done much in the Holy Land, in besieging the city; he had likewise rendered a great many services and given much help. By the authority of his presence as the most powerful of Christian kings and by merit of his most excellent dignity he had made it necessary to hasten the execution of the work toward the taking of the city. . . .

* Henry II of England, Richard's father.

When it became known, in fact, that it was the inflexible wish of the French King to leave and that he would not yield either to lamentations or to tearful supplications, the French renounced, if they could, their costly subjection to him and repudiated their lord. They called down upon the man who was now about to depart every adversity or misfortune which could happen to any mortal man in this miserable life. The King nonetheless hurried up his journey as speedily as he could. He left behind as his replacement in the Holy Land the Duke of Burgundy with many men. He asked King Richard to put some galleys at his disposal and Richard graciously ordered two of the best to be given to him. Philip's ingratitude for this offer was later sufficiently apparent.

King Richard asked the French King for an agreement for the preservation of mutual faith and security. They, like their fathers, disliked keeping up a rivalry and, though they looked for mutual love, it was never considered sufficient to exclude fear. King Richard was eager for a pact, for he had been stung by the nettle of fear. He demanded that the French King take an oath to keep faith and that he promise that he would not knowingly or maliciously trespass on King Richard's lands or the lands of his followers while Richard remained on Crusade. But if King Richard should seem to be incorrigibly at fault in some particular, he would be called upon by the French within forty days after he had returned home to correct whatever grievances there might be and he was to be warned by the French King before that monarch sought any revenge. The King of France took an oath and swore to King Richard that he would observe all of these conditions. The French King gave as hostages the Duke of Burgundy and Count Henry* and five or more others whose names are not given. How faithfully the French King stood by this agreement and oath is known well enough to everyone. For, as soon as he reentered his homeland, he stirred up the country and threw Normandy into disorder. What more? The King of France took leave and departed from the army at Acre. Instead of blessings, everyone had bad wishes and curses for him.

* Duke Hugh III of Burgundy and Henry of Troyes, Count of Champagne.

On the feast of St. Peter in Chains[53] the King of France boarded a ship and sailed toward Tyre. He left the larger part of his army, however, with King Richard.

[Trans. James A. Brundage]

After the departure of Philip Augustus from the Holy Land, Richard took command of the remaining Crusaders there. The fulfillment of the truce conditions at Acre was the first consideration now and Richard pressed Saladin to deliver the prisoners whose release had been promised. The Moslem arrangements, however, proved too slow for the impatient English king.

MOSLEM HOSTAGES SLAUGHTERED AT ACRE[54]

King Richard awaited the expiration of the time set by the agreement between him and the Turks, as mentioned earlier. Meanwhile, he had the siege machines and mangonels loaded into packs for transport. Even after the period set by the Saracens for the return of the Holy Cross and the freeing of the hostages [on the conditions mentioned before] had ended, he waited three weeks beyond the time limit to see if Saladin would remain faithful to what had been done or if the treaty-maker would further violate his agreement. King Richard thought that since Saladin seemed to care nothing about it, perhaps God would so arrange things that something even better might come of it. Too, the Saracens might need a delay in order to fulfill their promise and to seek for the Holy Cross.

Frequently you could hear the Christians seeking for news of when the Holy Cross would come. God, however, did not wish it to be returned at that time for the liberation of those whose freedom had been promised for its return. Rather, he wished them to perish. One man said to another: "The Cross has come now!" Another man said to someone else: "It has been seen in the Saracen army." But all of them were mistaken.

Saladin had not arranged for the return of the Holy Cross. Instead, he neglected the hostages who were held as security for its return. He hoped, indeed, that by using the Holy Cross he could gain much greater concessions in negotiation. Saladin meanwhile was sending gifts and messengers to the King, gaining time by false and clever words. He fulfilled none of his promises, but by an increasing use of graceful and ambiguous words

*Attack
and
Counterattack*

183

he attempted for a long time to keep the King from making up his mind. . . .

Later, indeed, after the time limit had more than passed, King Richard determined that Saladin had hardened his heart and cared no longer about ransoming the hostages. He assembled a council of the greater men among the people and they decided that they would wait in vain no longer, but that they would behead the captives. They decided, however, to set apart some of the greater and more noble men on the chance that they might be ransomed or exchanged for some other Christian captives.

King Richard always hoped to overwhelm the Turks completely, to crush their impudent arrogance, to confound the Moslem law, and to vindicate Christianity.

On the Friday next after the feast of the Assumption of Blessed Mary,[55] he ordered that two thousand seven hundred of the vanquished Turkish hostages be led out of the city and decapitated. Without delay his assistants rushed up and quickly carried out the order. They gave heartfelt thanks, since with the approval of divine grace, they were taking vengeance in kind for the death of the Christians whom these people had slaughtered with the missiles of their bows and ballistas.

[Trans. James A. Brundage]

Two days later the Crusading army left Acre and marched south along the coast, trailed by Saladin's forces. An unsuccessful attempt at negotiation between Saladin and Richard broke down early in September and on September 7 battle was joined near Arsuf. The Crusading army, though hard-pressed, held its ground and at the end of the fray Richard's men retained control of the battlefield.

The army proceeded from Arsuf to Jaffa, which the Crusaders took and fortified strongly. Jaffa, they hoped, would be the base of operations in a drive to reconquer Jerusalem itself. As the winter of 1191-1192 approached, active campaigning was abandoned and further sporadic negotiations between Richard and Saladin were taken up, though without any immediate result. During the winter months Richard's men occupied and refortified Ascalon, whose fortifications had earlier been razed by Saladin.

The spring of 1192 saw continued negotiations and further skirmishing between the opposing forces. During this period

Richard began to receive disturbing news of the activities of his brother John and of Philip Augustus, and as the spring gave way to summer it became evident that Richard must soon return to Europe to safeguard his own interests there. Saladin several times attacked Jaffa and once was on the point of taking the city during Richard's absence; the plan, however, was foiled by Richard's unexpected return.

During the summer Richard fell ill and this, added to the news of the rapidly deteriorating situation in Europe, brought him finally to accept Saladin's peace terms.[56]

RICHARD THE LION-HEARTED MAKES PEACE
WITH SALADIN[57]

As his illness became very grave, the King despaired of recovering his health. Because of this he was much afraid, both for the others as well as for himself. Among the many things which did not pass unnoted by his wise attention, he chose, as the least inconvenient course, to seek to make a truce rather than to desert the depopulated land altogether and to leave the business unfinished as all the others had done who left the groups in the ships.

The King was puzzled and unaware of anything better that he could do. He demanded of Saif ad-Din, Saladin's brother, that he act as go-between and seek the best conditions he could get for a truce between them. Saif ad-Din was an uncommonly liberal man who had been brought, in the course of many disputes, to revere the King for his singular probity. Saif ad-Din carefully secured peace terms on these conditions: that Ascalon, which was an object of fear for Saladin's empire so long as it was standing, be destroyed and that it be rebuilt by no one during three years beginning at the following Easter.[58] After three years, however, whoever had the greater, more flourishing power, might have Ascalon by occupying it. Saladin allowed Joppa to be restored to the Christians. They were to occupy the city and its vicinity, including the seacoast and the mountains, freely and quietly. Saladin agreed to confirm an inviolate peace between Christians and Saracens, guaranteeing for both free passage and access to the Holy Sepulcher of the Lord without the exaction of any tribute and with the freedom of bringing

*Attack
and
Counterattack*

185

objects for sale through any land whatever and of exercising a free commerce.

When these conditions of peace had been reduced to writing and read to him, King Richard agreed to observe them, for he could not hope for anything much better, especially since he was sick, relying upon scanty support, and was not more than two miles from the enemy's station. Whoever contends that Richard should have felt otherwise about this peace agreement should know that he thereby marks himself as a perverse liar.

Things were thus arranged in a moment of necessity. The King, whose goodness always imitated higher things and who, as the difficulties were greater, now emulated God himself, sent legates to Saladin. The legates informed Saladin in the hearing of many of his satraps, that Richard had in fact sought this truce for a three year period so that he could go back to visit his country and so that, when he had augmented his money and his men, he could return and wrest the whole territory of Jerusalem from Saladin's grasp if, indeed, Saladin were even to consider putting up resistance. To this Saladin replied through the appointed messengers that, with his holy law and God almighty as his witnesses, he thought King Richard so pleasant, upright, magnanimous, and excellent that, if the land were to be lost in his time, he would rather have it taken into Richard's mighty power than to have it go into the hands of any other prince whom he had ever seen. *[Trans. James A. Brundage]*

The departure of Richard the Lion-Hearted from the Holy Land in October 1192 ended the third major Western invasion of the East. On this expedition three great armies had toiled to conquer Jerusalem and the whole of Palestine for the West. But, in 1192, Jerusalem was still in Saladin's hands and the deliverance of the East from the Moslems was still a pious hope. The positive achievement of this Crusade was modest: it had re-established a tiny Latin Kingdom on the Palestinian coast. The major task of the Crusade, however, was left undone.

CHAPTER X
[1] Joseph Stevenson (ed.), *De Expugnatione Terrae Sanctae per Saladinum* ("Rolls Series"
[London: Longmans 1875]), pp. 218-28.
[2] Matt. 17:1-8.
[3] Eccles. 10:16.

4 The Saracen host is meant. Esau was the elder brother of Jacob; for his descendants see Gen. 36.

5 The army of the Latin Kingdom.

6 Isa. 30:20.

7 *Pullani;* the word is used here to distinguish those who, like Raymond of Tripoli, Balian d'Ibelin, and Reginald Garnier, had been long resident in the East from new arrivals, such as Reginald of Chatillon and his friends.

8 Stevenson, *De Expugnatione,* pp. 241-51.

9 On the northwest side of the city.

10 September 26.

11 Also known as Nebi-Samed. This elevation lay on the direct path to the city and was the point from which Crusaders and pilgrims ordinarily caught their first sity of the Holy City. *Cf.* "The Book of Sir John de Maundeville," in Wright, *Early Travels in Palestine,* p. 175.

12 Saladin.

13 *Ruptores murorum:* literally, wall-breakers.

14 Ps. 76:1.

15 While the purchasing-power value of this sum would be extremely difficult to estimate, it clearly represented a small fortune.

16 *Sapientibus nostris Alphacinis;* the noun is a Latinization of the Arabic *al-fakih,* meaning a learned man, especially a theologian, lawyer, or casuist. I am indebted to Sir H. A. R. Gibb for this information.

17 See below, p. 163.

18 Both members of the Ibelin family.

19 *Cassini* in the text is a Latinization of *Kadi* (pronounced *Kazi* by the Persians and Turks). The *Kadis* were primarily secular judges, rather than religious officials as the author apparently thought. I am indebted to Sir. H. A. R. Gibb for this information.

20 Here, as above, the chronicler makes an erroneous equation between these Moslem dignitaries and what he thinks were their Christian counterparts.

21 *Quabat as-Sakhrah.*

22 "God is great God is great!"

23 There were, in addition, a number of secondary strongholds still in Latin hands, *e.g.,* Antioch, Krak, Tortosa.

24 Runciman, *Crusades,* II, 468-71; Setton, *Crusades,* I, 617-19; see also Smail, *Crusading Warfare,* pp. 64-75, on the Turkish *iqta* and the army.

25 J.-D. Mansi, *Sacrorum conciliorum nova et amplissima collectio* (new ed.; 53 vols.; Paris: Hubert Welter, 1903-27), XXIV, 527-30.

26 Mansi, *Concilia,* XXIV, 531.

27 William Stubbs (ed.), *Itinerarium Peregrinorum et Gesta Regis Ricardi,* ("Rolls Series" [London: Longmans, 1864]), II, 140-47; Ambroise, *The Crusade of Richard Lion-Heart,*ed. and trans. Merton Jerome Hubert and John L. LaMonte (New York: Columbia University Press, 1941), II. 1-276 (pp. 31-40)—hereafter cited as Ambroise, *The Crusade;* Runciman, *Crusades,* III, 5-9; Grousset, *Croisades,* III, 45; Adolf Waas, *Geschichte der Kreuzzüge* (2 vols.; Freiburg: Herder, 1956), I, 186-87.

28 Stubbs, *Itinerarium*, I, 18-24 (pp. 34-57); Runciman, *Crusades*, III, 10-15; Grousset, *Croisades*, III, 10-18; Waas, *Geschichte der Kreuzzüge*, I, 192-95.

29 *Historia de Expeditione Friderici Imperatoris*, A. Chroust (ed.), in *Quellen zur Geschichte des Kreuzzügges Kaiser Friedrichs I, MGH, SSRG,* new series, V, pp. 91-92.

30 Frederick Barbarossa.

31 Cf. Eccles. 4:32.

32 II Kings 16:10.

33 Lam. 5:16-17.

34 The rightful claimant of the Sicilian throne was Barbarossa's elder son, Henry VI of Germany, who was also the husband of Constance, the daughter and heiress of William II of Sicily (d. November 1189). Tancred of Lecce, a bastard son of William II, seized the throne, however, with the support of the Sicilian nobility, who abhorred the thought of a German ruler.

35 Stubbs, *Itinerarium*, II, 9-29 (pp. 150-83); Ambroise, 11. The Crusade, 277-1,400 (pp. 41-83); Runciman, *Crusades*, III, 34-43; Grousset, *Croisades*, III, 45-47; Waas, *Geschichte der Keruzzüge*, I, 197-200.

36 Stubbs, *Itinerarium*, II, 30-33, 38, 40 (pp. 184-85, 187-94, 199-203).

37 Wednesday, April 24, 1191.

38 Thursday, May 2, 1191.

39 May 5, 1191.

40 May 6.

41 May 7.

42 *Ptrut, sire,* in the original.

43 The night of May 7-8.

44 Friday, May 31.

45 Stubbs, *Itinerarium*, III, 1, 5, 13, 17-18 (pp. 210-11, 214-17, 224-26, 231-34).

46 Acts, 2:5.

47 This would be July 1, 1191, which seems too late a date; probably the Monday before the feast of St. John, i.e., June 17, is meant.

48 Matt. 12:45.

49 The feast of the translation of St. Benedict occurred on Thursday, July 11; the next Friday would have been the following day, July 12.

50 Luke 1:58.

51 Luke 2:68.

52 Stubbs, *Itinerarium*, III, 21-23 (pp. 236-39).

53 Thursday, August 1, 1191.

54 Stubbs, *Itinerarium*, IV, 2, 4 (pp. 240-41, 243).

55 The date given here, August 16, 1191, may have been the day on which the decision to massacre the prisoners was made. The execution took place on August 20.

56 Stubbs, *Itinerarium*, IV, 5-VI, 26 (pp. 244-426); Ambroise, *The Crusades,* II. 5, 720-11,764 (pp. 235-429; Runciman, *Crusades*, III, 53-73; Grousset, *Croisades*, III, 62-116; Waas, *Geschichte der Kreuzzüge*, I, 211-15.

57 Stubbs, *Itinerarium*, VI, 27-28 (pp. 427-30).

58 March 28, 1193.

Chapter XI

The TuRNiNG poiNT:
The fouRTh cRusaDe

The Third Crusade solved none of the basic problems of
the Western communities in the Near East. Still needed if
these communities were to continue to exist were permanent
garrisons far larger than any Europe seemed inclined to send
them. The Western colonies in Palestine needed to make
further conquests to establish themselves safely; further conquests meant more men, both for the work of fighting and for
the business of governing and garrisoning the Eastern outposts. So long as these needs were not met, the position of
the Western colonists in Syria and Palestine would continue
to be precarious.

The wealth of the Latin colonies, however, depended
upon continued peace, not more war. The areas conquered
by the First Crusaders and still retained in the late twelfth
century were not very productive agriculturally. Their economic well-being depended upon trade with the Moslem
hinterland, and this trade was largely in the hands of the
Italian merchant communities settled in the Christian cities
of the Holy Land. These merchant communities, whose members were drawn principally from Genoa and Pisa, were a
strong force in the polity of the Latin states. The mercantile
interests used their strength to encourage the continuance of
peaceful coexistence amid the tangled religious passions of

The
Turning
Point:
The Fourth
Crusade

189

Christians and Moslems in the Holy Land. The merchant communities were basically opposed to war.

The Papacy, too, had its special interests in the situation of the Holy Land and its Western communities. The Crusades had been launched originally by the Popes and the appeal of these expeditions to Western knights and soldiers lay in the fact that papal sanction, papal privileges, and papal indulgences were bestowed upon participants in these holy wars. The popes of the late twelfth century were eager to see the culmination of so much past Crusading zeal in a permanent conquest of the East. The popes were eager also to keep the Crusading armies under their own special control.

In 1197, this papal control of the Crusading movement was seriously threatened by the German Emperor, Henry VI, who raised a formidable army and prepared to lead an expedition of his own to the Holy Land. Henry's power in Europe was already redoubtable, for he controlled both Germany and southern Italy and had claims, as well, to suzerainty over northern Italy, Hungary, Bohemia, and Denmark. The extension of his power to the East Mediterranean area was a development which the Papacy could regard only with trepidation. Fortunately, from the papal point of view, Henry died suddenly and unexpectedly in Sicily in September 1197. The Emperor left his lands and powers to his wife, Constance, and to their infant son, Frederick II. When Constance died in 1198, the young German king became a ward of the Pope.

In 1198, too, Pope Innocent III, one of the most able and ambitious of the medieval pontiffs, came to the papal throne. Innocent set out shortly after his coronation to raise a Crusading host which would re-establish Western Christendom's claims in the East and also refurbish papal prestige in the West.[1]

THE ORGANIZATION OF THE FOURTH CRUSADE[2]

Bt it known to you that eleven hundred and ninety-seven years after the Incarnation of our Lord Jesus Christ, in the time of Innocent, Pope of Rome, and Philip, King of France, and Richard, King of England, there was in France a holy man named Fulk of Neuilly—which Neuilly is between Lagni-sur-Marne and

Paris—and he was a priest and held the cure of the village. And this said Fulk began to speak of God throughout the Isle of France, and the other countries round about; and you must know that by him the Lord wrought many miracles.

Be it known to you further, that the fame of this holy man so spread, that it reached the Pope of Rome, Innocent; and the Pope sent to France, and ordered the right worthy man to preach the cross (the Crusade) by his authority. And afterward the Pope sent a cardinal of his, Master Peter of Capua, who himself had taken the cross, to proclaim the indulgence of which I now tell you, viz., that all who should take the cross and serve in the host for one year, would be delivered from all the sins they had committed, and acknowledged in confession. And because this indulgence was so great, the hearts of men were much moved, and many took the cross for the greatness of the pardon.

The other year after that right worthy man Fulk had so spoken of God, there was held a tourney in Champagne, at a castle called Ecri, and by God's grace, it so happened that Thibaut, Count of Champagne and Brie, took the cross, and the Count Louis of Blois and Chartres likewise; and this was at the beginning of Advent (28th November 1199). Now you must know that this Count Thibaut was but a young man, and not more than twenty-two years of age and the Count Louis not more than twenty-seven. . . .

With these two counts there took the cross two very high and puissant Barons of France, Simon of Montfort, and Renaud of Montmirail. Great was the fame thereof throughout the land when these two high and puissant men took the cross. . . .

Afterward the Barons held a parliament at Soissons, to settle when they should start, and whither they should wend. But they could come to no agreement, because it did not seem to them that enough people had taken the cross. So during all that year (1200) no two months passed without assemblings in parliament at Compiegne. There met all the counts and barons who had taken the cross. Many were the opinions given and considered; but in the end it was agreed that envoys should be sent, the best that could be found, with full powers, as if they were the lords in person, to settle such matters as needed settlement. . . .

The Turning Point: The Fourth Crusade

To these six envoys the business in hand was fully committed, all the Barons delivering to them valid charters, with seals attached, to the effect that they would undertake to maintain and carry out whatever conventions and agreements the envoys might enter into, in all sea ports, and withersoever else the envoys might fare.

Thus were the six envoys despatched, as you have been told; and they took counsel among themselves, and this was their conclusion: that in Venice they might expect to find a greater number of vessels than in any other port. So they journeyed day by day, till they came thither in the first week of Lent (February 1201).

The Doge of Venice, whose name was Henry Dandolo, and who was very wise and very valiant, did them great honor, both he and the other folk, and entertained them right willingly, marveling, however, when the envoys had delivered their letters, what might be the matter of import that had brought them to that country. For the letters were letters of credence only and declared no more than that the bearers were to be accredited as if they were the Counts in person, and that the said Counts would make good whatever the six envoys should undertake.

So the Doge replied: "Signors, I have seen your letters; well do we know that of men uncrowned your lords are the greatest, and they advise us to put faith in what you tell us, and that they will maintain whatsoever you undertake. Now, therefore, speak, and let us know what is your pleasure."

And the envoys answered: "Sire, we would that you should assemble your council; and before your council we will declare the wishes of our lords; and let this be tomorrow, if it so pleases you." And the Doge replied asking for respite till the fourth day, when he would assemble his council, so that the envoys might state their requirements.

The envoys waited then till the fourth day, as had been appointed them, and entered the palace, which was passing rich and beautiful; and found the Doge and his council in a chamber. There they delivered their message after this manner: "Sire, we come to thee on the part of the high Barons of France, who have taken the sign of the cross to avenge the shame done to Jesus Christ, and to reconquer Jerusalem, if so be that God will suffer it. And because they know that no people have such great power to help them as you and your people, therefore we pray you by God that you take pity on the land oversea, and the shame of Christ, and use diligence that our lords have ships for transport and battle."

"And after what manner should we have diligence?" said the Doge. "After all manners that you may advise and propose," rejoined the envoys, "in so far as what you propose may be within our means." "Certes," said the Doge, "it is a great thing that your lords require of us, and well it seems that they have in view a high enterprise. We will give you our answer eight days from today. And marvel not if the term be long, for it is meet that so great a matter be fully pondered."

When the term appointed by the Doge was ended, the envoys returned to the palace. Many were the words then spoken which I cannot now rehearse. But this was the conclusion of that parliament: "Signors," said the Doge, "we will tell you the conclusions at which we have arrived, if so be that we can induce our great council and the commons of the land to allow of them; and you, on your part, must consult and see if you can accept them and carry them through.

"We will build transports to carry four thousand five hundred horses, and nine thousand squires, and ships for four thousand five hundred knights, and twenty thousand sergeants of foot. And we will agree also to purvey food for these horses and people during nine months. This is what we undertake to do at the least, on condition that you pay us for each horse four marks, and for each man two marks.

"And the covenants we are now explaining to you, we undertake to keep, wheresoever we may be, for a year, reckoning from the day on which we sail from the port of Venice in the service of God and of Christendom. Now the sum total of the expenses above named amounts to 85,000 marks.

"And this will we do moreover. For the love of God, we will add to the fleet fifty armed galleys on condition that, so long as we act in company, of all conquests in land or money, whether at sea or on dry ground, we shall have the half, and you the other half. Now consult together to see if you, on your parts, can accept and fulfill these covenants."

The envoys then departed, and said that they would consult together and give their answer on the morrow. They consulted, and talked together that night, and agreed to accept the terms offered. . . .

The Venetians had fulfilled all their undertakings, and above measure, and they now summoned the Barons and Counts to fulfill theirs and make payment, since they were ready to start.

The cost of each man's passage was now levied throughout the host; and there were people enough who said they could not pay for their passage, and the Barons took from them such moneys as they had. So of the passages, and when the payments had been collected, the moneys came to less than the sum due —yea, by more than one half.

Then the Barons met together and said: "Lords, the Venetians have well fulfilled all their undertakings, and above measure. But we cannot fulfill ours in paying for our passages, seeing we are too few in number; and this is the fault of those who have journeyed by other ports. For God's sake, therefore, let each contribute all that he has, so that we may fulfill our covenant; for better is it that we should give all that we have, than lose what we have already paid, and prove false to our covenants; for if this host remains here, the rescue of the land oversea comes to naught."

Great was then the dissension among the main part of the Barons and the other folk, and they said: "We have paid for our passages, and if they will take us, we shall go willingly; but if not, we shall inquire and look for other means of passage." And they spoke thus because they wished that the host should fall to pieces and each return to his own land. But the other party said, "Much rather would we give all that we have and go penniless with the host, then that the host should fall to pieces and fail; for God will doubtless repay us when it so pleases Him."

Then the Count of Flanders began to give all that he had and all that he could borrow, and so did Count Lewis and the marquis, and the Count of Saint-Paul, and those who were of their party.

Then might you have seen many a fine vessel of gold and silver borne in payment to the palace of the Doge. And when all had been brought together, there was still wanting, of the sum required, 34,000 marks of silver. Then those who had kept back their possessions and not brought them into the common stock, were right glad, for they thought now surely the host must fail and go to pieces. But God, who advises those who have been ill-advised, would not so suffer it.

Then the Doge spoke to his people, and said unto them: "Signors, these people cannot pay more; and in so far as they have paid at all, we have benefited by an agreement which they cannot now fulfill. But our right to keep this money would not everywhere be acknowledged; and if we so kept it we should be greatly blamed, both us and our land. Let us therefore offer them terms.

"The King of Hungary has taken from us Zara in Sclavonia, which is one of the strongest places in the world; and never shall we recover it with all the power that we possess, save with the help of these people. Let us therefore ask them to help us to reconquer it, and we will remit the payment of the debt of 34,000 marks of silver, until such time as it shall please God to allow us to regain the moneys by conquest, we and they together." Thus was agreement made. Much was it contested by those who wished that the host should be broken up. Nevertheless the agreement was accepted and ratified.

Then, on a Sunday, was assemblage held in the Church of St. Mark. It was a very high festival, and the people of the land were there, and the most part of the Barons and pilgrims.

Before the beginning of high mass, the Doge of Venice, who bore the name of Henry Dandolo, went up into the reading-desk, and spoke to the people, and said to them: "Signors, you are associated with the most worthy people in the world, and for the highest enterprise ever undertaken; and I am a man old and feeble, who should have need of rest, and I am sick in body; but I see that no one could command and lead you like myself, who am your lord. If you will consent that I take the sign of the cross to guard and direct you, and that my son remain in my place to guard the land, then shall I go to live or die with you and with the pilgrims."

And when they had heard him, they cried with one voice: "We pray you by God that you consent, and do it, and that you come with us!"

Very great was then the pity and compassion on the part of the people of the land and of the pilgrims; and many were the tears shed, because that worthy and good man would have had so much reason to remain behind, for he was an old man, and albeit his eyes were unclouded, yet he saw naught, having lost his sight through a wound in the head. He was of a great heart. Ah! how little like him were those who had gone to other ports to escape the danger.

Thus he came down from the reading-desk, and went before the altar, and knelt upon his knees greatly weeping. And they sewed the cross to a great cotton hat, which he wore, in front, because he wished that all men should see it. And the Venetians began to take the cross in great numbers, a great multitude, for up to that day very few had taken the cross. Our pilgrims had much joy in the cross that the Doge took, and were greatly moved, because of the wisdom and the valour that were in him.

Thus did the Doge take the cross, as you have heard. Then the Venetians began to deliver the ships, the galleys, and the transports to the Barons for departure; but so much time had already been spent since the appointed term, that September drew near (1202).

[Trans. Sir Frank Marzials]

Now began one of the strangest and most baffling enterprises in the history of the whole Crusading movement. The army assembled under papal auspices to wrest the Holy Land from the Moslems was turned against the Christians of the East Mediterranean.

The first to feel the power of the Crusading army were the subjects of the Christian King of Hungary at Zara, a port city, once the property of the Venetians, on the east coast of the Adriatic Sea. The Venetian leaders of the expedition proposed that part of the sum owed by the Crusaders to Venice might properly be paid if the Crusaders would assist Venice in recapturing Zara. The proposal was agreed to and Zara thus became the first target of this strange Crusade.

THE CRUSADERS TAKE ZARA[3]

On the Eve of St. Martin (10th November) they came before Zara in Sclavonia, and held the city enclosed by high walls and high towers; and vainly would you have sought for a fairer city, or one of greater strength, or richer. And when the pilgrims saw it, they marveled greatly, and said one to another, "How could such a city be taken by force, save by the help of God himself?"

The first ships that came before the city cast anchor and waited for the others; and in the morning the day was very fine and very clear, and all the galleys came up with the transports, and the other ships which were behind; and they took the port by force, and broke the chain that defended it and [which] was very strong and well-wrought;* and they landed in such sort that the port was between them and the town. Then might you have seen many a knight and many a sergeant swarming out of the ships, and taking from the transports many a good war horse, and many a rich tent and many a pavilion. Thus did the host encamp. And Zara was besieged on St. Martin's Day (11th November 1202). . . .

On the day following the feast of St. Martin, certain of the people of Zara came forth, and spoke to the Doge of Venice, who was in his pavilion, and said to him that they would yield up the city and all their goods—their lives being spared—to his mercy. And the Doge replied that he would not accept these conditions, nor any conditions, save by consent of the Counts and Barons, with whom he would go and confer.

While he went to confer with the Counts and Barons, that party, of whom you have already heard, who wished to disperse the host, spoke to the envoys and said, "Why should you surrender your city? The pilgrims will not attack you—have no care of them. If you can defend yourselves against the Venetians, you will be safe enough." And they chose one of themselves, whose name was Robert of Boves, who went to the walls of the city, and spoke the same words, therefore the envoys returned to the city, and the negotiations were broken off.

The Doge of Venice, when he came to the Counts and Barons, said to them: "Signors, the people who are therein desire to yield the city to my mercy, on condition only that their lives are spared. But I will enter into no agreement with them—neither this nor any other—save with your consent." And the Barons answered: "Sire, we advise you to accept these conditions, and we even beg of you so to do." He said he would do so; and they all returned together to the pavilion of the Doge to make the agreement, and found that the envoys had gone away by the advice of those who wished to disperse the host.

* In medieval ports, a chain was customarily drawn across the entrance to the harbor to block the entry of unauthorized vessels.

Then rose the Abbot of Vaux, of the order of the Cistercians, and said to them: "Lords, I forbid you, on the part of the Pope of Rome, to attack this city; for those within it are Christians, and you are pilgrims." When the Doge heard this, he was very much wroth, and much disturbed, and he said to the Counts and Barons: "Signors, I had this city, by their own agreement, at my mercy, and your people have broken that agreement; you have covenanted to help me to conquer it, and I summon you to do so."

Whereupon the Counts and Barons all spoke at once, together with those who were of their party, and said: "Great is the outrage of those who have caused this agreement to be broken, and never a day has passed that they have not tried to break up the host. Now are we shamed if we do not help to take the city." And they came to the Doge, and said: "Sire, we will help you to take the city despite those who would let and hinder us."

Thus was the decision taken. The next morning the host encamped before the gates of the city, and set up their petraries and mangonels, and other engines of war, which they had in plenty, and on the side of the sea they raised ladders from the ships. Then they began to throw stones at the walls of the city and at the towers. So did the assault last for about five days. Then were the sappers set to mine one of the towers, and began to sap the wall. When those within the city saw this, they proposed an agreement, such as they had before refused by the advice of those who wished to break up the host.

Thus did the city surrender to the mercy of the Doge, on condition only that all lives should be spared. Then came the Doge to the Counts and Barons, and said to them: "Signors, we have taken this city by the grace of God and your own. It is now winter, and we cannot stir hence till Eastertide; for we should find no market in any other place; and this city is very rich, and well furnished with all supplies. Let us therefore divide it in the midst, and we will take one half, and you the other."

As he had spoken, so was it done. The Venetians took the part of the city toward the port, where were the ships, and the Franks took the other part. There were quarters assigned to each, according as was right and convenient. And the host raised the camp, and went to lodge in the city. [Trans. Sir Frank Marzials]

While the soldiers of the Crusading host rested after their exertions at Zara in 1202, they were led to take a further step to turn the Crusade away from its original purpose. The Crusaders became entangled in the web of recent Byzantine history.

In 1195, the aged and incompetent Byzantine Emperor, Isaac Angelus, was deposed by his brother, Alexius III, who took the imperial throne at Constantinople for himself. Isaac Angelus, blinded and imprisoned by his brother, hoped for his own restoration to the throne. In 1201, Isaac's son, young Alexius, escaped from Constantinople and came to western Europe to seek help from his brother-in-law, Philip of Suabia, the German King. Philip was occupied with domestic difficulties in Germany and could do nothing to assist young Alexius' plans. The German monarch did, however, direct Alexius to Zara, where the Crusading army and the Venetian fleet might prove more able to lend Alexius the aid he required.[4]

DIVERSION OF THE FOURTH CRUSADE
TO CONSTANTINOPLE[5]

And after another fortnight came also the envoys from Germany, sent by King Philip and the heir of Constantinople. Then the Barons, and the Doge of Venice assembled in a palace where the Doge was lodged. And the envoys addressed them and said: "Lords, King Philip sends us to you, as does also the brother of the King's wife, the son of the Emperor of Constantinople.

" 'Lords,' says the King, 'I will send you the brother of my wife; and I commit him into the hands of God—may he keep him from death!—and into your hands. And because you have fared forth for God, and for right, and for justice, therefore you are bound, in so far as you are able, to restore to their own inheritance those who have been unrighteously despoiled. And my wife's brother will make with you the best terms ever offered to any people, and give you the most puissant help for the recovery of the land oversea.

" 'And first, if God grant that you restore him to his inheritance, he will place the whole empire of Roumania[6] in obedience to Rome, from which it has long been separated. Further, he knows that you have spent of your substance and that you are poor, and he will give you 200,000 marks of silver, and food for

The
Turning
Point:
The Fourth
Crusade

199

all those of the host, both small and great. And he, of his own person, will go with you into the land of Babylon,* or, if you hold that that will be better, send thither 10,000 men, at his own charges. And this service he will perform for one year. And all the days of his life he will maintain, at his own charges, five hundred knights in the land oversea, to guard that land.'"

"Lords, we have full power," said the envoys, "to conclude this agreement, if you are willing to conclude it on your parts. And be it known to you, that so favorable an agreement has never before been offered to any one; and that he that would refuse it can have but small desire of glory and conquest."

The Barons and the Doge said they would talk this over; and a parliament was called for the morrow. When all were assembled, the matter was laid before them.

Then arose much debate. The Abbot of Vaux, of the order of the Cistercians, spoke, and that party that wished for the dispersal of the host; and they said they would never consent; that it was not to fall on Christians that they had left their homes, and that they would go to Syria.

And the other party replied: "Fair lords, in Syria you will be able to do nothing; and that you may right well perceive by considering how those have fared who abandoned us, and sailed from other ports. And be it known to you that it is only by way of Babylon, or of Greece, that the land oversea can be recovered, if so be that it ever is recovered. And if we reject this covenant we shall be ashamed to all time."

There was discord in the host, as you hear. Nor need you be surprised if there were discord among the laymen, for the white monks of the order of Citeaux were also at issue among themselves in the host. The Abbot of Loos, who was a holy man and a man of note, and other abbots who held with him, prayed and besought the people, for pity's sake, and the sake of God, to keep the host together, and agree to the proposed convention, in that "it afforded the best means by which the land oversea might be recovered"; the Abbot of Vaux, on the other hand, and those who held with him, preached full oft, and declared that all this was naught, and that the host ought to go to the land of Syria, and there do what they could.

* I.e., Egypt. Babylon is the customary Western name for Cairo in this period.

Then came the Marquis of Montferrat, and Baldwin, Count of Flanders and Hainault, and Count Louis, and Count Hugh of St. Paul, and those who held with them, and they declared that they would enter into the proposed covenant, for that they should be ashamed if they refused. So they went to the Doges' hostel, and the envoys were summoned, and the covenant, in such terms as you have already heard, was confirmed by oath, and by charters with seals appended.

And the book tells you that only twelve persons took the oaths on the side of the Franks, for more (of sufficient note) could not be found. Among the twelve were first the Marquis of Montferrat, the Count Baldwin of Flanders, the Count Louis of Blois and of Chartres, and the Count of St. Paul, and eight others who held with them. Thus was the agreement made, and the charters prepared, and a term fixed for the arrival of the heir of Constantinople; and the term so fixed was the fifteenth day after the following Easter.   [*Trans. Sir Frank Marzials*]

The agreement made at Zara committed the Crusaders to attack Constantinople, a maneuver utterly incompatible with the legitimate business of the Crusade. The agreement, though halfheartedly denounced by the Pope, had the power of Venice behind it and the Crusaders, conscious of the debt still owed to the Venetians, went forward with their preparations. The army embarked from Zara late in April 1203 and, after pausing at Durazzo and Corfu, sailed on to Constantinople where they arrived late in June.

An attack upon the city began forthwith. In mid-July a breach in the walls was made. Alexius III fled quickly from the city and the aged Isaac Angelus was released from prison to become coemperor with his son, Alexius the younger (Alexius IV).

Now the reinstated Emperor and his son had the task of fulfilling the promises made by young Alexius to the Crusaders. While the Crusaders camped near the city, Alexius endeavored to raise the money and the men whose delivery he had rashly and irresponsibly promised. Neither money nor men were forthcoming, however, and the citizens of Constantinople were aggrieved by the actions of the Crusaders in their midst. By January 1204, the situation was grave. The Crusaders were impatient to be on their way

The Turning Point: The Fourth Crusade

and the Byzantines were eager to be rid both of their new Emperor and of the Crusaders.

A riot in the city against the Crusaders and against the government of Isaac Angelus and Alexius IV resulted in the deposition of the two Emperors and the elevation of still another emperor to the throne, Alexius V Murzuphlus. Young Alexius IV was quietly strangled and his father also perished in the revolution.

The Crusaders panicked. The new government was openly hostile to them and there was now no chance that the promised money and reinforcements would be given to them. The Venetians urged another attack upon Constantinople and the advice was quickly taken.[7]

THE CAPTURE OF CONSTANTINOPLE[8]

Then those of the host spoke together, and took counsel what they should do. Much was advanced this way and that, but in the end, they devised that if God granted them entry into the city by force, all the booty taken was to be brought together, and fittingly distributed; and further, if the city fell into their power, six men should be taken from among the Franks, and six from among the Venetians, and these twelve should swear, on holy relics, to elect as emperor the man who, as they deemed, would rule with most profit to the land. And whosoever was thus elected emperor, would have one quarter of whatever was captured, whether within the city or without, and moreover would possess the palace of Bucoleon and that of Blachernae; and the remaining three parts would be divided into two, and one of the halves awarded to the Venetians and the other to those of the host.

And there should be taken twelve of the wisest and most experienced men among the host of the pilgrims, and twelve among the Venetians, and those twenty-four would divide fiefs and honors, and appoint the service to be done therefore to the emperor.

This covenant was made sure and sworn to on the one side and the other by the Franks and the Venetians; with provision that at the end of March, a year hence, any who so desired might depart thence and go their way, but that those who remained in the land would be held to the service of the emperor in such manner as might be ordained. Thus was the covenant devised and made sure; and such as should not observe it were excommunicated by the clergy.

The fleet was very well prepared and armed, and provisions were got together for the pilgrims. On the Thursday after mid-Lent,[9] all entered into the vessels, and put their horses into the transports. Each division had its own ships, and all were ranged side by side; and the ships were separated from the galleys and transports. A marvelous sight it was to see; and well does this book bear witness that the attack, as it had been devised, extended over full half a French league.

On the Friday morning the ships and the galleys and the other vessels drew near to the city in due order, and then began an assault most fell and fierce. In many places the pilgrims landed and went up to the walls, and in many places the scaling ladders on the ships approached so close that those on the towers and on the walls and those on the ladders crossed lances, hand to hand. Thus lasted the assault, in more than a hundred places, very fierce, and very dour, and very proud, till near upon the hour of nones.[10]

But, for our sins, the pilgrims were repulsed in that assault, and those who had landed from the galleys and transports were driven back into them by main force. And you must know that on that day those of the host lost more than the Greeks, and much were the Greeks rejoiced thereat. And some there were who drew back from the assault, with the ships in which they were. And some remained with their ships at anchor so near to the city that from either side they shot at one another with petraries and mangonels.

Then, at vesper time, those of the host and the Doge of Venice called together a parliament, and assembled in a church on the other side of the straits—on the side where they had been quartered. There were many opinions given and discussed; and much were those of the host moved for the mischief that had that day befallen them. And many advised that they should attack the city on another side—the side where it was not so well fortified. But the Venetians, who had fuller knowledge of the sea, said that if they went to that other side, the current would carry them down the straits, and that they would be unable to stop their ships. And you must know that there were those who would have been well pleased if the current had borne them down the straits, or the wind, they cared not whither, so long as they left that land behind, and went on their way. Nor is this to be wondered at, for they were in sore peril.

Enough was there spoken, in this way and in that; but the conclusion of their deliberation was this: that they would repair and refit on the following day, which was Saturday, and during the whole of Sunday, and that on the Monday they would return to the assault; and they devised further that the ships that carried the scaling ladders should be bound together, two and two, so that two ships should be in case to attack one tower; for they had perceived that day how only one ship had attacked each tower, and that this had been too heavy a task for the ship, seeing that those in the tower were more in number than those on the ladder. For this reason it was well seen that two ships would attack each tower with greater effect than one. As had been settled, so it was done, and they waited thus during the Saturday and Sunday.

Before the assault the Emperor Murzuphlus had come to encamp, with all his power, in an open space, and had there pitched his scarlet tents. Thus matters remained till the Monday morning[11] when all those on the ships, transports, and galleys were all armed. And those of the city stood in much less fear of them than they did at the beginning and were in such good spirits that on the walls and towers you could see nothing but people. Then began an assault proud and marvelous, and every ship went straight before it to the attack. The noise of the battle was so great that it seemed to rend the earth.

Thus did the assault last for a long while, till our Lord raised a wind called Boreas which drove the ships and vessels further up on the shore. And two ships that were bound together, of which the one was called the *Pilgrim* and the other the *Paradise*, approached so near to a tower, the one on the one side and the other on the other—so as God and the wind drove them—that the ladder of the *Pilgrim* joined on to the tower. Immediately a Venetian, and a knight of France, whose name was Andrew of Urboise, entered into the tower, and other people began to enter after them, and those in the tower were discomfited and fled.

When the knights see this, who are in the transports, they land, and raise their ladders against the wall, and scale the top of the wall by main force, and so take four of the towers. And all begin to leap out of the ships and transports and galleys, helter-skelter, each as best he can; and they break in some three of the gates and enter in; and they draw the horses out of the transports; and the knights mount and ride straight to the quarters of the Emperor Murzuphlus. He had his battalions arrayed before his tents, and when his men see the mounted knights coming, they lose heart and fly; and so goes the Emperor flying through the streets to the castle of Bucoleon.

Then might you have seen the Greeks beaten down; and horses and palfreys captured, and mules, and other booty. Of killed and wounded there was neither end nor measure. A great part of the Greek lords had fled toward the gate of Blachernae. And vesper time was already past, and those of the host were weary of the battle and of the slaying. And they began to assemble in a great open space that was in Constantinople, and decided that they would take up their quarters near the walls and towers they had captured. Never had they thought that in a whole month they should be able to take the city, with its great churches, and great palaces, and the people that were in it.

As they had settled, so it was done, and they encamped before the walls and before the towers by their ships. Count Baldwin of Flanders and Hainault quartered himself in the scarlet tents that the Emperor Murzuphlus had left standing, and Henry his brother before the palace of Blachernae; and Boniface, Marquis of Montferrat, he and his men, toward the thickest part of the city. So were the host encamped as you have heard, and Constantinople taken on the Monday after Palm Sunday.[12] *[Trans. Sir Frank Marzials]*

The Latin knights and soldiers who took Constantinople had now to create a government for the city and for the Balkan territory which soon fell to them. They chose to create a Latin Empire of Constantinople: the Byzantine emperor was replaced by an elected Latin emperor and the professional bureaucratic machinery of the Byzantine state was largely replaced by a hodgepodge of feudal vassals of the new emperor. The Crusaders at Constantinople created a government fashioned along the same lines as the feudal states which earlier Crusaders had established in the Holy

Land. One of the first acts of the conquerors, once they were firmly in control of the city, was to proceed to the election of their emperor.

ELECTION AND CORONATION OF THE FIRST LATIN EMPEROR OF CONSTANTINOPLE[13]

Then a parliament assembled, and the commons of the host declared that an emperor must be elected, as had been settled aforetime. And they parliamented so long that the matter was adjourned to another day, and on that day would they choose the twelve electors[14] who were to make the election. Nor was it possible that there should be lack of candidates, or of men covetous, seeing that so great an honor was in question as the imperial throne of Constantinople. But the greatest discord that arose was the discord concerning Count Baldwin of Flanders and Hainault and the Marquis Boniface of Montferrat; for all the people said that either of those two should be elected.

And when the chief men of the host saw that all held either for Count Baldwin or for the Marquis of Montferrat, they conferred together and said: "Lords, if we elect one of these two great men, the other will be so filled with envy that he will take away with him all his people. And then the land that we have won may be lost, just as the land of Jerusalem came nigh to be lost when, after it had been conquered, Godfrey of Bouillon was elected King, and the Count of St. Giles became so fulfiled with envy that he enticed the other barons, and whomsoever he could, to abandon the host. Then did many people depart, and there remained so few that, if God had not sustained them, the land of Jerusalem would have been lost. Let us therefore beware lest the same mischance befall us also, and rather bethink ourselves how we may keep both these lords in the host. Let the one on whom God shall bestow the Empire so devise that the other is well content; let him grant to that other all the land on the further side of the straits, toward Turkey, and the Isle of Greece, and that other shall be his liegemen. Thus shall we keep both lords in the host."

As had been proposed, so was it settled, and both consented right willingly. Then came the day for the parliament, and the parliament assembled. And the twelve electors were chosen, six on one side and six on the other; and they swore on holy relics to elect, duly and in good faith, whomsoever would best meet the needs of the host and bear rule over the Empire most worthily.

Thus were the twelve chosen, and a day appointed for the election of the emperor; and on the appointed day the twelve electors met at a rich palace, one of the fairest in the world, where the Doge of Venice had his quarters. Great and marvelous was the concourse, for everyone wished to see who should be elected. Then were the twelve electors called, and set in a very rich chapel within the palace, and the door was shut, so that no one remained with them. The barons and knights stayed without in a great palace.

The council lasted till they were agreed; and by consent of all they appointed Nevelon, Bishop of Soissons, who was one of the twelve, to act as spokesman. Then they came out to the place where all the barons were assembled, and the Doge of Venice. Now you must know that many set eyes upon them, to know how the election had turned. And the Bishop, lifting up his voice— while all listened intently—spoke, as he had been charged, and said: "Lords, we are agreed, let God be thanked! upon the choice of an emperor; and you have all sworn that he whom we shall elect as emperor shall be held by you to be emperor indeed, and that if any one gainsay him, you will be his helpers. And we name him now at the selfsame hour when God was born, THE COUNT BALDWIN OF FLANDERS AND HAINAULT!"

A cry of joy was raised in the palace, and they bore the Count out of the palace, and the Marquis Boniface of Montferrat bore him on one side to the church and showed him all the honor he could. So was the Count Baldwin of Flanders and Hainault elected Emperor, and a day appointed for his coronation, three weeks after Easter.[15]   [Trans. Sir Frank Marzials]

While the knights of the Latin Empire under their newly crowned leader planned to subject the remnants of the Byzantine Empire to themselves, the news of the Crusaders' attack upon the city was carried to Pope Innocent III. The Pope was astounded and furious. In his first flush of anger, he wrote sharply to the papal legate who had accompanied the Crusaders:

The
Turning
Point:
The Fourth
Crusade

207

POPE INNOCENT III REPRIMANDS A PAPAL LEGATE[16]

To Peter, Cardinal Priest of the Title of St. Marcellus, Legate of the Apostolic See.

We were not a little astonished and disturbed to hear that you and our beloved son the Cardinal Priest of the Title of St. Praxida and Legate of the Apostolic See, in fear of the looming perils of the Holy Land, have left the province of Jerusalem (which, at this point is in such great need) and that you have gone by ship to Constantinople. And now we see that what we dreaded has occurred and what we feared has come to pass. . . . For you, who ought to have looked for help for the Holy Land, you who should have stirred up others, both by word and by example, to assist the Holy Land—on your own initiative you sailed to Greece, bringing in your footsteps not only the pilgrims, but even the natives of the Holy Land who came to Constantinople, following our venerable brother, the Archbishop of Tyre. When you had deserted it, the Holy Land remained destitute of men, void of strength. Because of you, its last state was worse than the first, for all its friends deserted with you; nor was there any admirer to console it. . . . We ourselves were not a little agitated and, with reason, we acted against you, since you had fallen in with this counsel and because you had deserted the Land which the Lord consecrated by his presence, the land in which our King marvelously performed the mystery of our redemption. . . .

It was your duty to attend to the business of your legation and to give careful consideration, not to the capture of the Empire of Constantinople, but rather to the defense of what is left of the Holy Land and, with the Lord's leave, the restoration of what has been lost. We made you our representative and we sent you to gain, not temporal, but rather eternal riches. And for this purpose, our brethren provided adequately for your needs.

We have just heard and discovered from your letters that you have absolved from their pilgrimage vows and their crusading obligations all the Crusaders who have remained to defend Constantinople from last March to the present. It is impossible not to be moved against you, for you neither should nor could give any such absolution.

Whoever suggested such a thing to you and how did they ever lead your mind astray? . . .

How, indeed, is the Greek church to be brought back into ecclesiastical union and to a devotion for the Apostolic See when she has been beset with so many afflictions and persecutions that she sees in the Latins only an example of perdition and the works of darkness, so that she now, and with reason, detests the Latins more than dogs? As for those who were supposed to be seeking the ends of Jesus Christ, not their own ends, whose swords, which they were supposed to use against the pagans, are now dripping with Christian blood—they have spared neither age nor sex. They have committed incest, adultery, and fornication before the eyes of men. They have exposed both matrons and virgins, even those dedicated to God, to the sordid lusts of boys. Not satisfied with breaking open the imperial treasury and plundering the goods of princes and lesser men, they also laid their hands on the treasures of the churches and, what is more serious, on their very possessions. They have even ripped silver plates from the altars and have hacked them to pieces among themselves. They violated the holy places and have carried off crosses and relics. . . .

Furthermore, under what guise can we call upon the other Western peoples for aid to the Holy Land and assistance to the Empire of Constantinople? When the Crusaders, having given up the proposed pilgrimage, return absolved to their homes; when those who plundered the aforesaid Empire turn back and come home with their spoils, free of guilt; will not people then suspect that these things have happened, not because of the crime involved, but because of your deed? Let the Lord's word not be stifled in your mouth. Be not like a dumb dog, unable to bark. Rather, let them speak these things publicly, let them protest before everyone, so that the more they rebuke you before God and on God's account, the more they will find you simply negligent. As for the absolution of the Venetian people being falsely accepted, against ecclesiastical rules, we will not at present argue with you. . . .

Given July 12.

[Trans. James A. Brundage]

Despite these bitter words, there was little that the Pope could do to alter what had happened and so, as his initial anger subsided, Innocent first recognized and then embraced the new order in Constantinople.

The Fourth Crusade marks the turning point of the whole Crusading endeavor. By destroying the only major Christian power of the East, this misbegotten expedition effectively determined that, despite occasional local victories, the Holy Land would remain largely in Moslem hands. The power of Byzantium was gone, never to return. The Latin Empire which replaced it was weak, amorphous, and unstable. The Crusade had crippled Christian power in the East Mediterranean. The capture of Constantinople and the greedy orgies which accompanied it determined once and for all the resolution of the Greeks to avoid any association, doctrinal or organizational, with the Papacy or with any part of the Western Church.

The Latin Empire's history was as inglorious as it was brief. While the emperors and their Latin vassals struggled vainly to establish themselves in the Balkans, Greek governments were formed at three separate centers within the former territory of Byzantium. Of these Byzantine governments in exile, the one established by Theodore Lascaris at Nicaea was destined to win out over its competitors, both Greek and Latin. Despite heroic efforts by the Latin emperors, one of whom ultimately was forced to pawn his son in order to secure money to support his government,[17] the Empire soon disappeared. Wracked by dissensions within the Empire and attacked by Greeks, Bulgars, and Saracens, the Empire fell in 1261 to the Nicaean Emperor, Michael Paleologus, whose victorious army was materially assisted by Genoese merchants. The restored Byzantine Empire after 1261, however, was never more than a pallid ghost of the great Christian state destroyed by the Fourth Crusade.[18]

CHAPTER XI

[1] Runciman, *Crusades*, III, 76-109; Waas, *Geschichte der Kreuzzüge*, I, 216-27.

[2] Geoffrey of Villehardouin, "De la conqueste de Constantinople," trans. Sir Frank Marzials in *Memoirs of the Crusades*, (London: Dent 1908), pp. 1-2, 4-7, 15-17—hereafter

cited as Villehardouin, *Memoirs*.

[3] Villehardouin, *Memoirs*, pp. 19-22.

[4] Runciman, *Crusades*, III, 111-17; Letter of Dandalo to Innocent III, Migne, *P.L.*, CCXV, 511-12; Henri Gregoire, "The Question of the Diversion of the Fourth Cru-

sade, Or, An Old Controversy Solved by a Latin Adverb," *Byzantion*, XV (1940-41), 158-66, contends that the diversion was planned long ahead of time by the ambitious Boniface of Montferrat; see, too, A.A. Vasiliev, *History of the Byzantine Empire* (Madison, Wis.: University of Wisconsin Press, 1952), pp. 452-58; also A. Frolow, *Recherches sur la deviation de la IVᵉ croisade vers Constantinople* (Paris, 1955).

5 Villehardouin, *Memoirs*, pp. 22-24.

6 The Byzantine Empire, i.e., the Roman Empire. See Robert Lee Wolf, "Romania: The Latin Empire of Constantinople," *Speculum*, XXIII (1948), 1-34, for a discussion of the uses and meanings of the term at various periods.

7 Villehardouin, *Memoirs*, pp. 24-56; Robert af Clari, *The Conquest of Constantinople*, trans. Edgar Holmes McNeal ("Columbia University Records of Civilization" [New York: Columbia University Press, 1936]), pp. 45-86; Runciman, *Crusades*, III, 117-21.

8 Villehardouin, *Memoirs*, pp. 59-63.

9 April 8, 1204.

10 That is, until mid-afternoon.

11 April 12, 1204.

12 Villehardouin here means the Monday *before* Palm Sunday, i.e., April 12, 1204, not the Monday *after* Palm Sunday, which would have been April 19.

13 Villehardouin, *Memoirs*, pp. 67-68.

14 Clari, *The Conquest of Constantinople*, speaks of ten, rather than twelve, electors.

15 Sunday, May 16, 1204.

16 Pope Innocent III, Epist. 136, Migne, *P.L.*, CCXV, 699-702.

17 Robert Lee Wolff, "Mortgage and Redemption of an Emperor's Son: Castile and the Latin Empire of Constantinople," *Speculum*, XXIX (1954), 45-84.

18 For the Latin Empire, see Vasiliev, *History of the Byzantine Empire*, pp. 463-69, 506-39, and the literature cited there, especially William Miller, *Latins in the Levant* (London: John Murray, 1908). See also the many articles by Robert Lee Wolff on this theme, especially "Baldwin of Flanders and Hainaut, First Latin Emperor of Constantinople; His Life, Death and Resurrection, 1172-1225," *Speculum*, XXVII (1952), 281-322; "Footnote to an Incident of the Latin Occupation of Constantinople," *Traditio*, VI (1948), 319-28; "The Latin Empire of Constantinople and the Franciscans," *Traditio* II (1944), 213-37; "The Organization of the Latin Patriarchate of Constantinople, 1204-1261; Social and Administrative Consequences of the Latin Conquest," *Traditio*, VI (1948), 33-60; "Politics in the Latin Patriarchate of Constantinople," *Dumbarton Oakes Papers*, VIII (1954), 225-304; "Romania: The Latin Empire of Constantinople," *Speculum*, XXIII (1948), 1-34.

The Turning Point: The Fourth Crusade

211

Chapter XII

THE THIRTEENTH-CENTURY CRUSADES

After 1204 the character and direction of the European Crusades were fundamentally altered. The Crusades which followed the expeditions of 1202-1204 were most commonly directed against Egypt rather than against the Moslems in the Holy Land itself. Thirteenth-century Crusaders saw that, as Richard the Lion-Hearted had pointed out, Egypt was the source of Moslem strength in the East, and they felt that control of Egypt was necessary to insure the continuance of any Western states in the East at all.

Never in the thirteenth century was there to be a general coalition of Western kings for a Crusade, as there had been in 1187. This was in part due, no doubt, to the internal politics of thirteenth century Europe, in part to the gradual decline of the Crusading movement itself. That the spirit of the Crusade was not dead is amply proved by the eight large expeditions from various quarters of Europe during the thirteenth century.[1] The survival of the Crusading spirit during the century is further shown by the extraordinary movement in 1212 which is known as the Children's Crusade. This expedition—which, of course, was not a Crusade at all in the strict sense of the term—attracted thousands of children and young adults from northern France and western Germany to its banners. The "Crusade" was preached in France by a peasant boy named Stephen from a village near Vendome. In Germany, a boy named Nicholas from Cologne started the movement.[2] The sorry business was summarized by a chronicler in these terms:

THE CHILDREN'S CRUSADE[3]

In this year occurred an outstanding thing and one much to be marveled at, for it is unheard of throughout the ages. About the time of Easter and Pentecost,[4] without anyone having preached or called for it and prompted by I know not what spirit, many thousands of boys, ranging in age from six years to full maturity, left the plows or carts which they were driving, the flocks which they were pasturing, and anything else which they were doing. This they did despite the wishes of their parents, relatives, and friends who sought to make them draw back. Suddenly one ran after another to take the cross. Thus, by groups of twenty, or fifty, or a hundred, they put up banners and began to journey to Jerusalem. They were asked by many people on whose advice or at whose urging they had set out upon this path. They were asked especially since only a few years ago many kings, a great many dukes, and innumerable people in powerful companies had gone there and had returned with the business unfinished. The present groups, morever, were still of tender years and were neither strong enough nor powerful enough to do anything. Everyone, therefore, accounted them foolish and imprudent for trying to do this. They briefly replied that they were equal to the Divine will in this matter and that, whatever God might wish to do with them, they would accept it willingly and with humble spirit. They thus made some little progress on their journey. Some were turned back at Metz, others at Piacenza, and others even at Rome. Still others got to Marseilles, but whether they crossed to the Holy Land or what their end was is uncertain. One thing is sure: that of the many thousands who rose up, only very few returned.

[Trans. James A. Brundage]

The defense of the Holy Land against the Moslems could not depend upon such spasmodic, uncontrolled demonstrations of popular enthusiasm as were manifested in the Children's expedition. A few years later, at the Fourth Lateran Council of the Church in 1215, Pope Innocent III called for further Crusades. At the same time the Pope took care to see that the hoped-for expedition would be under papal authority and bound by papal controls. The thirteenth-century

The Thirteenth- Century Crusades

popes saw the Crusades as instruments of papal policy, for which they were responsible and over which papal authority must be paramount.

PAPAL REGULATIONS FOR THE CRUSADE[5]

As we hope, with a burning desire, for the liberation of the Holy Land from the hands of the impious, on the advice of prudent men who are fully aware of the temporal and geographical circumstances and with the approval of the Holy Council,* we have decreed that:

The Crusaders shall so prepare themselves that on the first day of next June all those who are going to travel by sea shall assemble in the kingdom of Sicily. Some, as shall be convenient or handy, shall be at Brundisium and others shall be at Messana and the environs of both places. We have determined that we personally—with the Lord's permission—shall be there at that time so that with our aid and counsel the Christian army shall be arrayed advantageously to set out with the Divine and Apostolic blessing. Those who propose to go by land shall also strive to be ready at the same time. In the meantime they shall inform us of their plans, so that we may give them the aid and counsel of a suitable legate *a latere*.† The priests and other clerics, both prelates and others, who may be in the Christian army shall diligently devote themselves to prayer and exhortation. The priests shall teach the soldiers, both by word and by example, to have Divine love and fear ever before their eyes, lest the army do or say anything which might offend the Divine Majesty. If the soldiers should at any time lapse into sin, let them quickly rise again through true penance. They shall act humbly in heart and body. Let them observe moderation both in their dress and in their manner of living. They shall entirely foreswear dissension and emulation and they shall put off any spite or rancor. Thus, let them

* I.e., the Fourth Lateran Council, meeting at Rome in 1215.

† A Legate *a latere* is a Cardinal or other high-ranking cleric sent "from the side of" the Pope, i.e., he possesses in the province to which he is sent a full and ample power to exercise in the Pope's name the same jurisdiction possessed by the Pope. A recent discussion of the legate *a latere* with ample references to the literature is found in Franz Wasner, "Fifteenth Century Texts on the Ceremonial of the Papal Legatus a Latere,'" *Traditio* XIV (1958), 295-358.

fight, secure in faith, with both spiritual and material weapons ✓
against the foe. They are not to presume in their own power, but
to hope for Divine strength.

We allow these clerics to participate in their benefices for
three years, as if they were resident at their churches* and, should
it be necessary, they may pledge their benefices as security for
the same length of time.†

Lest anything happen to delay or impede this holy enterprise,
we strictly order all the prelates of the Church that each of them
in his own territory shall arrange to renew the decision of those
who have taken the cross, and they shall diligently warn and remind both them and the other Crusaders who have already taken
the cross to fulfill their vow to the Lord. Should it be necessary,
the prelates may press them through personal excommunication
and sentences of interdict against their lands, so that there be no
turning back. Those alone are to be excepted who are so impeded
that, according to the providence of the apostolic see, their vow
may for good reason be commuted or postponed.

In this connection, lest any contingencies be overlooked in an
undertaking pertaining to Jesus Christ, we wish and order that
the Patriarchs, Archbishops, Bishops, Abbots, and others who have
the care of souls, carefully explain the message of the Crusade
to those committed to them. Let them, through the Father, Son,
and Holy Spirit, the one, only, true, eternal God, beseech the
kings, dukes, princes, marquises, counts, barons, and other magnates, as well as the common people of the towns, villages, and
castles so that those who do not personally go to the aid of the
Holy Land may send a like number of warriors with their necessary expenses for three years, according to their means and for
the remission of their sins, as has been set forth in the general
letters. Let even the lesser people be pressed, for greater security.

We wish not only those who provide their own ships, but also
those who help to build ships for this purpose to participate in

---

* Clerics are ordinarily required by Roman canon law to be personally resident in their parishes or benefices in order to receive the full
income accruing to their posts. This privilege, however, would allow
those clerics who went on Crusade to enjoy their full income, even
though they might be nonresident for as long as three years.
† I.e., the clergy who went on Crusade might mortgage their benefices
as security for loans for a three-year period.

this remission of sins. As for those who refuse, should there be any so ungrateful to our Lord God, let them be firmly warned on behalf of the Apostolic See, so that they may know that they will have to answer to us in a strict examination on this matter on the last day before the Great Judge. Let them first consider what kind of conscience, what security they will be able to have before Jesus Christ, the only-begotten son of God, into whose hands the Father has given all things, if they refuse to serve him, the Crucified, for the remission of sins, in this enterprise, which is properly his own, by whose protection they live, by whose benificence they are sustained, by whose blood, indeed, they have been redeemed.

Lest it seem that we place upon men's shoulders a grave and unbearable burden, which we are unwilling to move our finger to lift, and that we are like those who talk but do nothing: be it known that from what we can set aside above and beyond necessary and moderate expenses, we have given and donated thirty thousand pounds for this undertaking. This is in addition to the ship which we have given to the Crusaders from Rome and its environs. To this latter will be assigned no less than three thousand silver marks, which remain to us from the alms of certain of the faithful. The remainder of those alms has faithfully been allocated for other things useful and necessary in the Holy Land by the hands of the Patriarch of Jerusalem, Alberic of happy memory, and the Masters of the Temple and the Hospital.

We desire further that the other prelates of the Church, as well as all the clergy, shall participate and be associated both in the merit and in the toil of the expedition. We have ordained by the common consent of the Council that all the clergy whatever, both prelates and their subjects, shall give a twentieth part of the income of the churches for three years for aid to the Holy Land. This income shall be given through the agency of those appointed by apostolic provision. Only those religious shall be exempted from this levy who are singled out by reason of merit, as well as those who have taken or are taking the cross and who are going personally on the Crusade.

We, however, and our brethren, the cardinals of the Holy Roman Church, will pay a full tenth. Be it known to all that they are bound to observe this duty faithfully under pain of excommunication, so that those who knowingly perpetrate any fraud in this matter shall incur the sentence of excommunication. . . .

We excommunicate and place under anathema those false and impious Christians who, contrary to the interests of Christ and Christian people, carry arms, iron, or wood for ships to the Saracens; also those who sell galleys or ships to them. Those who command pirate ships for the Saracens or give them aid of technical assistance with engines or anything else, to the damage of the Holy Land, we order to be deprived of their goods. When captured, they are to become slaves. We direct that this sentence be expounded in all maritime cities on Sundays and feast days and that such people are not to be admitted into the Church unless they shall have paid full damages from their pockets and have sent the damages thus paid to aid the Holy Land, so that, by a just judgment, the punishment fits the crime. If perchance they do not pay, let some other such sentence be imposed, so that by their punishment others may be averted from presuming to try similar impudent behavior.

We furthermore enjoin all Christians and forbid them under pain of anathema to send their ships or to sail for four years into the lands of the Saracens who live in the East. A great abundance of ships will thereby be prepared for those who wish to cross over to aid the Holy Land and the aforesaid Saracens will thereby be deprived of the not inconsiderable help which normally accrues to them.

It has happened that tournaments have been generally forbidden under certain penalties by various councils. Since, however, at this time the business of the Crusade would be greatly impeded by them, we absolutely forbid tournaments to be held for a period of three years, under penalty of excommunication.

Since for the pursuit of this undertaking it is most essential that the princes and Christian people keep peace with one another, on the advice of the holy universal synod, we have decreed that a general peace is to be observed in the whole Christian world for at least four years. Disputing parties are to be brought by the prelates of the Church to observe inviolate a full peace or a firm truce. Those who shall perchance refuse to abide by this shall be firmly forced to do so, meanwhile, by excommunication of their persons and their lands, unless the hatred of the injured is so great that they ought not rejoice in such a peace. But if, by chance, they contemn an ecclesiastical censure, they may rightly be terrified lest, through the authority of the Church, the secular power be arrayed against them, as disturbers of the Crusade.

We, therefore, relying upon the mercy of God and by the authority of the blessed apostles Peter and Paul, by the power of binding and loosing given to us (though unworthy) by God, grant to all who assist the labor in their own persons and at their own expense a plenary indulgence of their sins for which they shall have been truly contrite of heart and which they shall have confessed orally. We are promised an increase of eternal salvation as the reward of the just.

To those who do not take part in the Crusade in their own persons, but at least furnish the expenses of suitable men, according to their means and quality; and to those, likewise, who shall go in their own persons but at the expense of another, we grant a plenary indulgence for their sins. We wish and grant that those also shall be partakers of this remission who shall have ministered suitably with their goods to the needs of the Holy Land, according to the quality of their assistance, as well as those who shall have given useful aid and counsel.

To all those who piously take part in this endeavor, the common universal synod has given its approbation for all their good works, that it may worthily assist them to salvation. Amen.

[Trans. James A. Brundage]

Pope Innocent III died in 1216, before the planned expedition materialized. Innocent's successor, Pope Honorius III, was no less eager than Innocent for a Crusade which would seize Egypt and strengthen the precariously placed Latin Kingdom. Honorius stirred up King Andrew II of Hungary, who had taken the cross some time previously. Preachers in various parts of Europe reported a gratifying response to the appeal for a Crusade, but various delays arose. In 1217, the Hungarian King and the Duke of Austria, with their respective armies, finally sailed to Acre. In Palestine this Crusading expedition cooperated with the Eastern knights just long enough to capture the minor fortress of Beisan, late in 1217. From that point onward, however, the expedition foundered for lack of discipline, lack of manpower, and lack of food. The Hungarian King returned to Europe early in 1218, having accomplished virtually nothing.

Other Crusaders, meanwhile, were assembling in Europe for a further expedition, hoping to surprise the Sultan, al-Adil, by attacking Egypt while the Sultan's army was still committed to guard against attacks from Syria and Palestine. In the spring of 1218, further Crusading forces sailed to Acre, where they joined the Austrian Duke and the Latin barons. In May, these combined forces sailed for Damietta, near the mouth of the Nile. After landing successfully on the Delta, the Crusaders began to fight their way to the city of Damietta itself. Their advance was opposed both by the Sultan's army and by the natural defenses of the Delta region. The initial attack soon bogged down. The numerous rivers of the Delta and the dogged resistance of the Egyptians made the Crusaders' slow advance an expensive one as well. In September, the Christian army was joined by reinforcements from Italy headed by the arrogant Cardinal Pelagius, the Papal Legate who assumed command of the whole expedition. More reinforcements arrived in October to swell the army's ranks, but through the winter of 1218-1219 little real progress was made. Floods, cold weather, and a mysterious wave of illness hampered the Crusaders. One-fifth of the army, it is said, died during the epidemic.

With the arrival of spring came further fighting and, at last, the Crusaders were able to isolate the city of Damietta, their immediate goal. During the summer of 1219 an all-out attack upon the city began.[6]

DAMIETTA IS CAPTURED[7]

On the first of May a great multitude of pilgrims began to withdraw, leaving us in the greatest danger. But our kind and merciful Father, our leader and comrade in arms, Jesus Christ, "the protector and defender of those who hope in him . . ."[8] did not permit the unbelievers to rush in upon us until new and recent pilgrims arrived with abundant aid; a supply of provisions and horses sent over by divine power gladdened the assembly of the faithful. Therefore, on the feast of the Ascension of the Lord,[9] when the number of the soldiers of Christ was renewed, the untrustworthy enemy, according to their custom, rushed upon us by land and by water. As they could not prevail, though they made many attempts, they challenged our men particularly near the camp, losing and inflicting losses. But, on July 31 they brought forward all the power which they could muster, and after many assaults, finally crossed the ramparts against the army of the Temple. Violently bursting the barriers, they put our foot soldiers to flight, to such an extent that the whole army of the Christians was then endangered. The knights and soldiery of France tried three times to drive them farther back beyond the rampart, but were unable to do so. The Saracens, when our wooden fortifications had been shattered, ranged lines of horsemen and foot soldiers within our walls; their shouts arose as they mocked us; the whole multitude prepared its retinue. Fear welled up in the Christians, but the spirit which came upon Gideon animated the Templars. The Master of the Temple, with the Marshal and other brothers who were then present, made an attack through a narrow approach and manfully put the unbelievers to flight. The House of the Teutons and the counts and other knights of different nations, seeing the army of the Temple placed in such danger, quickly brought aid through entrances opposite them; thus the foot soldiers of the Saracens threw away their shields and were killed, except those whose headlong flight had snatched them from their killers. Our foot soldiers went out after our horsemen. The enemy retreated a short distance, their armed ranks holding out here and there, until evening twilight put an end to the battle. The Saracens went away first. Bodies of massacred wretches lay strewn near our rampart in great numbers, except those who were wounded seriously or slightly, and were brought back to camp. . . . A few of our men were killed or captured.

Almost all the machines prepared against the city were burned in a many-sided sortie of the defenders of Damietta. The Pisans, the Genoese, and the Venetians stoutly affirmed that they would attack the city by means of four ships upon which ladders hung; "but they were not of the race of those men by whom salvation was brought to Israel,"[10] for they wished to make a name for themselves. . . . The Legate of the Apostolic See[11] supplied copious funds to them from the common store, the King and others produced ropes and anchors in abundance according as they needed them. And so, attacking the city, they killed and wounded many on the first day; and the more often they made an attack afterward, so much the more were the walls strengthened by wooden towers and palisades; the defenders resisted the oncomers even more vigorously and efficaciously, and thus the ladders, injured by fire and several times repaired, were forced to the bank, and the attempt was fruitless. And so it was truly understood that by divine power alone would Damietta be delivered into the hands of the Christians.

But we, insensible and unmindful of the benefits and wonderful deeds of God, which He had done, "provoked the eyes of his Divine Majesty"[12] against us through the idleness of the leaders and the complaints of the followers. . . . Therefore it happened that on the feast of the beheading of Saint John the Baptist,[13] with our common faults urging us on, although scarcely any were to be found who would remain in the custody of the camp, we led forth a naval and land army and proceeded to the camp of the Babylonians between the sea and the river, where fresh water could not be found to drink. But taking up their tents they pretended flight; and when our men had advanced to a point where it was clear that our adversaries did not wish to meet us in open combat, our leaders began a long debate whether they should advance or retreat. . . . Meanwhile the ranks were scattered except for a group of those whom obedience bound in military discipline. The knights of Cyprus,* who were on the right flank, showed their timidity to the Saracens as they made an attack from the side. The Italian foot soldiers fled first, after them horsemen of various nations, and certain Hospitallers of Saint John, while the Legate of the Roman See and the Patriarch,† who was carrying the Cross, begged them earnestly to stand their ground, but in vain. The heat of the sun was intense, the foot soldiers were burdened with the weight of their arms. The difficulty of the way increased the heat, and those who had brought wine with them drank it unmixed in the distress of their thirst because of the lack of water. With all these things happening at the same time, those who defended themselves as they stood their ground and turned their backs on those who fled first in their breathless course were wiped out, collapsing without wounds. But the King, with the Templars, and the House of the Teutons, and the Hospitallers of Saint John, and the counts of Holland, and of Wied, of Saarbrücken and Chester, with Walter of Berthout, several counts of France and of Pisa,

* There were about a hundred of these Cypriot knights under the command of Walter, Lord of Caesarea and Constable of Cyprus.
† Ralph of Merencourt, the Patriarch of Jerusalem.

and other knights, sustained the attack of the pursuers. The King was almost burned with Greek fire; these men all served as a protection for those who were fleeing. As often as they showed their faces to the enemy, so often did the enemy flee, but as they gradually returned, these men had to sustain the blows and weapons of the enemy. . . . Thirty-three Templars were captured or killed with the Marshal of the Hospital of Saint John, and certain other brothers of the same House. Nor did the House of the Teutons escape without loss. The army of the Temple, which is usually first to assemble, was last to retreat. Therefore, when it arrived last at our ramparts, it stayed without, so that it might bring those who were before it back within the walls as soon as it was possible. Our persecutors finally returned to lead off the captives and to gather their spoils, presenting, as we afterwards learned from a Saracen, five hundred heads of Christians to the Sultan. Gloom took possession of our men, but not despair. For we knew that this affliction was the punishment of sin, and that there was less in the punishment than our fault demanded, since He tempered the chastisement Who says to the soul of the sinner, "Thou hast prostituted thyself to many lovers; nevertheless return to me, and I will receive thee. . . ."[14] For the Sultan, sending one of our captives, began to negotiate with us concerning peace or a truce, during which negotiation we promptly repaired our ramparts and other fortifications. . . .

Meanwhile, the city, being grievously afflicted by the long siege by sword, famine, and pestilence even more than can be written, placed its hope solely in the peace which the Sultan had promised the citizens. For famine had grown so strong in it that desirable foods were lacking, although spoiled foods abounded. For the grain of Egypt is not lasting on account of the soft earth in which it grows . . . and as we heard, one fig was sold there for eleven besants. Because of the distress of the famine, various kinds of diseases harassed them; among the other grievances which they suffered, they were said to see nothing at night, as if struck by blindness, though their eyes were open.[15] The Sultan, dissuading them from surrender, deceived the wretched men from day to day by empty promises. Finally, however, they blockaded their gates from within so that no one coming to us from their number might tell us how the days of affliction beset them. But any who could escape through the postern gate or down the walls by ropes clearly proved the distress of their people by their swollen and famished condition. The supply of bread and fodder began to diminish even for those who were besieging us from without in the army of the Saracens. For the Nile, which usually overflows from after the feast of Saint John the Baptist[16] until the Exaltation of the Holy Cross[17] and irrigates the plains of Egypt, did not rise this year according to its custom, to the mark which the Egyptians usually place, but, as we learned, left a great part of the land dry, which could not be ploughed or sown at the proper season. Therefore the Sultan, fearing death and famine and also because of his desire to keep Damietta, offered the Christians a peace with Coradin his brother on these terms: that he would give back the Holy Cross which had formerly been captured in the victory of Saladin,[18] along with the Holy City and all the captives who could be found alive throughout the kingdoms of Babylonia and Damascus, and also funds to repair the walls of Jerusalem; in addition he would restore the kingdom of Jerusalem entirely, except Krak and Montreal,* for the possession of which he would offer tribute for as long as the truce would last.

Now there are two places located in Arabia, which have seven very strong fortresses through which merchants of the Saracens and of the pilgrims usually cross going to Mecca or returning from it; and whoever holds them in his power can very seriously injure Jerusalem with her fields and vineyards when he wishes. The King and the French and the Count of Chester with the leaders of the Germans firmly believed that this arrangement was of advantage to Christianity, and ought to be accepted. . . . But the Legate, with the Patriarch, the archbishops and bishops, the Templars and Hospitallers, and all the leaders of Italy and many other prudent men, effectively resisted this arrangement, showing reasonably that Damietta ought to be taken before everything.[19] Differences of opinion produced discord which was quickly settled because of the common need. Meanwhile the Sultan secretly sent a great multitude of foot soldiers through the marshy places to the city on the Sunday night after the feast of All Saints;[20] two

---

* These two castles, located in the desert east of the Dead Sea, commanded the vital caravan route which linked Syria with the south. Hence the unwillingness of the Moslems to lose them and the opposition of at least some of the Christian leaders to a truce which left these fortresses in Moslem hands.

hundred and forty of them attacked the palisades while the Christians were sleeping; but the outcry of the sentries roused us, and about two hundred or more, according to our count, were killed or captured.

On November 5, in the reign of the Savior of the world, and with Pelagius, Bishop of Albano, skillfully and vigilantly executing the office of Legate of the Apostolic See, Damietta was captured without treachery, without resistance, without violent pillage and tumult, so that the victory may be ascribed to the Son of God alone, who inspired his people to the entrance of Egypt and administered help there. And when the city was captured before the eyes of the King of Babylon, he did not dare, according to his usual custom, to attack through our ramparts the soldiers of Christ who were prepared for the attack. . . . But the Sultan himself, in confusion, burned his own camp and fled. But God, who on the third day gathered the waters under the firmament into one place, who himself brought his soldiers through the waters of the sea to the harbor of Damietta on the third day of the month of May, led them over the Nile to besiege the city on the third day of the month of February, and himself captured Damietta located amidst the waters, on the third day of the month of November. . . .

Damietta! Renowned among kingdoms, very famous in the pride of Babylon, ruler of the sea, plunderer of Christians, seized in the pride of your persecutors by means of a few small ladders, now you are "humbled under the mighty hand of God";[21] and casting out the adulterer whom you kept for a long time, you have returned to your former husband; and you who first brought forth bastards, now shall bear legitimate sons for the faith of the Son of God, being firmly held by the faithful of Christ. The Bishop of Acre released from you the first fruits of souls for God by cleansing in the sacramental waters of baptism your little ones, who were found in you, alive by His power, even though they were near death. You have been subjected to manifold punishments because besides those who were taken alive in you, your dead of both sexes from the time of the siege round about you are computed at thirty thousand and more. The Lord struck them down without sword and fire, scorning henceforth to endure the uncleanness committed in you.

[Trans. Rev. John J. Gavigan]

The capture of Damietta raised the hopes of the Crusaders that at last they could crush Islam by conquering Egypt. Damietta gave the Crusaders a strategic outpost for further operations and the arrival of still more reinforcements was anticipated. The town, however, also gave the Crusaders something over which they could fight among themselves, and quarrels about the distribution of the spoils together with the beginning of some necessary construction work within the town brought the Crusade to a standstill. During 1220-1221 no significant advance was made and meanwhile various Crusaders left the army to return to Europe. The army which the Emperor Frederick II had been gathering still failed to make its appearance in the East, for Frederick was busy trying to consolidate his own position in Germany and Italy.

By the summer of 1221 the Crusaders despaired of Frederick's arrival and the forces at Damietta set out to try their hands against the Moslems. The army advanced southward toward Cairo, but soon ran into fierce Moslem opposition. As the summer wore on, action slowed down and, by late August, the army was so short of food that it was forced to retreat. By this time the Nile was rising and, when the Moslems opened the sluices which held back the water, the Crusading army was trapped between the Moslem forces and a flood.

There was no alternative but to surrender. On August 30 an agreement was concluded. The Crusaders were forced to give up Damietta and retire from Egypt. On September 8, as the Sultan's army entered the city, the Crusaders sailed for Acre.[22]

Hope for a Christian reconquest of the East now centered upon Frederick II, the handsome, young Holy Roman Emperor. That Christendom should depend upon Frederick to rescue the Holy Land from Islam was ironic, for Frederick's religious sentiments seem to have been more closely akin to those of his Moslem enemies than to any Christian orthodoxy. Piety was not one of Frederick's failings and, though brilliant and accomplished in many fields, Frederick's understanding of the Crusade was somewhat warped. Frederick had vowed to go on Crusade as early as 1215, but the Crusader's vow for him seems to have been principally a method of shielding his precarious hold upon Germany and Sicily behind the papal protection which was extended to Crusaders. Frederick's concern was primarily to consolidate his own position as Emperor. To this end, he postponed the fulfillment of his Crusading vow time and time again. When finally pressed by Pope Honorius III in 1225, Frederick solemnly promised to depart for the East within two years. Meanwhile, he prepared to use his Crusade to extend his Empire into the East. In 1225 he married Yolanda, the young heiress of the Latin Kingdom. Shortly thereafter, Frederick claimed the title of Latin King for himself. After seducing one of Yolanda's cousins, Frederick banished his fourteen-year-old bride to the harem which he kept at Palermo, where she bore the Emperor a son, Conrad, in 1228. Yolanda died less than a week later, but formally the title to the Latin Kingdom had already passed to her infant son, and Frederick was forced to be content with the position of regent for his son—if, according to the customs of the Kingdom, the Latin barons could be persuaded to accept his regency.

A Crusading army, meanwhile, was raised and on September 8, 1227 the Emperor and his army embarked for the East, just before the expiration of the time limit set by the Pope. Almost immediately after the fleet set sail, Frederick fell ill. His physician advised him in strong terms that he must return to Sicily to recover before attempting to make the arduous voyage to Palestine. Frederick forthwith landed to recuperate.

In view of Frederick's repeated postponements of the Crusade during the past twelve years, it is not surprising that Pope Gregory IX took this situation to be another attempt to delay the Crusade. In anger, the Pontiff solemnly excommunicated Frederick. The Emperor replied with a manifesto in which he attacked the pretensions of the Papacy and then proceeded, once he had recovered his health, with his preparations for the expedition. On June 28, 1228 Frederick sailed once again for the East.

The Emperor was now determined to gain such power and prestige as he could in the East, to add the remnants of the Crusaders' states to his Empire.[23] He stopped first at

Cyprus, whose infant king, Henry, was nominally Frederick's vassal.

THE EMPEROR FREDERICK II IN CYPRUS[24]

In the year 1229[25] the Emperor Frederick, at the command of Pope Gregory,* crossed the sea to Cyprus. He first landed at the city of Limassol,[26] where he had with him seventy galleys, transports and other ships. Most of his army and his household, together with his marshall and the horses, had already landed at Acre. . . .

The Lord of Beirut† . . . went to the Emperor with his children, all his friends, and the whole of the Cypriot army, both knights and sergeants. They brought their little lord, King Henry,‡ to the Emperor and put themselves completely at his disposal. The Emperor received them with a great feast and with the semblance of great joy and it appeared that their enemies had been mistaken. The Emperor immediately asked of them a favor, namely that they would put off the black robes which they were still wearing in mourning for the death of Philip d'Ibelin, the Lord of Beirut's brother. For, the Emperor said, the joy of his arrival should be greater than their sorrow for the loss of their friend, the Lord of Beirut's brother, who had died, even though he had been a most brave and noble man. They acceded most cheerfully to his command and willingly thanked him. They offered to place their bodies, hearts, and goods wholly at his service. The Emperor joyfully thanked them, saying that he would repay them amply and richly. The Emperor then sent scarlet gowns to those who had worn black and to others he sent jewelry and he gave all of them a verbal invitation to dine with him on the following day. They hastily fixed up their gowns and on the following morning they all appeared, clad in scarlet, before the Emperor.

On the previous night, however, the Emperor had secretly opened a door in the wall of a room which led into a garden—this was in a gracious house in which my lord Philip had housed him in Limassol. The Emperor had three thousand or more armed men—sergeants, arbalesters, and sailors—enter secretly at night through this false postern, so that virtually all the men from his

---

* Pope Gregory IX had, of course, excommunicated Frederick before he actually left Sicily the second time.
† John d'Ibelin, Lord of Beirut, 1197-1226.
‡ Henry I, "the Fat," King of Cyprus, 1218-1252.

fleet were there. They were stationed throughout the stables and the rooms of the house, behind closed doors, until the dinner hour.

The tables were set and the water poured. The Emperor put the Lord of Beirut and the old Lord of Caesarea,* who was Constable of Cyprus, at his own table. He placed the King of Cyprus and the King of Salonika† at the first place at another long table, together with the Marquis of Lancia‡ and the other barons of Germany and of the Kingdom. He ordered all the Cypriot knights to be seated in such a way that the Lord of Beirut and the others could hear and see him when he spoke. He also arranged for the two sons of the Lord of Beirut to serve him, one with the cup, the other with the bowl, and for the young Lord of Caesarea and the Lord Anceau de Brie to carve before him. The Emperor had the four of them don tunics and doublets over their mantles, for such, he said, was the law and custom of the Empire. The young men served him very willingly and nobly and there were many courses and a variety of food. During the last course the armed men emerged from the places where they had been waiting and they took charge of the palace, the rooms, and the great court and placed guards there and elsewhere. There were well-armed men in the palace where the Emperor was and he had them seated before him with their weapons in their hands—some held their swords by the pommel, others grasped their daggers. The Cypriots were well aware of what was going on, but they said not a word and tried to appear at ease.

The Emperor turned to the Lord of Beirut and said aloud: "Sir John, I ask two things of you. You will be wise if you do them agreeably and well." The Lord of Beirut replied: "Sire, say what is your pleasure and I shall willingly do what is right, so far as I understand it or as it is understood by honorable men." "One of the two things," said the Emperor, "is this: You will give me the city of Beirut, for you do not have it or hold it rightfully. The other thing is this: You will give me the income you have received as regent and ruler of Cyprus since the death of King Hugh, that is the income for the past ten years, for it is mine by right according to the custom of Germany." The Lord of Beirut replied: "Sire,

* Gautier III, Count of Caesarea, and a brother-in-law of John d'Ibelin, the Lord of Beirut.
† Demetrius of Montferrat, titular King of Salonica.
‡ Manfred II, Marquis of Lancia, vicar-general of Lombardy.

I believe that you must be joking and making sport of me, as it may well be. Perchance some evil men who hate me have suggested that you demand these things of me and this is what has prompted you to do it. But, please God, you are such a good and wise lord that you know that we can and will serve you so willingly that you will not trust those evil men." The Emperor placed his hand upon his head and said: "By this head, which has many times worn a crown, I shall have my way in these two matters which I have mentioned or you will be taken prisoner." At this the Lord of Beirut rose up and his appearance was striking as he said loudly: "I have and hold Beirut as my fief by right. My lady, Queen Isabelle,[27] who was my sister on my mother's side and a daughter of King Amaury[28] and who is thus the rightful heir of the Kingdom of Jerusalem—she and her lord, King Amaury,[29] together gave me Beirut in exchange for the constableship when the Christians had recovered the city all destroyed. The Templars and the Hospitallers and all the barons of Syria had refused the town. I have restored its walls and have maintained it by the alms of Christendom and by my own labors. In it I have invested the income I had from Cyprus and elsewhere.[30] If you maintain that I hold it wrongfully, I will substantiate my reasons and my rights in the court of the Kingdom of Jerusalem. As for the income from the regency and governance of Cyprus which you demand of me, I never had it. My brother got from the regency only the headaches of governing and working for the Kingdom. But my niece, Queen Alice, had the income and did with it as she pleased, as the one who held the rights of regency according to our custom. If you demand this of me, I shall furnish you with proof according to the customs and the court of the Kingdom of Cyprus. And you may be certain that I shall do no more than this out of any fear of death or imprisonment, unless the judgment of the good and loyal court requires me so to do."

The Emperor grew very angry and swore and threatened him. Finally the Emperor said: "I heard and learned a long time ago across the sea that your words were handsome and polite and that you were very discreet and subtle with words, but I shall show you that your wit, your subtlety, and your words are worth nothing against my power."

The Lord of Beirut replied in such a way that those who were present were astounded and all of his friends were much afraid.

His reply was: "Sire, you heard tell long ago of my polite words; I, too, have heard often and for long of your deeds. When I planned to come here, my whole council, with one voice, warned me that you would do what you are now doing and worse, and that I was not to trust you in any way. I came under no illusions; I had good advice and I understood it. But I would much rather suffer death or imprisonment than to allow anyone to speak evil of us or to allow the help due to Our Lord, the help due to the conquest of the Holy Land, and your service to be hindered by me, my family, or my compatriots. . . ." He suddenly stopped and sat down.

The Emperor was very angry and changed color often. People stared at the Lord of Beirut and there were many words and threats. Religious men and other good people intervened to try to reach agreement, but no one could get the Lord of Beirut to alter what he had said he would do. The Emperor made many strange and sinister requests. At last they agreed to do what the Lord of Beirut had earlier proposed and he could now be forced to concede no more than this: that he would furnish the Emperor with twenty of the most noble vassals of Cyprus as hostages. These men would pledge by their bodies, their belongings, and their estates that the Lord of Beirut would serve the Emperor, would go to the Court of the Kingdom of Jerusalem, and would there prove his rights, and that, when he had appeared in court, the hostages would be freed and released.

[Trans. James A. Brundage]

From Cyprus Frederick sailed quickly to Acre to begin his Crusade. The Crusade in Frederick's hands, however, was to be a far different kind of affair from his predecessors. Instead of using his army against the Moslems, it was Frederick's intention to negotiate with the Egyptian Sultan for a peaceful territorial settlement in the Holy Land. Frederick proposed to use his army principally against the Latins in the East, to try to force them to acknowledge his position as regent and de facto ruler of the Latin states in the East. In short, Frederick's objective was the conquest, not of the Moslem-held territories of Palestine, but rather of the Crusading states.

In the year 1229[32] the Emperor came to Syria with his whole navy. The King[33] and all the Cypriots, together with the Lord of Beirut,[34] accompanied him. The Lord of Beirut went to Beirut, where he was joyfully received, for never was a lord more warmly loved by his men. He remained there but one day and then followed the Emperor to Tyre. The Emperor was very well received in Syria where all did homage to him as regent, because he had a little son called King Conrad, who was the rightful heir of the Kingdom of Jerusalem through his mother who was dead.[35] The Emperor and his men and all the Syrians left Acre to go to Jaffa. There they held truce conferences with al-Kamil, who was then Sultan of Babylon and Damascus,[36] and who held Jerusalem and the whole country. As a result of their agreement Jerusalem, Nazareth, and Lydda were thereby turned over to the Emperor.

In this same year,[37] amidst these events, the Emperor ordered Count Stephen of Gotron and other Longobards[38] as well, to come to Cyprus. He had all the fortresses and the royal revenues seized for his use. He claimed that he was regent and that this was his right. The Cypriots were much perplexed and had their wives and children placed in religious houses wherever they could. Some of them—namely Sir John d'Ibelin, later Count of Jaffa, who was then a child, his sister, and other gentlefolk—fled in the midst of the winter. It was a bad season and they barely escaped drowning, but, as it so pleased God, they finally arrived at Tortosa. The Emperor held Cyprus. The Cypriots who were in his army were very uncomfortable and, had the Lord of Beirut sanctioned it, they would have carried off and kidnapped the young King Henry and would have fled from the Emperor's camp.

The Emperor was now disliked by all the people of Acre. He was the object of the Templars' special disfavor. There was at that time a very brave Templar, Brother Peter de Montagu, a most valiant and noble man, as was also the master of the Teutonic Knights. The people of the lowlands[39] also had little use for the Emperor. The Emperor seemed to be delaying.[40] Every day, even in winter, he kept his galleys armed, with the oars in the locks. Many people said that he wished to seize the Lord of Beirut and his children, Sir Anceau de Bries and his other friends, the Master of the Temple and other persons and have them shipped to Apulia. Another said that he wished to have them killed at a

The Thirteenth-Century Crusades

231

council to which he had called and summoned them but that they had been aware of this and went to the council with such forces that he dared not do it.

He made his truce with the Saracens in all particulars as they wished it. He went to Jerusalem and then to Acre. The Lord of Beirut never left him and, though he was often advised to leave, he did not wish to do so. The Emperor assembled his people at Acre and had all the people of the city come and there were many who thought well of him. . . .

The Emperor secretly prepared to depart. At daybreak on the first of May, he boarded a galley before the Butchers' Street, without notifying anyone. Thus it happened that the butchers and the old people who lived on the street and who were very unfriendly saw his party and pelted him most abusively with tripe and scraps of meat. . . .

Thus the Emperor left Acre, cursed, hated, and despised.

[Trans. James A. Brundage]

By diplomacy and without spilling a drop of blood, Frederick won the goals for which the Crusade had been launched. Jerusalem and Bethlehem were restored to Christian hands and a corridor linking the cities with the sea was also ceded to the Latins. Moreover, a ten-year truce was arranged and trading rights were guaranteed to Christians and Moslems alike. But the Emperor, who had won so much, lost what he had come to gain. The Latin Kingdom was not to be a part of Frederick's Empire. The barons and clergy unanimously rejected him as regent and Frederick was forced to return to the West almost immediately to meet an attack which had been launched against his Sicilian Kingdom during his absence by his father-in-law and the Pope.[41]

Frederick's departure left the Latin states reconstituted but devoid of strong leadership. The barons of the Latin Kingdom cherished dearly their feudal independence, even though, in the final analysis, it might cost them the possession of the Kingdom itself. The decade of comparative peace which followed Frederick's departure saw nothing done to assure the permanence of the Latin states. At the expiration of the treaty period, small Crusading armies journeyed to the East, one in 1239, led by King Thibaud of Navarre, and another one in 1240, led by Richard of Cornwall. Neither of these expeditions accomplished anything important, and meanwhile the feudal families of the Latin Kingdom fought among themselves and with various Moslem foes.

In July 1244 Jerusalem was again attacked, this time by wild Khwarismian Turks in the employ of the Egyptians. The Khwarismian attack came as a surprise to the garrison of the city and, after a short defense, the Turks broke into the town. The garrison fled to the Tower of David and held out there for nearly six weeks. Then, on August 23, they surrendered. Thus began six hundred and fifty years of uninterrupted Moslem control of the Holy City.

The fall of Jerusalem presaged further disasters for the Latins in the Levant. In October 1244, a major Latin army was destroyed by the Egyptians and their allies at La Forbie, near Gaza. Egyptian attacks continued during the next three years and in 1247 the major city of Ascalon was also lost by the Latins. The need for renewed assistance from the West was obvious.

The saintly, steadfast King of France, Louis IX, rose to the occasion. In 1245 he declared his intention of raising an expedition to attack Egypt and, after three years of strenuous preparation, the army made ready to sail in 1248. One of King Louis' boon companions thus described his departure:

THE JOURNEY OF ST. LOUIS AND HIS CRUSADERS TO THE HOLY LAND[42]

The Abbot of Cheminon gave me my scrip and pilgrim's staff; and then I left Joinville, barefooted and in my shirt, never to enter the castle again until my return; and thus I went to Blecourt and Saint Urbain and to visit other relics of the saints in the neighborhood. On my road to Blecourt and Saint Urbain I would not looked back toward Joinville for fear lest my heart should weaken at the thought of the lovely castle I was leaving and of my two children.

I and my companions dined at Fontaine-l'Archeveque opposite Donjeux, and there Abbot Adam of Saint Urbain (God grant him his mercy) gave a great store of fine jewels to me and the nine knights I had with me. Thence we went to Auxonne; and from Auxonne we went down the Saone to Lyons with the equipment we had loaded into boats. The great warhorses were led beside the boats.

At Lyons we embarked on the Rhone to go to Arles-le-Blanc; and by the Rhone we saw a castle called Roche le Glun which the King had razed because Roger, the lord of the castle, was accused of robbing pilgrims and merchants.

In the month of August we embarked on our ships at the Rock of Marseilles. On the day we embarked, the entry port of the ship was opened and all the horses we had to take overseas were taken on board. Then the door was closed and well tamped, in the same way as you bung a cask, for when the ship is at sea the whole door is under water.

When the horses had been embarked, our master mariner called to his sailors, who were in the prow of the ship, "Is all fast?" "Aye, aye, sir," they answered; "the clerks and priests may come forward." As soon as they had done so, he called out to them, "In the name of God, strike up a song!" They all sang in unison *"Veni, Creator Spiritus"*; the master called to the sailors, "In the name of God, make sail." And so they set the sails.

Soon the wind filled the sails and had taken us out of sight of land, so that we could see nothing but sky and water; and every day the wind took us farther from the homes in which we were born. How foolhardy, then the man is who dares to run so grave a risk when he has in his possession what belongs to another, or is in mortal sin. For when you go to sleep at night you do not know whether you may find yourself in the morning at the bottom of the sea.

An awesome marvel befell us at sea; we sighted a mountain, off the Barbary Coast, which was quite round. It was about the time of Vespers when we sighted it, and all that night we sailed on and thought that we must have made over fifty leagues; but in the morning we found ourselves still off this same mountain; and this happened two or three times. The sailors were greatly perturbed when they saw it and told us that our ships were in great danger, as we were off the country of the Saracens of Barbary.

Then a good priest, who was known as the Dean of Maurupt, told us that in his parish, whenever he had had trouble from drought or too much rain—in any trouble, indeed—he had held three processions on three Saturdays, and immediately God and His Mother had rid them of the trouble. It was then a Saturday.

We made the first procession round the two masts of the ship. For my part, I had myself carried round, as I was very sick. That was the last we saw of the mountain, and on the third Saturday we arrived at Cyprus.

The King was already there when we arrived, and we found that a great store of provisions was ready for him—wine and money and corn. There was such a supply of wine that in the middle of the fields by the seashore his men had built great piles of barrels of wine which they had been buying for two years before his arrival; they had put them one on top of the other, so that when you looked at them from the front you would have thought that they were great wooden barns.

The wheat and barley were also heaped out in the fields. At first sight you thought they were hills; the rain had been beating on the grain for a long time and had made it sprout on the outside, so that all you could see was green grass. But when they were ready to ship it to Egypt they tore off the outside crust of grass, and inside the wheat and barley was as fresh as if they had been newly threshed.

The King would have been glad to press on to Egypt without delay—so I have heard him say when we were in Syria—had not his barons advised him to wait for those of his people who had not yet arrived.   [*Trans. René Hague*]

The strategy of this Crusade was the same as that of the Fifth Crusade in 1218-1221. Egypt was to be the immediate target of the expedition. Once Egypt was taken, the conquest of Jerusalem and the establishment of a strong, permanent Latin state would be simple.

The army sailed first to Cyprus and from there to the Egyptian delta.

ST. LOUIS SAILS TO EGYPT AND CAPTURES DAMIETTA[43]

At the beginning of March, by the King's order, the King, the barons, and the other pilgrims ordered the ships to be loaded again with wine and food, ready to sail when he should give the word. On the Friday before Pentecost[44] the King saw that everything was in order, and he and the Queen embarked. He told his barons to follow him in their ships and to set a straight course for Egypt. On the Saturday he sailed, and all the other ships with him. It was a beautiful sight; as far as your eye could see, the whole sea seemed to be covered with towels, by the canvas of ships' sails, whose number, large and small, was given as eighteen hundred vessels.

The King anchored off a hill called the Point of Limassol, with all the other ships around him. On Whitsunday he landed; but after we had heard Mass a violent and gusty wind from Egypt rose with such force that of the two thousand eight hundred knights the King was leading to Egypt there were only seven hundred left with him; the rest were scattered and driven to Acre or other distant places and were unable to rejoin him for a long time.

On the Monday after Pentecost the wind had fallen. The King and those of us who, by God's grace, had not been separated from him set sail again and met the Prince of the Morea and the Duke of Burgundy, who had been staying in the Morea. On the Thursday after Pentecost, the King arrived off Damietta. There we found all the Sultan's forces on the seashore: fine people to look upon, for all the Sultan's arms are gold and the sun shone on the golden blazonry. The noise they made with their trumpets and Saracen horns was terrifying to hear.

The King summoned his barons to receive their advice about what he should do. Many thought that he should wait until the rest of his people had returned, for he had hardly a third part of his force left with him. But he would not listen to them. The reason he gave was that to do so would put heart into his enemies; more, there is no safe anchorage off Damietta where he could wait for his people without the risk of a strong wind driving the fleet away from their objective, as had happened to the others on Whitsunday.

It was accordingly agreed that the King should land on the Friday before Trinity Sunday[45] and give battle to the Saracens unless they declined it. The King told my Lord John of Beaumont to lend a galley to my Lord Erard of Brienne and me, to land us and our knights, since the big ships were unable to reach the shore. . . .

When the King heard that the ensign of St. Denis was ashore, he strode across the galley, refusing even for the Legate[46] who was with him to lag behind the standard, and leapt into the water, which came up to his armpits. His shield around his neck, his helmet on his head, lance in hand, he joined his men on the beach.

When he had landed and could see the Saracens he asked what people they were. He was told that they were Saracens. He couched his lance under his arm and put his shield before him, and would have flung himself upon them had not his wiser companions held him back.

Three times the Saracens sent the Sultan a message by carrier pigeons to say that the King had landed; but he was suffering from an attack of his disease, and they had no answer from him. When they heard nothing, they thought that the Sultan must be dead and abandoned Damietta. The King sent on a knight to discover what had happened. He came back and told the King he had been into the Sultan's palace and the news was true. Then the King sent for the Legate and all the prelates in the army, and a high "Te Deum Laudamus" was sung. The King and all of us mounted and we went to camp outside Damietta.

The Turks were most unwise to abandon the city without cutting the bridge of boats, which would have greatly hampered us. But when they left they did a great deal of damage to us by setting fire to the market, where all the goods and merchandise were stored. It was as bad as though tomorrow someone—which God forbid—were to set fire to the Petit-Pont in Paris.

But now we must admit that Almighty God was most gracious to us in saving us from death and hunger when we landed, for we had to come in on foot and attack a mounted enemy. Our Lord was again gracious to us in giving us Damietta, which we could not have taken except by starvation, as we may realize when we remember that it was only so that King John took it in our fathers' time.[47]   [Trans. René Hague]

The speedy capture of Damietta was followed by a long period of comparative inactivity. The flooding of the Nile was partly responsible for this, but St. Louis was also anxious to await the arrival of further reinforcements before moving on. At last, on November 20, 1249, the army left Damietta and moved south toward Mansurah. The march was slow, impeded by the canals and Nile tributaries which crisscross the Delta region. In December the campaign bogged down altogether for six weeks in the face of rugged Egyptian resistance. In February 1250 the Crusaders forced their way into the Egyptian camp, killed the commander and very nearly routed their foes. The Egyptian troops were regrouped, however, and, amid fierce fighting, the Crusaders were driven back to their original positions. Losses on both sides were heavy, but the Western leaders hoped that the Egyptian government would crumble as a result of the slaughter at Mansurah. Their hopes were in vain. After eight more weeks of waiting, it was evident that the army could proceed no further and a general retreat toward Damietta began.

ST. LOUIS AND HIS ARMY ARE CAPTURED[48]

When the King saw that to stay where we were meant death for himself and his people, he gave orders and made arrangements to move at nightfall on the Tuesday after the octave of Easter[49] in an attempt to reach Damietta. He sent word to the sailors in charge of the galleys to gather all the sick and convey them to Damietta; and he ordered Jocelyn of Cornaut and his brothers and the other engineers to cut the ropes which fastened the bridge between us and the Saracens; but this they failed to do.

We embarked on the Tuesday, in the afternoon after dinner, myself and the two knights that were left to me, and my servants. When night began to fall I told my sailors to raise the anchor so that we could go downstream; they answered that they were afraid to do so, because the Sultan's galleys, which were between us and Damietta, would kill us. The sailors had built large fires to give them light while they collected the sick into their galleys, and the sick had gathered on the river bank. While I was telling the sailors that we should be moving, the Saracens made their way into the camp, and by the light of the fires I saw them slaughtering the sick on the bank.

While my sailors were raising the anchor, those who were to bring off the sick cut the anchor cables and mooring ropes of their galleys and ran alongside our little vessel, hemming us in on both sides, so that they nearly capsized us in the water. When we had extricated ourselves from this danger and were making our way downstream, the King, who was suffering from the camp fever and a very severe dysentery, could well have found safety in the galleys had he wished. But he said that, please God, he would not desert his people. That night he fainted several times, and his dysentery was so bad that it was necessary, so often was he obliged to go to the latrine, to cut away the lower part of his drawers.

As we were going downstream we were shouted at to wait for the King, and when we refused to do so we were fired on with crossbows. We had to stop, accordingly, until they gave us permission to sail.

I must break off at this point and tell you how the King was captured, as he described it to me himself. He said that he had left his own division and, with my Lord Geoffrey of Sargines, joined that of my Lord Walter of Chatillon, who commanded the rear guard.

The King told me, too, that he was riding a cob, covered with a silken housing, and that behind him, of all his knights and men-at-arms, there remained only my Lord Geoffrey of Sargines, who led the King as far as the village in which he was taken. Speaking of the way in which he escorted him, the King told me that my Lord Geoffrey of Sargines protected him from the Saracens like a good servant protecting his master's cup from flies; every time the Saracens approached, he took his spear, which he kept between himself and his saddlebow, couched it under his armpit, and charged them again and drove them away from the King.

So he conducted the King as far as the village. There they took him into a house and laid him in the lap of a woman, a Parisian, and he almost like a dead man so that they thought that he would not see that night. There came my Lord Philip of Montfort and told the King that he could see the emir with whom he had discussed the truce; if the King wished, he would go to him and arrange a truce again on the terms the Saracens offered. The King said that he agreed, and begged him to go. He went to the Saracen, who had his turban off his head and took the ring from his finger as an assurance that he would respect the truce.

Meanwhile a great misfortune had befallen our people. A treacherous man-at-arms called Marcel began to shout to them, "My lords, knights, surrender yourselves, for it is the King's order, and do not cause the King to be slain!" They all believed that it was indeed the King's order and surrendered their swords to the Saracens. The emir saw that the Saracens were already leading off our men as prisoners and told my Lord Philip that there was no need for him to grant terms of truce to them, since he could see that they were already captured.

Although all our people were taken prisoner, my Lord Philip himself was left free in virtue of being an envoy. But they have

The Thirteenth-Century Crusades

239

a bad custom in the country of the infidels, by which, when the King sends envoys to the Sultan, or the Sultan to the King, should the King or the Sultan die before their return the envoys are imprisoned or enslaved, to whichever party they may belong, Christian or Saracen.

While our people on land had the misfortune of being taken prisoner, the same happened to us on the river, as you will shortly hear. The wind was blowing in our direction from Damietta and deprived us of the advantage of the current. The knights, too, whom the King had embarked in his boats to protect the sick, fled. Our sailors missed the main stream of the river and took a backwater from which we had to return toward the Saracens.

A little before dawn broke, we who were going by water came to the stretch in which were the Sultan's galleys which had prevented provisions from coming to us from Damietta. There was a tremendous hubbub. They were firing such a quantity of bolts armed with Greek fire at us and at those of our mounted men who were on the river bank that it seemed as though the stars were falling from the sky.

When our sailors had brought us back from the arm of the river into which they had turned, we met—flying towards Damietta—the boats which the King had given us for the defense of the sick. A wind then rose from that direction, of such force that the current was of no service to us.

By both banks of the river there was a great number of our people's vessels which were unable to go downstream and had been held up and captured by the Saracens. They were killing the men and throwing them into the water, and robbing our ships of their chests and baggage. Their cavalry on the banks were firing bolts at us because we were refusing to pull into them. My people had put a jousting hauberk over me to save me from being wounded by the bolts which were falling into our vesesel.

At that moment my people who were forward in the bows called out to me, "Sir, sir, the sailors are frightened by the Saracens' threats and mean to put you on shore." Weak as I was, I had myself hoisted up by the arms and drew my sword on them and told me that if they put me on shore I should kill them. They answered that I could make my own choice: either they could put me on shore, or they could anchor for me in the midddle of the stream until the wind should fall. I told them that I would rather they anchored than put me on shore where I could see our men being slaughtered; and they accordingly anchored.

It was not long before we saw four of the Sultan's galleys approaching, with a good thousand men on board. Then I called my knights and my men and I asked them which they would prefer that we should do: surrender to the Sultan's galleys or surrender to the enemy on land. We all agreed that we should prefer to surrender to the galleys, where we would be kept all together, rather than to the Saracens on land, who would divide us up and sell us to the Bedouins.

Then one of my storekeepers, who was born at Doulevant, said, "Sir, I cannot agree with that advice." I asked him to what he would agree, and he answered, "I think that we should all allow ourselves to be killed and thus we shall all go to Paradise." But we paid no attention to him.

When I saw that we were bound to be captured I took my jewel box and jewels and threw them in the river, and my relics with them. One of my sailors then said to me, "Sir, unless you allow me to say that you are the King's cousin you will all be killed, and we too." I told him that he might say what he pleased. When the men in the first galley, who were preparing to ram our vessel, heard what he said, they anchored close by us.

It was then that God sent me a Saracen, a man who came from one of the Emperor's possessions. He was dressed in a pair of drawers of unbleached linen and swam across the river to our vessel. He took me by the waist and said, "Sir, unless you look to yourself quickly, you are lost; you must jump—their minds are on what they can loot in your ship." They threw me a rope from the galley, and by God's grace I jumped into the bows. But I may tell you that I was trembling so much that if the Saracen had not jumped after me and supported me I should have fallen into the water.

They took me into the galley, in which there were at least two hundred and eighty of their men, and all the time he held me firmly. Then I was thrown on the ground and they fell on me to cut my throat, for whoever murdered me would have thought to win honor for himself. But the Saracen continued to hold me firm and shouted, "The King's cousin!" In this way I was twice thrown to the ground, and once to my knees, and it was then I felt the knife at my throat. From this extremity God saved me through

The Thirteenth-Century Crusades

the help of the Saracen, who brought me to the aftercastle in which were the Saracen knights.

When I came among them they took off my hauberk, and, taking pity on my condition, they threw over me a scarlet blanket I had, lined with miniver, which my Lady, my mother had given me, and someone else brought me a white belt. I tied it round the blanket I had put on, in which I had made a hole. Another brought me a hood, which I drew over my head. But then, from the state of terror I was in, I began to tremble violently, though this was also due to my sickness. I asked them for something to drink, and they brought me some water in a jar, but as soon as I filled my mouth to swallow it, it poured out of my nostrils.

When I saw this I sent for my people and told them I was a dead man, for I had a tumor in my throat. They asked me how I knew, and I showed them; as soon as they saw the water pouring out of my mouth and nostrils they began to weep. When the Saracen knights who were present saw my folk weeping they asked the Saracen who had saved us why they were doing so. He answered that he thought that I had a tumor in my throat from which I should not recover. Then one of the knights told the man who had looked after us to console us, since he would give me something to drink which would cure me in two days. And this he did.

[Trans. René Hague]

Bargaining began at once between captors and prisoners to set the ransom terms for Saint Louis and his army.

ST LOUIS AND HIS MEN ARE RANSOMED[50]

The Sultan's Council tested the King in the same way as they had tested us, to see whether he would promise to surrender any of the castles of the Temple or the Hospital or of the Syrian barons. By God's will, the King gave them the same answer as we had done. They threatened him and said that as he would not agree they would have him put in the bernicles.

The bernicles are the most cruel torture you can suffer. They consist of two pliable lengths of wood, armed at the end with teeth. They fit together and are lashed at the end with strong oxhide thongs. When they wish to put people in them they lay the victims on their sides and insert their legs between the teeth. They then have a man sit on the planks. The result is that there is not six inches of unbroken bone left in the legs. To make the torture as severe as possible, at the end of three days, when the legs are swollen, they place them in the bernicles again and break them afresh. To these threats the King answered that he was their prisoner and that they could do with him as they wished.

When they saw that their threats could not master the good King, they asked him how much money he would pay the Sultan, Damietta to be surrendered in addition. The King answered that if the Sultan would accept a reasonable sum from him he would send and ask the Queen to pay it for their release. "How is it," they said, "that you will not undertake yourself to pay the ransom?" The King answered that the Queen was his lady and mistress and he did not know whether she would be willing. The Council then went back to consult the Sultan and returned with a message to the King that he [the Sultan] would set the King free if the Queen would pay one million gold besants, which was the equivalent of five hundred thousand pounds. The King asked them, on their oath whether the Sultan would release them for that sum if the Queen was willing. They went back to consult the Sultan, and when they returned they swore to the King that they would release him on those terms. As soon as they had sworn, the King spoke and promised the emirs freely to pay the five hundred thousand pounds for the freedom of his people, and Damietta for the release of his own person, since a man of his position should not be ransomed for money. When the Sultan heard this, he said, "By my faith, it is liberal of the Frank not to have haggled over so large a sum of money. Go tell him," said the Sultan, "that I make him a present of one hundred thousand pounds toward the ransom."

Then the Sultan had the men of rank embarked on four galleys, to take them to Damietta. In the galley in which I was put were also the good Count Peter of Brittany, Count William of Flanders, the good Count John of Soissons, my Lord Humbert of Beaujeu, the Constable of France, the good knight my Lord Baldwin of Ibelin, and my Lord Guy, his brother.

Those who were taking us in the galley brought us opposite a lodging which the Sultan had put up by the river. I will explain how it was made. In front of the lodging was a tower of fir poles covered with dyed cloth. This was the entrance to the lodging. Beyond this door a pavilion was erected in which the emirs, when they went to speak with the Sultan, left their swords and equipment. Beyond this pavilion there was another entrance like the first, and through this, one went into a large pavilion which was the Sultan's hall. Beyond the hall was a tower like the first one, through which one entered the Sultan's chamber.

Behind the chamber was a courtyard, and in the middle of it a tower higher than the others; this the Sultan used to climb to look over all the countryside and the camp. From the courtyard an alley ran to the river, where the Sultan had a pavilion erected in the water for bathing. The whole lodging was enclosed by wooden trelliswork covered with indigo cloth, so that those outside could not see within, and all four towers were also covered with cloth.

We arrived at this place in which the Sultan's quarters had been built on the Friday before the Ascension,[51] and the four galleys in which they were all confined together were anchored off it. The King was landed and taken to a pavilion close by. The Sultan had arranged that on the Saturday before the Ascension, Damietta should be surrendered to him and he should release the King. . . . [Further difficulties ensued, however, when the Sultan was himself assassinated by his emirs. The terms of the agreement with St. Louis were confirmed by the emirs who had conspired in the murder, and the arrangements for the payment of the ransom and the release of the prisoners then went forward.]

After the terms between the King and the emirs had been settled and sworn, it was agreed that they should release us the day after Ascension Day;[52] and that as soon as Damietta had been surrendered to the emirs the King himself and the persons of importance who were with him should, as was said before, be released. On the Thursday evening, those in charge of our four galleys anchored in midstream, by the bridge at Damietta; there they had a pavilion erected, and the King landed.

At sunrise my Lord Geoffrey of Sargines went into the town and arranged for it to be handed over the emirs. The Sultan's banners were hoisted on the towers. The Saracen knights entered the town; they began to drink the wine and soon they were all drunk. One of them came to our galley, drew his sword dripping with blood, and told us that for his own share he had killed six of our people.

Before Damietta was surrendered, the Queen, with all our people in the town except the sick, had been put on board our ships. By the terms of their oath the Saracens should have looked after the sick; they killed them all.

The King's engines of war, also, which they should have kept for him, they broke to pieces; nor did they keep the salt meats, as, not being eaters of pork, they should have done. They made a pile of the engines, another of the salt meat, and another of the corpses, and set fire to them. The blaze was so huge that it lasted all the Friday, Saturday and Sunday.

The King and us, whom they should have released at sunrise, they held until sunset. We had no food to eat, nor had the emirs, who spent the whole day in arguing. . . .

By the will of God, who is never forgetful of his own, it was agreed, about sunset, that we should be released. We were brought back again and our four galleys moored at the bank. We then asked to be allowed to go, but they told us that they could not allow us to do so until we had eaten, "for the emirs would be shamed if you were to leave our hands fasting."

We then asked to be given food, and we would eat, and they told us that food had been sent for from the camp. What they gave us was little round cheeses baked in the sun to keep the worms out, and hard-boiled eggs four or five days old; the shells of these they had painted, in our honor, in different colors.

We were landed and went to join the King, whom they were escorting to the river from the pavilion where they had held him. Twenty thousand Saracens at least, swords at their belts, marched on foot behind them. In the stream there was a Genoese galley, facing the King, and there appeared to be only one man on board. As soon as he saw the King on the bank he blew a whistle, and at the signal eighty or so fully armed crossbowmen, their bows at the ready, leapt out of the hold and straightaway loaded their bolts in the notches. When the Saracens saw them, they scattered like sheep, until only two or three were left with the King.

A plank was passed to the shore for the King to come on board, with his brother the Count of Anjou, my Lord Geoffrey of Sargines, my Lord Philip of Nemours, the Marshal of France, who was known as du Mez, the Minister of the Trinity, and me. They were holding the Count of Poitiers in confinement until the King should have paid them the two hundred thousand pound ransom that was due before he left the river. . . .

The Thirteenth-Century Crusades

245

That Saturday morning, the business of making up the money was begun, and continued all day Saturday and Sunday, until Sunday evening. For the payment was made in scales by weight and each scale represented the value of ten thousand pounds. At vespers time on Sunday the King's men who were making up the money sent a message to the King that they were still a good thirty thousand pounds short. With the King were only the King of Sicily, the Marshal of France, the Minister of the Trinity, and I. All the others were at the weighing.

Then I told the King that he would do well to send for the Commander and the Marshal of the Temple (for the Master was dead) and ask them to lend him the thirty thousand pounds needed to release his brother. The King sent for them and asked me to speak to them. When I had given them the message, Brother Stephen of Otricourt, the Commander, said to me, "My Lord of Joinville, this advice you have given the King is neither good nor reasonable, for you know that we receive deposits only on the sworn understanding that we shall not hand them over to any person except those who deposited them in our keeping"—and this led to plenty of hard words between him and me.

Then Brother Renaud of Vichiers, who was the Marshal of the Temple, spoke. "My Lord," he said, "enough of this dispute between the Lord of Joinville and our Commander. As our Commander says, we could not hand over any money without being false to our oath. But when the Seneschal suggests that if we are unwilling to lend you the money you should simply take it; there is nothing extraordinary in this suggestion, and you may do as you please about it. If you take any of our moneys we have sufficient of yours at Acre for you to reimburse us."

I told the King that I was ready to go if he wished, and he bade me do so. I went then to one of the Templars' galleys, the flagship, and as I was about to go down into the hold where the treasure was kept I asked the Commander of the Temple to come and see what I took, but he haughtily refused. The Marshal said that he would come and see what I took by force.

As soon as I had gone down to the place where the treasure was I asked the Treasurer of the Temple, who was there, to give me the keys of a chest which was facing me. Seeing how lean and wasted by disease I was, and that I was still wearing the clothes I had worn in captivity, he refused to give them to me. I saw a hatchet lying on the ground, picked it up, and said that I would use that as a key for the King. Seeing this, the Marshal took me by the hand and said, "My Lord, we see that you are set on taking what you need by force; we will give you the keys." Then he ordered the Treasurer to have them given to me, which he did; and when he told him who I was the Treasurer was greatly disconcerted.

I found that the chest I opened belonged to Nicholas of Soisy, one of the King's men-at-arms. I turned out all the money I found inside it and went and sat in the bows of the boat that had brought me out. I put the Marshal of France and the Minister of the Trinity on board the galley and left the Marshal below with the money. Once on board, the Marshal handed the money up to the Minister who passed it down to me in the boat. As we approached the King's galley I began to call out to him, "Sir, sir, see what I have got!" The Saint was overjoyed to see me, and we gave my load to the men who were weighing out the money.

When it had all been weighed the King's Council who had been in charge of the work came and told him that the Saracens refused to release his brother until the money was in their hands; some of them thought that the King should not actually pay the money until he had his brother back. The King answered that he would hand it over, as he had agreed to do, and if the Saracens wished to do what was right they should keep their part of the agreement. My Lord Philip of Nemours then told the King that in the count they had cheated the Saracens of one balance of ten thousand pounds.

The King was extremely angry and said that he wished the ten thousand pounds to be returned to them, since he had promised to pay the two hundred thousand before he left the river. I then trod on my Lord Philip's foot and told the King not to believe him, for he was mistaken, the Saracens being the most skillful reckoners in the world. My Lord Philip said that I was right and that he had only been joking. The King said that such a joke was untimely. "I order you," he said to my Lord Philip, "on the faith you owe me, being my own man, if the ten thousand pounds have not been paid, to see that they are made up in full."

Many had advised the King to transfer to his ship, which was waiting out at sea for him, so as to remove himself from Saracen hands; but he would have none of that advice, saying that he would not leave the river until, as he had agreed, he had paid them two hundred thousand pounds. As soon as the payment was complete, without anyone suggesting it again, he told us that now he had fulfilled his oath and that we were to leave and go on board the ship, which was out at sea.

[Trans. René Hague]

St. Louis and his army now sailed to Acre, where the French King spent the next four years rebuilding fortifications and attempting to secure the Latin Kingdom's defenses, both military and diplomatic. Although Frederick II's son, Conrad, was still the nominal King of Jerusalem, he had never come to the East to claim his crown and both he and his father were too deeply engrossed in their quarrels with the Papacy to make it likely that either of them would attempt the voyage to Palestine. There were no prospects of further large-scale aid from the West and, when St. Louis was finally forced to leave for France in 1254, the best protection he could arrange for the Latin states before he left was to secure a truce with the Moslem rulers of Cairo and Damascus.

St. Louis' departure from the East was forced upon him by the necessity of attending to the affairs of the French Kingdom, but Louis kept in mind the possibility of returning some day to the East. Sixteen years after his departure, Louis set out on another Crusade. His objective this time was Tunis, for his brother, Charles of Anjou, who now controlled Sicily, had persuaded Louis that the Tunisian emir was a prospective candidate for conversion to Christianity. Despite the remonstrances of Joinville and his other old counsellors, St. Louis determined to make the expedition.[53] Joinville describes the circumstances:

ST. LOUIS' CRUSADE TO TUNIS[54]

One Lent . . . the King summoned all his barons to Paris. I sent him my excuses, pleading a quartan fever I then had, and asked him to forgive me, but he told me that he insisted on my coming, because he had good physicians with him who were skilled in curing the fever.

To Paris, then, I went. I arrived on the evening of the Vigil of Our Lady's feast in March,[55] and I could find no one, neither the Queen nor anyone else, who could tell me why the King had sent for me. It happened, however, by the will of God, that at matins I fell asleep. As I slept, I thought that I saw the King kneeling before an altar, and that I saw some bishops in their vestments dressing him in a red chasuble of Rheims serge. After this vision I called my Lord William, my priest, who was a man of great understanding, and described it to him. He answered, "Sir, you will see that tomorrow the King will take the cross." I asked him why he thought so, and he told me that it was because of the dream I had had, for the red chasuble stood for the cross, which was red with the blood which God shed from his side and his hands and his feet. "And the chasuble's being of Rheims serge means that the Crusade will not achieve great things, as you will see if God lets you live long enough."

After I had heard Mass at the Madeleine at Paris, I went to the King's chapel and found that the King had gone up to the relics in the gallery and was having the True Cross brought down. As the King was descending, two knights of this Council began to talk to one another, and one said, "Never believe me again, if the King does not take the cross here." The other answered that "if he does, this will be one of the most distressful days that ever dawned in France, for if we do not take the cross, too, we shall lose the favor of the King; but if we do take it, we shall lose that of God, since we shall be doing so not for his sake but through fear of the King."

The King, in fact, did take the cross on the next day,[56] and his three brothers with him, and in the event the Crusade, as my priest foretold, achieved little. Both the King of France and the King of Navarre pressed me earnestly to take the cross.

To this I answered, that while I was in the service of God and the King overseas and after my return the officers of the King of France and of the King of Navarre had so ruined and impoverished my people that the day would never come when they and I would not suffer the effect. I told them, too, that if I wished to do God's will I should stay at home to help and protect my people; for were I to endanger my person in the pilgrimage of the cross, knowing full well that it would be at the expense of my people's well-being, I should incur the anger of God, who gave his life to save his people.

I thought that all who advised him to go committed a mortal sin, for while he was still in France the whole Kingdom enjoyed peace at home and with all its neighbors, but after his departure its condition grew constantly worse.

In view also of his great bodily weakness it was very wrong of them to give him such advice; for he could not endure either to go in a carriage or to ride; he was so weak that he allowed himself to be carried in my arms, when I took leave of him, from the Count of Auxerre's house to the Grey Friars. Weak though he was, had he stayed in France he might still have lived for some time longer and done much good and profitable work.

Of his expedition to Tunis I do not wish to give any account nor to say anything, since, thank God, I was not there, and I would not put in my book anything of which I am not certain. Let me confine myself, then, to speaking of our holy King and simply say that after arriving at Tunis before the castle of Carthage he succumbed to a dysentery of the belly (his eldest son Philip was sick with a quartan fever and the same dysentery as the King), which forced him to take to his bed, with the knowledge that soon he would have to pass from this world to the next.

Then he sent for my Lord Philip, his son, and bade him respect, as he would his will, all the precepts that he bequeathed to him. . . .

After the good King had given his instructions to his son, my Lord Philip, his sickness grew dangerously worse. He asked for the sacraments of Holy Church and received them, it could be seen, in sound mind and with full understanding, for when he was anointed and they said the seven penitential psalms he recited the verses in his turn.

I have heard his son, my Lord the Count of Alençon, describe how at the approach of death he called on the saints to help and succor him, and especially on my Lord St. James, saying his prayer which begins "Esto, Domine," which means, "God, be the sanctifier and protector of Your people." He then called on my Lord St. Denis of France to help him, saying that prayer of his, which means "Lord God, grant that we may so despise the prosperity of this world that we may fear no adversity."

I have also heard my Lord of Alençon (God grant him his mercy) say that his father then prayed to my Lady St. Genevieve. Afterward the holy King had himself laid on a bed covered with ashes, crossed his hands on his breast, and, looking up to heaven, gave back his spirit to our Creator, at the very hour when the Son of God died on the Cross for the salvation of the world.

Well may we, and with piety, mourn the death of this holy Prince, who held his Kingdom with such sanctity and truth, and did in it such great deads of alms and gave it such good ordinances. As the scribe, when he has written his book, illuminates it with gold and azure, so did the King illuminate his Kingdom with the fine abbeys he built and the great number of hospitals and convents of Friars Preachers, and Grey Friars, and of other religious of which I have already told you.

On the day after the feast of St. Bartholomew the Apostle[57] there passed from this world the good King Louis, in the year of the Incarnation of our Lord, the year of grace one thousand two hundred and seventy, and his bones were kept in a casket and brought for burial to St. Denis in France, where he had chosen his place of burial; and in that place he was buried, where God has since, through his merits, done many fine miracles for him.

[Trans. René Hague]

CHAPTER XII

1 These expeditions were: (1) 1218, Andrew of Hungary's Crusade; (2) 1218-1221, the Fifth Crusade; (3) 1228-1229, Frederick II's Crusade; (4) 1239, the Crusade of Thibaut of Navarre; (5) 1240-1241, the Crusade of Richard of Cornwall; (6) 1248-1254, the first Crusade of St. Louis (the Sixth Crusade); (7) 1270-1272, the Crusade of Edward of England (later King Edward I); (8) 1270, the second Crusade of St. Louis (the Seventh Crusade). In addition to these major Crusades there were countless minor ventures of various kinds which claimed the status of Crusades.

2 The best summary of the movement is given in Dana Carleton Monro's article, "The Children's Crusade," *AHR*, XIX (1913-14), 516-24. See also Runciman, *Crusades*, III, 139-44; Waas, *Geschichte der Kreuzzüge*, I, 253-57.

3 *Chronica Regiae Coloniensis Continuatio prima, s.a.* 1213, *MGH, SS*, XXIV, 17-18.

4 Easter fell on March 25, Pentecost on May 13 in 1212.

5 The Canon *Ad Liberandum* of the Fourth Lateran Council; the text is in J. D. Mansi, *Sacrorum conciliorum nova et amplissima collechio*, (new ed.; 53 vols.; Paris: Hubert Welker, 1903-27), XXII, 1057-78.

6 Oliver of Paderborn, *The Capture of Damietta*, trans. John J. Gavigan ("University of Pennsylvania, Translation and Reprints" [Philadelphia: University of Pennsylvania Press, 1948]), chaps. I-XXVI (pp. 12-39); Joseph P. Donovan, *Pelagius and the Fifth Cru-*

sade (Philadelphia: University of Pennsylvania Press, 1950), pp. 25-68; Runciman, *Crusades*, III, 145-62.

[7] Oliver of Paderborn, *The Capture of Damietta*, chaps. XXVII-XXIX, 31-33 (pp. 39-48).

[8] Ps. 17:31.

[9] May 16, 1219.

[10] I Macc. 5:62.

[11] Cardinal Pelagius of St. Lucia.

[12] Isa. 3:8.

[13] August 29.

[14] Jer. 3:1.

[15] The night blindness described here is known as nyctalopia and is a classic symptom of severe and prolonged vitamin A deficiency.

[16] June 24.

[17] September 14.

[18] At the Battle of Hattin; see above p. 158.

[19] The Italian merchants undoubtedly coveted Damietta for its commercial possibilities. This account makes clear Oliver's partisanship for Pelagius and his ecclesiastical brethren.

[20] November 2-3.

[21] I Pet. 5:6.

[22] Donovan, *Pelagius*, pp. 69-97; Runciman, *Crusades*, III, 162-70.

[23] Runciman, *Crusades*, III, 171-80; Grousset, *Croisades*, III, 272-90; Waas, *Geschichte der Kreuzzüge*, I, 274-78. The classic biography of Frederick II is Ernst Kantorowicz, *Frederick the Second, 1194-1250*, trans. E. O. Lorimer (New York: Ungar, 1957), see especially pp. 167-81.

[24] Philippe de Novare, *Les Gestes*

des Chiprois no. 126-28 ed. Gaston Reynaud, (ed.), Geneva: Jules-Guillaumefick, 1887), pp. 37-43.

[25] Novare is mistaken. Frederick sailed from Brindisis on June 28, 1228.

[26] Frederick landed on July 21, 1228.

[27] There is a lacuna here in the manuscript of the text.

[28] Isabelle Plantagenet, Queen of Jerusalem, 1190-1205/6.

[29] Amaury I, King of Jerusalem, 1162-1174.

[30] John was Constable of Jerusalem, 1194-1200, and traded this post for Beirut, as stated above. Beirut had been conquered by Saladin in 1187 and was restored to Christian hands in 1197.

[31] de Novare, *Les Gestes des Chiprois*, no. 135-37, pp. 48-50.

[32] Actually, 1228.

[33] The infant Conrad IV, titular king of Jerusalem.

[34] John d'Ibelin.

[35] Yolanla, Frederick's deceased wife, the mother of Conrad IV.

[36] Al-Kamil was, of course, Sultan of Egypt, but he was not at this time Sultan of Demascus, for that state was held by his nephew, an-Nasir Dawud.

[37] Really, the following year, 1229.

[38] I.e. Frederick's troops from southern Italy, as distinct from the Lombards, a Germanic tribe which had settled in northern Italy but which had long since ceased to exist as a cultural entity.

[39] "[C] eaus de vau la terre":

probably the inhabitants of the coastal plain around Acre.

[40] A conjectural emandation of *delais* for *de lais* in the rather cryptic phrase: *fist mout de lais semblans,* which LaMonte renders "did much that seemed evil," *The Wars of Frederick II Against the Ibelins in Syria and Cyprus* (New York: Columbia University Press, 1936), p. 90.

[41] Runciman, *Crusades,* II, 205-54; Grousset, *Croisades,* III, 323-426; Waas, *Geschichte der Kreuzzüge,* I, 290-96.

[42] Jean de Joinville, *The Life of Saint Louis,* trans. René Hague (New York: Sheed and Ward 1955), chaps. XVII-XXIX (pp. 54-57).

[43] Joinville, *Life of Saint Louis,* chaps. XXXII-XXXIII, XXXV (pp. 60,61, 64).

[44] May 21, 1249.

[45] May 28, 1249.

[46] Cardinal Olo of Chatelerault, Bishop of Tusculum.

[47] A reference to the capture of the city in the Fifth Crusade; see above, p. 224.

[48] Joinville, *Life of Saint Louis,* LXI-LXIV (pp. 100-05).

[49] April 5, 1250.

[50] Joinville, *Life of Saint Louis,* chaps. LXVII-LXVIII, LXXII, LXXIV-LXXVI (pp. 109-11, 116-17, 118-22).

[51] April 29, 1250.

[52] Friday, May 6.

[53] LXXIX-CXXI (pp. 125-82); Runciman, *Crusades,* III, 274-92; Grousset, *Croisades,* III, 493-530, 651-54; Waas, *Geschichte der Kreuzzüge,* I ,307-09, 312-13.

[54] Joinville, *Life of Saint Louis,* chaps. CXLIV-CXLVI (pp. 213-17).

[55] March 24, 1267.

[56] March 25, 1267.

[57] August 25, 1270.

Chapter XIII

THE FALL OF THE LATIN KINGDOM

While St. Louis was still in the Holy Land on the first of his Crusades, men sensed the first faint premonitions of a major change in the politics of the Near East. The change was to come with the invasion of the area by the Mongols.

Europeans were already dimly aware of the Mongols. Jenghiz Khan, who died in 1227, had first united the various Mongol clans in north central Asia and with their aid he had subjected to himself an enormous empire which ran west from Korea to Persia and north from the Indian Ocean to Siberia. The Mongol tribesmen who made this conquest possible were stalwart, rugged, and primitive. Their character was described by a thirteenth century Western missionary thusly:

THE CHARACTER AND CUSTOMS OF THE MONGOLS[1]

These men, that is to say the Tartars, are more obedient to their masters than any other men in the world, be they religious or seculars; they show great respect to them nor do they lightly lie to them. They rarely or never contend with each other in word, and in action never. Fights, brawls, wounding, murder are never met with among them. Nor are robbers and thieves who steal on a large scale found there; consequently their dwellings and the carts in which they keep their valuables are not secured by bolts and bars. If any animals are lost, whoever comes across them either leaves them alone or takes them to men appointed for this purpose; the owners of the animals apply for them to these men and they get them back without any difficulty. They show considerable respect to each other and are very friendly together, and they willingly share their food with each other, although there is little enough of it. They are also long-suffering. When they are without food, eating nothing at all for one or two days, they do not easily show impatience, but they sing and make merry as if they had eaten well. On horseback they endure great cold and they also put up with excessive heat. Nor are they men fond of luxury; they are not envious of each other; there is practically no litigation among them. No one scorns another but helps him and promotes his good as far as circumstances permit.

Their women are chaste, nor does one hear any mention among them of any shameful behavior on their part; some of them, however, in jest make use of vile and disgusting language. Discord among them seems to arise rarely or never, and although they may get very drunk, yet in their intoxication they never come to words or blows.

Now that the good characteristics of the Tartars have been described, it is time for something to be said about their bad. They are most arrogant to other people and look down on all, indeed they consider them as nought, be they of high rank or low born. . . .

They are quickly roused to anger with other people and are of an impatient nature; they also tell lies to others and practically no truth is to be found among them. At first indeed they are smooth-tongued, but in the end they sting like a scorpion. They are full of slyness and deceit, and if they can, they get round everyone by their cunning. They are men who are dirty in the way they take food and drink and do other things. Any evil they intend to do to others they conceal in a wonderful way so that the latter can take no precautions nor devise anything to offset their cunning. Drunkenness is considered an honorable thing by them and when anyone drinks too much, he is sick there and then, nor does this prevent him from drinking again. They are exceedingly grasping and avaricious; they are extremely exacting in their demands, most tenacious in holding on to what they have and most niggardly in giving. They consider the slaughter of other people as nothing. In short, it is impossible to put down in writing all their evil characteristics on account of the very great number of them.

The
Fall
of the
Latin
Kingdom

Their food consists of everything that can be eaten, for they eat dogs, wolves, foxes, and horses and, when driven by necessity, they feed on human flesh. For instance, when they were fighting against a city of the Kitayans, where the emperor was residing, they besieged it for so long that they themselves completely ran out of supplies and, since they had nothing at all to eat, they thereupon took one out of every ten men for food. They eat the filth which comes from mares when they bring forth foals. Nay, I have even seen them eating lice. They would say, "Why should I not eat them since they eat the flesh of my son and drink his blood?" I have also seen them eat mice.

They do not use tablecloths or napkins. They have neither bread nor herbs nor vegetables nor anything else, nothing but meat, of which, however, they eat so little that other people would scarcely be able to exist on it. They make their hands very dirty with the grease of the meat, but when they eat they wipe them on their leggings or the grass or some other such thing. It is the custom for the more respectable among them to have small bits of cloth with which to wipe their hands at the end when they eat meat. One of them cuts the morsels and another takes them on the point of a knife and offers them to each, to some more, to some less, according to whether they wish to show them greater or less honor. They do not wash their dishes, and, if occasionally they rinse them with the meat broth, they put it back with the meat into the pot. Pots also or spoons or other articles intended for this use, if they are cleaned at all, are washed in the same manner. They consider it a great sin if any food or drink is allowed to be wasted in any way; consequently they do not allow bones to be given to dogs until the marrow has been extracted. They do not wash their clothes nor allow them to be washed, especially from the time when thunderstorms begin until the weather changes. They drink mare's milk in very great quantities if they have it; they also drink the milk of ewes, cows, goats and even camels. They do not have wine, ale, or mead unless it is sent or given to them by other nations. In the winter, moreover, unless they are wealthy, they do not have mare's milk. They boil millet in water and make it so thin that they cannot eat it but have to drink it. Each one of them drinks one or two cups in the morning and they eat nothing more during the day; in the evening, however, they are all given a little meat, and they drink the meat broth. But in the summer, seeing they have plenty of mare's milk, they seldom eat meat, unless it happens to be given to them or they catch some animal or bird when hunting.

They also have a law or custom of putting to death any man and woman they find openly committing adultery; similarly if a virgin commits fornication with anyone, they kill both the man and the woman. If any is found in the act of plundering or stealing in the territory under their power, he is put to death without any mercy. Again, if anyone reveals their plans, especially when they intend going to war, he is given a hundred stripes on his back, as heavy as a peasant can give with a big stick. If any of the lower class offend in any way, they are not spared by their superiors, but are soundly beaten. There is no distinction between the son of a concubine and the son of a wife, but the father gives to each what he will; and if they are of a family of princes, then the son of a concubine is a prince just the same as the son of a legitimate wife. When a Tartar has many wives, each one has her own dwelling and her household, and the husband eats and drinks and sleeps one day with one, and the next with another. One, however, is chief among the others and with her he stays more often than with the others. In spite of their numbers, they never easily quarrel among themselves.

The men do not make anything at all, with the exception of arrows, and they also sometimes tend the flocks, but they hunt and practice archery, for they are all, big and little, excellent archers, and their children begin as soon as they are two or three years old to ride and manage horses and to gallop on them, and they are given bows to suit their stature and are taught to shoot; they are extremely agile and also intrepid.

Young girls and women ride and gallop on horseback with agility like the men. We even saw them carrying bows and arrows. Both the men and the women are able to endure long stretches of riding. They have very short stirrups; they look after their horses very well, indeed they take the very greatest care of all their possessions. Their women make everything, leather garments, tunics, shoes, leggings, and everything made of leather; they also drive the carts and repair them, they load the camels, and in all their tasks they are very swift and energetic. All the women wear breeches and some them shoot like the men.

[Trans. by a nun of Stanbrook Abbey]

The
Fall
of the
Latin
Kingdom

257

In the fourth and fifth decades of the thirteenth century these people began to turn their attention to the West. Jenghiz Khan's grandson, Batu, invaded and ravaged a large part of Eastern Europe in 1240-1241 and inspired terror in the hearts of millions of Europeans. Fortunately for the West, however, Batu was forced for political reasons to return to the Far East, to Karakorum, before he could capitalize on his earlier successes and drive deep into central Europe.[2]

In 1245, Pope Innocent IV, who was greatly impressed with the dimensions of the Mongol menace, sent an ambassador to the court of the Great Khan to try to bargain with him for the future safety of the West. The Pope also hoped that the Mongols might prove ripe for conversion to Christianity.

A BULL OF POPE INNOCENT IV TO THE
EMPEROR OF THE TARTARS[3]

Seeing that not only men but even irrational animals, nay, the very elements which go to make up the world machine, are united by a certain innate law after the manner of the celestial spirits, all of which God the Creator had divided into choirs in the enduring stability of the peaceful order, it is not without cause that we are driven to express in strong terms our amazement that you, as we have heard, have invaded many countries belonging both to Christians and to others and are laying them waste in a horrible desolation, and with a fury still unabated you do not cease from stretching out your destroying hand to more distant lands, but, breaking the bond of natural ties, sparing neither sex nor age, you rage against all indiscriminately with the sword of chastisement. We, therefore, following the example of the King of Peace, and desiring that all men should live united in concord in the fear of God, do admonish, beg, and earnestly beseech all of you that for the future you desist entirely from assaults of this kind and especially from the persecution of Christians, and that after so many and such grievous offenses you conciliate by a fitting penance the wrath of Divine Majesty, which without doubt you have seriously aroused by such provocation; nor should you be emboldened to commit further savagery by the fact that when the sword of your might has raged against other men Almighty God has up to the present allowed various nations to fall before your face; for sometimes he refrains from chastising the proud in this world for the moment, for this reason, that if they neglect to humble themselves of their own accord he may not only no longer put off the punishment of their wickedness in this life but may also take greater vengeance in the world to come. On this account, we have thought fit to send to you our beloved son [John of Plano Carpini] and his companions, the bearers of this letter, men remarkable for their religious spirit, comely in their virtue, and gifted with a knowledge of Holy Scripture; receive them kindly and treat them with honor out of reverence for God, indeed as if receiving us in their persons, and deal honestly with them in those matters of which they will speak to you on our behalf, and when you have had profitable discussions with them concerning the aforesaid affairs, especially those pertaining to peace, make fully known to us through these same friars what moved you to destroy other nations and what your intentions are for the future, furnishing them with a safe conduct and other necessities on both their outward and return journey, so that they can safely make their way back to our presence when they wish.

Lyons, March 13, 1245
[Trans. by a nun of Stanbrook Abbey]

The Great Khan, realist that he was, was not impressed by the fulminations of the Pope. All that Innocent gained from the mission was this unsatisfactory reply:

GUYUK KHAN'S REPLY TO POPE INNOCENT IV[4]
We, by the power of the eternal heaven,
    Khan of the great Ulus
Our command:

This is a version sent to the great Pope, that he may know and understand in the [Moslim] tongue, what has been written. The petition of the assembly held in the lands of the emperor [for our support] has been heard from your emissaries.

If he reaches [you] with his own report, thou who art the great Pope, together with all the princes, come in person to serve us. At that time I shall make known all the commands of the *Yasa.*

*The
Fall
of the
Latin
Kingdom*

259

You have also said that supplication and prayer have been offered by you, that I might find a good entry into baptism. This prayer of thine I have not understood. Other words which thou hast sent me: "I am surprised that thou has seized all the lands of the Magyar and the Christians. Tell us what their fault is." These words of thine I have also not understood. The eternal God has slain and annihilated these lands and peoples, because they have neither adhered to Jenghiz Khan, nor the Khagan, nor to the command of God. Like thy words, they also were impudent, they were proud and they slew our messenger-emissaries. How could anybody seize or kill by his own power contrary to the command of God?

Though thou likewise sayest that I should become a trembling Nestorian Christian, worship God, and be an ascetic, how knowest thou whom God absolves, in truth to whom He shows mercy? How dost thou know that such words as thou speakest are with God's sanction? From the rising of the sun to its setting, all the lands have been made subject to me. Who could do this contrary to the command of God?

Now thou should say with a sincere heart: "I will submit and serve you." Thou thyself, at the head of all the princes, come at once to serve and wait upon us! At that time I shall recognize your submission.

If you do not observe God's command, and if you ignore my command, I shall know you as my enemy. Likewise, I shall make you understand. If you do otherwise, God knows what I know.

At the end of Jumada the second in the year 644.[5]

The Seal

We, by the power of the eternal Tengri, universal Khan of the great Mongol Ulus—our command. If this reaches peoples who have made their submission, let them respect and stand in awe of it. *[Trans. by D. A. Maitland Muller]*

In view of the Mongol Khan's haughty rejection of the Pope's proposals, it was fortunate indeed that the Mongol threat to continental Europe faded quickly after 1242. A decade later, however, the Mongols were again on the march, this time into the Near East.

The military prowess of the Mongol hordes was impressive. In the East, no less than in the West, their successes were astounding and very nearly uniform. In part this was due to a long-standing traditional discipline which the Pope's representative to the Great Khan described in these terms:

THE MILITARY METHODS OF THE MONGOLS[6]

Jenghiz Khan ordained that the army should be organized in such a way that over ten men should be set one man and he is what we call a captain of ten; over ten of these should be placed one, named a captain of a hundred; at the head of ten captains of a hundred is placed a soldier known as a captain of a thousand, and over ten captains of a thousand is one man, and the word they use for this number means "darkness."[7] Two or three chiefs are in command of the whole army, yet in such a way that one holds the supreme command.

When they are in battle, if one or two or three or even more out of a group of ten run away, all are put to death; and if a whole group of ten flees, the rest of the group of a hundred are all put to death, if they do not flee too. In a word, unless they retreat in a body, all who take flight are put to death. Likewise if one or two or more go forward boldly to the fight, then the rest of the ten are put to death if they do not follow and, if one or more of the ten are captured, their companions are put to death if they do not rescue them.

They all have to possess the following arms at least: two or three bows or at least one good one, three large quivers full of arrows, and an axe and ropes for hauling engines of war. As for the wealthy, they have swords pointed at the end but sharp only on one side and somewhat curved, and they have a horse with armor; their legs also are covered and they have helmets and cuirasses. Some have cuirasses, and protection for their horses, fashioned out of leather in the following manner: They take strips of ox hide, or of the skin of another animal, a hand's breadth wide and cover three or four together with pitch, and they fasten them with leather thongs or cord; in the upper strip they put the lace at one end, in the next they put it in the middle and so on to the end; consequently, when they bend, the lower strips come up over the upper ones and thus there is a double or triple thickness over the body.

They make the covering for their horses in five sections, one on one side of the horse and one on the other, and these stretch from the tail to the head and are fastened to the saddle and behind the saddle on its back and also on the neck; another section they put over its hindquarters where the ties of the two parts are fastened and in this last named place they make a hole for the tail to come through; covering the breast there is another section. All these pieces reach down as far as the knees or joints of the leg. On its forehead they put an iron plate which is tied to the aforementioned sections on each side of the neck.

The cuirass is made in four parts. One piece stretches from the thigh to the neck, but is shaped to fit the human figure, being narrow across the chest and curved around the body from the arms downwards; behind, over the loins, they have another piece which reaches from the neck and meets the first piece encircling the body; these two sections, namely the front and the back, are fastened with clasps to two iron plates, one on each shoulder; also on each arm they have a piece stretching from the shoulder to the hand and open at the bottom and on each leg another piece. All these sections are fastened together by clasps.

The upper part of the helmet is of iron or steel, but the part affording protection to the neck and throat is of leather. All these leather sections are made in the manner described above.

Some of the Tartars have all the things we have mentioned made of iron in the following fashion: They make a number of thin plates of the metal, a finger's breadth wide and a hand's breadth in length, piercing eight little holes in each plate; as a foundation they put three strong narrow straps; they then place the plates one on top of the other so that they overlap, and they tie them to the straps by narrow thongs which they thread through the aforementioned holes; at the top they attach a thong, so that the metal plates hold together firmly and well. They make a strap out of these plates and then join them together to make sections of armor as has been described above. They make these into armor for horses as well as men and they make them shine so brightly that one can see one's reflection in them.

Some of them have lances which have a hook in the iron neck, and with this, if they can, they will drag a man from his saddle. The length of their arrows is two feet, one palm and two digits. Since feet are not all the same, we will give the measurement of a geometrical foot; the length of a digit is two grains of barley, and sixteen digits make a geometrical foot. The heads of the arrows are very sharp and cut on both sides like a two-edged sword—the Tartars always carry files at the side of their quiver for sharpening their arrows. The iron heads have a pointed tail, a digit's breadth in length and this they stick into the shaft.

They have a shield made of wicker or twigs, but I do not think they carry it except in camp and when guarding the emperor and the princes, and this only at night. They also have other arrows for shooting birds and animals and unarmed men; these are three digits wide; in addition they have various other kinds of arrows for shooting birds and animals.

When they are going to make war, they send ahead an advance guard and these carry nothing with them but their tents, horses, and arms. They seize no plunder, burn no houses, and slaughter no animals; they only wound and kill men or, if they can do nothing else, put them to flight. The army follows after them, taking everything they come across, and they take prisoner or kill any inhabitants who are to be found. Not content with this, the chiefs of the army next send plunderers in all directions to find men and animals, and they are most ingenious at searching them out.

When they come to a river, they cross it in the following manner, even if it is wide. The nobles have a circular piece of light leather, round the edge of which they make numerous loops, through which they thread a rope; they draw this up so that it makes a pouch, which they fill with their clothes and other things, pressing them down very tightly together; on top of these, in the middle, they put their saddles and other hard things. The men also sit in the middle and they tie the boat they have made in this way to the tail of a horse. They make one man swim in front with the horse to guide it, or sometimes they have a couple of oars with which they row to the other side of the water and so cross the river. The horses, however, they drive into the water, and a man swims by the side of one horse, which he guides, and the others all follow it; in this way they cross both narrow and wide rivers. The poorer men have a leather bag securely sewn—everybody is expected to possess one of these—and into this bag or satchel they put their clothes and all their belongings; having tied the sack tightly at the top, they hang it on to a horse's tail and cross in the manner described above.

It should be known that when they come in sight of the enemy they attack at once, each one shooting three or four arrows at their adversaries; if they see that they are not going to be able to defeat them, they retire, going back to their own line. They do this as a blind to make the enemy follow them as far as the places where they have prepared ambushes. If the enemy pursues them to these ambushes, they surround and wound and kill them. Similarly if they see that they are opposed by a large army, they sometimes turn aside and, putting a day's or two day's journey between them, they attack and pillage another part of the country and they kill men and destroy and lay waste the land. If they perceive that they cannot even do this, then they retreat for some ten or twelve days and stay in a safe place until the army of the enemy has disbanded, whereupon they come secretly and ravage the whole land. They are indeed most cunning in war, for they have now been fighting against other nations for forty years and more.

When, however, they are going to join battle, they draw up all the battle lines just as they are to fight. The chiefs or princes of the army do not take part in the fighting but take up their stand some distance away facing the enemy, and they have beside them their children on horseback and their womenfolk and horses; and sometimes they make figures of men and set them on horses. They do this to give the impression that a great crowd of fighting-men is assembled there. They send a detachment of captives and men of other nationalities who are fighting with them to meet the enemy head-on, and some Tartars may perhaps accompany them. Other columns of stronger men they dispatch far off to the right and the left so that they are not seen by the enemy and in this way they surround them and close in and so the fighting begins from all sides. Sometimes when they are few in number they are thought by the enemy, who are surrounded, to be many, especially when the latter catch sight of the children, women, horses, and dummy figures described above, which are with the chief or prince of the army and which they think are combatants; and alarmed by this they are thrown into disorder. If it happens that the enemy fight well, the Tartars make a way of escape for them; then as soon as they begin to take flight and are separated from each other they fall upon them and more are slaughtered in flight than could be killed in battle. However, it should be known that, if they can avoid it, the Tartars do not like to fight hand to hand but they wound and kill men and horses with their arrows; they only come to close quarters when men and horses have been weakened by arrows.

They reduce fortresses in the following manner. If the position of the fortress allows it, they surround it, sometimes even fencing it round so that no one can enter or leave. They make a strong attack with engines and arrows and they do not leave off fighting by day or night, so that those inside the fortress get no sleep; the Tartars however have some rest, for they divide up their forces and they take it in turns to fight so that they do not get too tired. If they cannot capture it in this way they throw Greek fire; sometimes they even take the fat of the people they kill and, melting it, throw it on to the houses, and wherever the fire falls on this fat it is almost inextinguishable. It can, however, be put out, so they say, if wine or ale is poured on it. If it falls on flesh, it can be put out by being rubbed with the palm of the hand.

If they are still unsuccessful and the city or fort has a river, they dam it or alter its course and submerge the fortress if possible. Should they not be able to do this, they undermine the city and armed men enter it from underground; once inside, some of them start fires to burn the fortress while the rest fight the inhabitants. If, however, they are not able to conquer it even in this way, they establish a fort or fortification of their own facing the city, so as not to suffer any injury from the missiles of the enemy; and they stay for a long time over against the city, unless by chance it has outside help from an army which fights against the Tartars and removes them by force. While they are pitched before the fortification they speak enticing words to the inhabitants making them many promises to induce them to surrender into their hands. If they do surrender to them, they say: "Come out, so that we may count you according to our custom," and when they come out to them they seek out the artificers among them and keep these, but the others, with the exception of those they wish to have as slaves, they kill with the ax. If they do spare any others, they never spare the noble and illustrious men, so we are told, and if by chance the unexpected happens and some nobles are kept, they can never afterwards escape from captivity either by entreaty or by bribe.

All those they take prisoner in battle they put to death unless they happen to want to keep some as slaves. They divide those who are to be killed among the captains of a hundred to be executed by them with a battle-ax; they in turn divide them among the captives, giving each slave to kill ten or more or less as the officers think fit. *[Trans. by a nun of Stanbrook Abbey]*

As the Mongol armies began their advance into the Near East, there was for a time some hope that they might cooperate with the Christian powers of the Near East against the Moslem armies of that area. St. Louis, in fact, continued to cherish the hope—not entirely without foundation—that the Mongols might in time become Christian converts.

That the hope for Christian-Mongol cooperation against Islam was not unfounded was demonstrated when a large Mongol host under the Great Khan's brother, Hulagu, moved into Persia in 1256, destroying first the Assassin headquarters and then, in 1258, Baghdad itself. In the following year Hulagu's army moved into Syria, destroying Aleppo and taking Damascus as they went.

In 1260 word came to the Mongol armies in Syria that the Great Khan was dead. Hulagu anticipated trouble over the succession and withdrew his forces from Syria to hold them ready for fighting in the East. The Egyptian Sultan, meanwhile, had been preparing to fight off the Mongol horde. When the Sultan's armies advanced into Syria, they found only a relatively small Mongol rear guard there. At Ain Jalud on September 2, 1260 the Sultan defeated this Mongol army decisively.

The battle of Ain Jalud was of major importance, for it demonstrated both the prowess of the Egyptians and the vincibility of the Mongols. True, the Mongol force at Ain Jalud was comparatively small, but since no major Mongol forces were sent to Syria in the years immediately after the battle, Sultan Baibars was left free to attack the Latins in Palestine. The hope of joint Latin-Mongol cooperation in Palestine had failed.

Egyptian campaigns against the Latin kingdom came thick and fast. In 1265 Caesarea, Haifa, and Arsuf all fell to the Sultan. The following year saw the loss of all the important Latin holdings in Galilee. In 1268 Antioch was taken.

To help redress these losses, a number of minor Crusading expeditions left Europe for the East. The abortive Crusade of St. Louis to Tunis in 1270 was one such attempt. The tiny Crusade of Prince Edward (later King Edward I) of England in 1271-1272 was another. Neither of these expeditions was capable of giving any sound assistance to the beleaguered Latin states. The forces involved were too small, the duration of the Crusades too short, the interests of the participants too diverse to allow of any solid accomplishment.

Pope Gregory X (1271-1276) labored valiantly to excite some general enthusiasm for another great Crusade, but he labored in vain. The failure of his appeal was variously ascribed by the Pope's advisors to the laziness and vice of the European nobility and to clerical corruption. Though each of these factors may have been in part to blame, a more basic reason for the failure seems to have been the debasement of the ideal of the Crusade itself. The use by Gregory X's predecessors of the label and privileges of the Crusade to recruit armies which could fight the Papacy's European armies had done much to throw the whole movement into disrepute.

In any event, no Crusade of any major importance was forthcoming, despite the Pope's best efforts. Meanwhile the attacks on the Latin East continued, as did also the internal difficulties within what was left of the Latin Kingdom. By 1276 the situation of the Kingdom, both external and internal, had become so perilous that the "King of Jerusalem" withdrew from Palestine altogether to take up his abode on the Island of Cyprus.

The desperate plight of the Latin Kingdom worsened. In 1278 Lattakieh fell. In 1289 Tripoli was lost, too. Frantic efforts once again to conclude an alliance between Europe and the Mongols failed.[8] At last, in 1291, the Egyptian Sultan, al-Ashraf, began an assault upon the last major Latin city left in Palestine.

*The
Fall
of the
Latin
Kingdom*

267

After having told of the glories and beauties of Acre, I will now shortly tell you of its fall and ruin, and the cause of its loss, even as I heard the tale told by right truthful men, who well remembered it. While, then, the grand doings of which I have spoken were going on in Acre, at the instigation of the devil these arose a violent and hateful quarrel in Lombardy between the Guelfs and the Ghibellines, which brought all evil upon the Christians. Those Lombards who dwelt at Acre took sides in this same quarrel, especially the Pisans and Genoese, both of whom had an exceedingly strong party in Acre. These men made treaties and truces with the Saracens, to the end that they might the better fight against one another within the city. When Pope Urban[10] heard of this, he grieved for Christendom and for the Holy Land, and sent twelve thousand mercenary troops across the sea to help the Holy Land and Christendom. When these men came across the sea to Acre they did no good, but abode by day and by night in taverns and places of ill-repute, took and plundered merchants and pilgrims in the public street, broke the treaty, and did much evil. Melot Sapheraph, Sultan of Babylon,[11] an exceedingly wise man, most potent in arms and bold in action, when he heard of this, and knew of the hateful quarrels of the people of Acre, called together his counselors and held a parliament in Babylon, wherein he complained that the truces had frequently been broken and violated, to the prejudice of himself and his people. After a debate had been held upon this matter, he gathered together a mighty host, and reached the city of Acre without any resistance, because of their quarrels with one another, cutting down and wasting all the vineyards and fruit trees and all the gardens and orchards, which are most lovely thereabout. When the Master of the Templars,[12] a very wise and brave knight, saw this, he feared that the fall of the city was at hand, because of the quarrels of the citizens. He took counsel with his brethren about how peace could be restored, and then went out to meet the Sultan, who was his own very especial friend, to ask him whether they could by any means repair the broken truce. He obtained these terms from the Sultan, to wit, that because of his love for the Sultan and the honor in which the Sultan held him, the broken truce might be restored by every man in Acre paying one Venetian penny. So the Master of the Templars was glad, and, departing from the Sultan, called together all the people and preached a sermon to them in the Church of St. Cross, setting forth how, by his prayers, he had prevailed upon the Sultan to grant that the broken treaty might be restored by a payment of one Venetian penny by each man, that therewith everything might be settled and quieted. He advised them by all means so to do, declaring that the quarrels of the citizens might bring a worse evil upon the city than this —as indeed they did. But when the people heard this, they cried out with one voice that he was the betrayer of the city, and was guilty of death. The Master, when he heard this, left the church, hardly escaped alive from the hands of the people, and took back their answer to the Sultan. When the Sultan heard this, knowing that, owing to the quarrels of the people, none of them would make any resistance, he pitched his tents, set up sixty machines, dug many mines beneath the city walls, and for forty days and nights, without any respite, assailed the city with fire, stones, and arrows, so that [the air] seemed to be stiff with arrows. I have heard a very honorable knight say that a lance which he was about to hurl from a tower among the Saracens was all notched with arrows before it left his hand. There were at that time in the Sultan's army six hundred thousand armed, divided into three companies; so one hundred thousand continually besieged the city, and when they were weary another hundred thousand took their place before the same, two hundred thousand stood before the gates of the city ready for battle, and the duty of the remaining two hundred thousand was to supply them with everything that they needed. The gates were never closed, nor was there an hour of the day without some hard fight being fought against the Saracens by the Templars or other brethren dwelling therein. But the numbers of the Saracens grew so fast that after one hundred thousand of them had been slain two hundred thousand came back. Yet, even against all this host, they would not have lost the city had they but helped one another faithfully; but when they were fighting without the city, one party would run away and leave the other to be slain, while within the city one party would not defend the castle or palace belonging to the other, but purposely let the other party's castles, palaces, and strong places be stormed and taken by the enemy, and each one knew and believed his own castle and place to be so strong that he cared not for any other's castle or strong place. During this confusion the masters and brethren of the Orders alone defended themselves, and fought unceasingly against the Saracens, until they were nearly all slain; indeed, the Master and brethren of the house of the Teutonic Order, together with their followers and friends, all fell dead at one and the same time. As this went on with many battles and thousands slain on either side, at last the fulfillment of their sins and the time of the fall of the city drew near; when the fortieth day of its siege was come, in the year of our Lord one thousand two hundred and ninety-two, on the twelfth day of the month of May, the most noble and glorious city of Acre, the flower, chief and pride of all the cities of the East, was taken. The people of the other cities, to wit, Jaffa, Tyre, Sidon and Ascalon, when they heard this, left all their property behind and fled to Cyprus. When first the Saracens took Acre they got in through a breach in the wall near the King of Jerusalem's castle, and when they were among the people of the city within, one party still would not help the other, but each defended his own castle and palace, and the Saracens had a much longer siege, and fought at much less advantage when they were within the city than when they were without, for it was wondrously fortified. Indeed, we read in the stories of the loss of Acre that because of the sins of the people thereof the four elements fought on the side of the Saracens. First the air became so thick, dark, and cloudy that, while one castle, palace, or strong place was being stormed or burned, men could hardly see in the other castles and palaces, until their castles and palaces were attacked, and then for the first time they would have willingly defended themselves, could they have come together. Fire fought against the city, for it consumed it. Earth fought against the city, for it drank up its blood. Water also fought against the city, for it being the month of May, wherein the sea is wont to be very calm, when the people of Acre plainly saw that because of their sins and the darkening of the air they could not see their enemies, they fled to the sea, desiring to sail to Cyprus, and whereas at first there was no wind at all at sea, of a sudden so great a storm arose that no other ship, either great or small, could come near the shore, and many who essayed to swim off to the ships were drowned. Howbeit, more than one hundred thousand men escaped to Cyprus. I have heard from a most honorable Lord, and from other truthful men who were present, that more than five hundred most noble ladies and maidens, the daughters of kings and princes, came down to the seashore, when the city was about to fall, carrying with them all their jewels and ornaments of gold and precious stones, of priceless value, in their bosoms, and cried aloud, whether there were any sailor there who would take all their jewels and take whichever of them he chose to wife, if only he would take them, even naked, to some safe land or island. A sailor received them all into his ship, took them across to Cyprus, with all their goods, for nothing, and went his way. But who he was, whence he came, or whither he went, no man knows to this day. Very many other noble ladies and damsels were drowned or slain. It would take long to tell what grief and anguish was there. While the Saracens were within the city, but before they had taken it, fighting from castle to castle, from one palace and strong place to another, so many men perished on either side that they walked over their corpses as it were over a bridge. When all the inner city was lost, all who still remained alive fled into the exceeding strong castle of the Templars, which was straightway invested on all sides by the Saracens; yet the Christians bravely defended it for two months, and before it almost all the nobles and chiefs of the Sultan's army fell dead. For when the city inside the walls was burned, yet the towers of the city, and the Templars' castle, which was in the city, remained, and with these the people of the city kept the Saracens within the city from getting out, as before they had hindered their coming in, until of all the Saracens who had entered the city not one remained alive, but all fell by fire or by the sword. When the Saracen nobles saw the others lying dead, and themselves unable to escape from the city, they fled for refuge into the mines which they had dug under the great tower, that they might make their way through the wall and so get out. But the Templars and others who were in the castle, seeing that they could not hurt the Saracens with stones and the like, because of the mines wherein they were, undermined the great tower of the castle, and flung it down upon the mines and the Saracens therein, and all perished alike. When the other Saracens without the city saw that they had thus, as it were, failed utterly, they treacherously made a truce with the Templars and Christians on the condition that they should yield up the

The
Fall
of the
Latin
Kingdom

271

castle, taking all their goods with them, and should destroy it, but should rebuild the city on certain terms, and dwell therein in peace as heretofore. The Templars and Christians, believing this, gave up the castle and marched out of it, and came down from the city towers. When the Saracens had by this means got possession both of the castle and of the city towers, they slew all the Christians alike, and led away the captives to Babylon. Thus Acre has remained empty and deserted even to this day. In Acre and the other places nearly a hundred and six thousand men were slain or taken, and more than two hundred thousand escaped from thence. Of the Saracens more than three hundred thousand were slain, as is well known even to this day. The Saracens spent forty days over the siege of the city, fifty days within the city before it was taken, and two months over the siege of the Templars' castle. When the glorious city of Acre thus fell, all the Eastern people sung of its fall in hymns of lamentation, such as they are wont to sing over the tombs of their dead, bewailing the beauty, the grandeur, and the glory of Acre even to this day. Since that day all Christian women, whether gentle or simple, who dwell along the eastern shore [of the Mediterranean] dress in black garments of mourning and woe for the lost grandeur of Acre, even to this day.   *[Trans. Aubrey Stewart]*

CHAPTER XIII

[1] John of Plano Carpini, *"History of the Mongols,"* IV, trans. by a nun of Stanbrook Abbey in *The Mongol Mission,* Christopher Lawson (ed.) (New York: Sheed and Ward 1955), pp. 14-18.

[2] Runciman, *Crusades,* III, 237-54.

[3] Trans. by a nun of Stanbrook Abbey in *The Mongol Mission,* pp. 75-76.

[4] Trans. from the Persian by a nun of Stanbrook Abbey in *The Mongol Mission,* pp. 85-86.

[5] November 1246.

[6] John of Plano Carpini, *"History of the Mongols,"* VI, in *The Mongol Mission,* pp. 32-38.

[7] John here confuses the Mongol *duman* (darkness) with *tuman* (ten thousand).

[8] Runciman, *Crusades,* III, 293-348, 387-412; Grousset, *Croisades,* III, 518-30, 562-750; Waas, *Geschichte der Kreuzzüge,* I, 315-23.

[9] Ludolph of Suchem, *Description of the Holy Land and of the Way Thither,* trans. Aubrey Stewart (London: Palestine Pilgrims' Text Society, 1895), XII, 54-61.

[10] There is some confusion here. Perhaps Pope Nicholas IV (1288-1292) is meant.

[11] Al-Ashraf Khalil, Sultan of Egypt.

[12] William of Beaujeu.

Chapter XIV

ᚦһᴇ ᴇɴᴅ ᴏꜰ ᚦһᴇ ᴄʀᴜꜱᴀᴅᴇꜱ

The fall of Acre closed an era. No effective Crusade was raised to recapture the Holy Land after Acre's fall, though talk of further Crusades was common enough. By 1291 other ideals had captured the interest and enthusiasm of the monarchs and nobility of Europe and even strenuous papal efforts to raise expeditions to liberate the Holy Land met with little response. The ideal of the Crusade was irretrievably tarnished.

The Latin Kingdom continued to exist, theoretically, on the Island of Cyprus. There the Latin Kings schemed and planned to recapture the mainland, but in vain. Money, men, and the will to do the task were all lacking. One last effort was made by King Peter I in 1365, when he successfully landed in Egypt and sacked Alexandria. Once the city was pillaged, however, the Crusaders returned as speedily as possible to Cyprus to divide their loot. As a Crusade, the episode was utterly futile.

The fourteenth century saw some other so-called Crusades organized, but these enterprises differed in many ways from the eleventh and twelfth century expeditions which are properly called Crusades. The "Crusades" of the fourteenth century aimed not at the recapture of Jerusalem and the Christian shrines of the Holy Land, but rather at checking the advance of the Ottoman Turks into Europe. While many of the "Crusaders" in these fourteenth century undertakings looked upon the defeat of the Ottomans as a preliminary to the ultimate recapture of the Holy Land, none of the later expeditions attempted any direct attack upon Palestine and Syria.[1]

By the end of the fourteenth century, the Crusaders were a dead letter. The name and notion of the Crusade lived on and, even in the twentieth century, the name alone enjoys sufficient popular appeal to be used as a label by propagandists of varied social and political hues.

The Crusades in their heyday were a manifestation of European idealism, an idealism, however, which to many twentieth-century observers seems hopelessly wrongheaded, incorrigibly vicious, and irretrievably futile.

If the sole outcome of the Crusades had been the establishment of the paltry, short-lived Kingdom of Jerusalem and of its smaller, shorter-lived sister states, the movement might justifiably be called "a vast fiasco." Such a judgment, however, does less than justice to the whole enterprise. The Crusades did, after all, have profound and lasting effects upon the political character of Europe. To a very considerable degree, the Crusades conditioned the domestic politics of Europe in the high medieval period. The expeditions to the East enhanced the prestige of the Papacy. In large measure they made possible the emergence, for better or worse, of such a figure as Innocent III. At the same time, the Crusades, by providing an acceptable outlet for the warriors of the West, assisted immeasurably the establishment of a more stable polity in Europe itself. The emergence of the European national monarchies (again, for better or worse) would doubtless have been immeasurably retarded without the Crusades and the existence of the Latin states in the high Middle Ages. Yet these very developments in the West, for which the Crusades were in some measure responsible, to a large extent crippled the Crusading movement in the thirteenth century.

The turning point of the whole movement came in 1204, with the sack of Constantinople and the creation of the Latin Empire. This development harmed the other Latin holdings in the East by diverting attention, manpower, and money from them. The founding of the Latin Empire ruined Byzantium and, in the final analysis, did even greater harm

bibLioGRApby

The bibliography below represents only a fraction of the literature concerning the Crusades. To compile a complete bibliography of the subject would mean duplicating Hans Mayer's *Bibliographie zur Gischichte der Kreuzzüge*—itself a 270 page book—and adding to it the items which Mayer omitted, or which have appeared since the publication of his work. This is neither feasible nor particularly desirable. A selective bibliography of the Crusades might be drawn up on any of a number of principles. Only items directly used in the writing of this book and cited in the footnotes might be listed. Such a selection, however, has the major drawback of being largely superfluous. Only items written in English might be listed or only items published, say, within the past two decades might be included, but this would mean omitting most of the primary sources and much of the significant secondary literature. The selection of items included here has been made on a simple subjective basis. The books and articles listed below are those which I have found particularly useful, stimulating, or important in my own studies of the Crusades. This is admittedly a rather flexible criterion of selection and widely varying lists might be made by other competent scholars. I hope, nonetheless, that this selection of titles may be useful as a guide to reading and to the further study of the Crusades.

I. PRIMARY SOURCES

A. *Collections of sources*

Acta Sanctorum, quotquot toto orbe coluntur. Antwerp, Paris, Rome, Brussels: various imprints, 1643- (in progress; 67 vols. to date).

Collection des documents inédits sur l'histoire de France. Paris: various imprints, (in progress; more than 300 vols. to date).

Corpus iuris canonici, ed. E. Friedberg. 2 vols. Leipzig: B. Tauchnitz, 1879 (rp. Graz: Akademische Druck- und Verlagsanstalt, 1959).

Corpus scriptorum ecclesiasticorum Latinorum. Vienna: various imprints, 1866- (in progress; 76 vols. to date).

Corpus scriptorum historiae Byzantinae. 50 vols. Bonn: E. Weber, 1828-97.

Documents relatifs à l'histoire des croisades. Paris: Paul Geuthner, 1945- (in progress; 6 vols. to date).

Florez, Enrique (ed.). *España sagrada. Teatro geographico-historico de la iglesia de España.* 51 vols. Madrid: M. F. Rodriguez, 1747-1879.

Fonti per la storia d'Italia. Rome: Instituto Storico Italiano, 1887- (in progress; 92 vols. to date).

Gabrieli, F. (ed.). *Storici arabi delle crociate.* Turin: Einaudi, 1957 (Scriti di storia, vol. 6).

Jaffé, P. *Regesta pontificum Romanorum ab condita*

ecclesia ad annum post Christi natum 1198. 2d ed. 2 vols. Berlin: Veit, 1885-88 (rp. Graz: Akademische Druck- und Verlagsanstalt, 1956).

Mansi, G. D. (ed.). Sacrorum conciliorum nova et amplissima collectio. New ed., 53 vols. Paris: Hubert Welter, 1903-27.

Migne, J. P. (ed.). Patrologiae cursus completus. Series Latina. [= P.L.] 221 vols. Paris: J. P. Migne, 1844-64.

_____.Patrologiae cursus completus. Series Graeco-Latina. 161 vols. Paris: J. P. Migne, 1857-66.

Monumenta Germaniae historica inde ab anno Christi quingentesimo usque ad annum millesimum et quingentesimum. [= MGH] Hannover, Weimar, Berlin, Stuttgart, and Köln: various imprints, 1826- (in progress.

Muratori, L. A. (ed.). Rerum Italicarum scriptores. New ed. Città di Castello and Bologna: S. Lapi, 1900- (in progress; 34 vols. to date).

Potthast, A. Regesta pontificum Romanorum inde ab anno post Christi natum 1198 ad annum 1304, 2 vols. Berlin: Rudolf de Decker, 1874-75 (rp. Graz: Akademiche Druck - und Verlagsanstalt, 1957).

Recueil des historiens des croisades. [= RHC] 16 vols. Paris: Academie des Inscriptians et Belles Lettres, 1841-1906. Divided into series, as follows:
Lois (2 vols.), 1841-43.
Documents Armeniens (2 vols.), 1869-1906.
Historiens Grecs (2 vols.), 1875-81.
Historiens Occcidentaux (5 vols.), 1844-95. [=RHC, Occ]
Historiens Orientaux (5 vols.), 1872-1906.

Recueil des historiens des Gaules et de la France. Nouvelle édition. 23 vols. Paris: Victor Palmé, 1840-94.

Röhricht, R. (ed.). Quinti belli sacri scriptores minores. Geneva: J.-G. Fick, 1879 (Société de l'Orient Latin, série historique, vol. 2).

_____.Regesta regni Hierosolymitani, 1097-1291. 2 vols. Innsbruck: Wagner, 1893-1904.(rp. New York: Burt Franklin, 1960).

_____.Testimonia minora de quinto bello sacro. Geneva: J.-G. Fick, 1882 (Société de l'Orient Latin, série historique, vol. 3).

Rolls Series: Rerum Britannicarum medii aevi scriptores. 251 vols. London: Longmans 1858-96.

B. Editions of individual sources
Aimé de Monte Cassino. L'Ystorie de li Normant

et la chronique de Robert Viscart, ed. O. Delarcq. Rouen: A. Lestrinant, 1892.

Ambroise: L'Estoire de la guerre sainte. Ed. G. Paris. Paris, 1897.

Anna Comnena. Alexiade Règne de l'Empereur Alexis I Comnène (1081-1118), ed. B. Leib. 3 vols. Paris: Les Belles Lettres, 1937-45.

Bernard of Clairvaux. Sancti Bernardi opera, ed. J. Leclercq, C. H. Talbot, and H. M. Rochais. Rome: Editiones Cistercienses, 1957- (in progress; 1 vol. to date).

La Chanson d'Antioche, ed. P. Paris. 2 vols. Paris: J. Techener, 1848.

Fulcher of Chartres. Historia Hierosolymitana, ed. H. Hagenmeyer. Heidelberg: Carl Winter, 1913.

Geoffroi de Villehardouin. La Conquête de Constantinople, ed. E. Faral. 2 vols. Paris: Les Belles Lettres, 1938-39 (Les Classiques de l'histoire de France au moyen âge, vol. 18-19).

Hagenmeyer, H. (ed.). Epistulae et chartae ad historiam primi belli sacri spectantes quae supersunt aevo aequales ac genuinae; Die Kreuzzugsbriefe aus den Jahren 1088-1100. Innsbruck: Wagner, 1901.

Les Gestes des Chiprois, ed. G. Raynaud. Geneva: Jules-Guillaume-Fick,

1887 (Société de l'Orient Latin, série historique, vol. 5).

Ordericus Vitalis. Historia ecclesiastica, ed. A. Le Prevost and L. Delisle. 5. vols. Paris: J. Renoliard, 1838-55.

Histoire anonyme de la première croisade, ed. L. Bréhier. Paris: Les Belles Lettres, 1924. (Les Classiques de l'histoire de France au moyen âge, vol. 4).

Jean de Joinville. Histoire de Saint Louis, ed. N. de Wailly. Paris: Hachette, 1874.

La Règle du Temple, ed. H. de Curzon. Paris: Renouard, 1886.

Robert de Clari. La Conquête de Constantinople, ed. P. Lauer. Paris: Edouard Champion, 1924 (Les Classiques de l'histoire de France au moyen âge).

Sugur de St.-Denis. Oeuvres complètes, ed. A. Lecoy de la Marche. Paris: Renouard, 1867.

Vincent de Beauvais. Speculum historiale. Strassburg: Johann Mentelin, 1473.

C. English translations of primary sources
1. Translations from Latin

St. Bernard of Clairvaux. The Letters of St. Bernard of Clairvaux, trans. B. S. James. London: Burns, Oates, 1953.

Dawson, C. (ed.). The Mongol Mission. Narratives and Letters of the

Franciscan Missionairies in Mongolia and China in the Thirteenth and Fourteenth Centuries, trans. by a nun of Stanbrook Abbey. New York: Sheed and Ward, 1955 (Makers of Christendom).

De expugnatione Lyxbonensi; The Conquest of Lisbon, ed. and trans. C. W. David. New York: Columbia University Press, 1936 (Records of Civilization, vol. 24).

DuBois, Pierre. The Recovery of the Holy Land, trans. W. I. Brandt. New York: Columbia University Press, 1956 (Records of Civilization, vol. 51).

Fulcher of Chartres. Chronicle of the First Crusade, trans. M. E. McGinty. Philadelphia: University of Pennsylvania Press, 1941. (Translations and Reprints from the Original Sources of History, 3d series, vol. 1).

Gesta Francorum: The First Crusade. The Deeds of the Franks and other Jerusalemites, trans. Somerset de Chair. London: Golden Cockerel Press, 1945.

Helmold. The Chronicle of the Slavs, trans. E. J. Tschan. New York: Columbia University Press, 1935 (Records of Civilization, vol. 21).

Henry of Livonia. The Chronicle of Henry of Livonia, trans. J. A. Brundage. Madison, Wis.: University of Wisconsin Press, 1961 (Documents From Medieval Latin, vol. 1).

Krey, A. C. (ed. and trans.). The First Crusade. Princeton: Princeton University Press, 1921.

Munro, D. C. (ed. and trans.). Letters of the Crusaders Written From the Holy Land. Philadelphia: University of Pennsylvania Press, n.d. (Translations and Reprints from the Original Sources of History, vol. 1, no. 4).

____.Urban and the Crusaders. Philadelphia: University of Pennsylvania Press, n.d. (Translations and Reprints from the Original Sources of History, vol. 1, no. 2).

Odo of Deuil. De profectione Ludovici VII in orientem. ed. and trans. V. G. Berry. New York: Columbia University Press, 1948 (Records of Civilization, vol. 42).

Oliver of Paderborn. The Capture of Damietta, trans. J. J. Gavigan. Philadelphia: University of Pennsylvania Press, 1948. (Translations and Reprints from the Original Sources of History, 3d series, vol. 2).

Otto of Freising. The Deeds of Frederick Barbarossa, trans. C. C. Mierow and R. Emery. New York: Columbia University

Press, 1953 (Records of Civilization, vol. 49).

———.*The Two Cities. A Chronicle of Universal History to the Year 1146 A.D.*, trans. C. C. Mierow; ed. A. P. Evans and C. Knapp. New York: Columbia University Press, 1928 (Records of Civilization, vol. 9).

Palestine Pilgrims' Text Society. 14 vols. London: Palestine Pilgrims' Text Society, 1896-1907.

William of Tyre. *A History of Deeds Done Beyond the Sea*, trans. E. A. Babcock and A. C. Krey. 2 vols. New York: Columbia University Press, 1943 (Records of Civilization, vol. 35).

Wright, T. (ed.). *Early Travels in Palestine*. London: Bohn, 1848 (Bohn's Antiquarian Library).

2. Translations from Old French

Ambroise. *The Crusade of Richard Lion-Heart*, ns. M. J. Hubert and LaMonte. New mbia Univer- ʼ41 (Rec- ʼn, vol.

.*aprois*: of Frederick ᵤinst the Ibelins in ᵤyria and Cyprus, trans. J. L. LaMonte and M. J. Hubert. New York: Columbia University Press, 1936. (Records of Civilization, vol. 25).

Jean de Joinville. *Life of St. Louis,* trans. Rene Hague. New York: Sheed and Ward, 1955. (Makers of Christendom).

Memoirs of the Crusades, trans. F. T. Marzials. London: J. M. Dent, 1907.

Munro, D. C. (ed. and trans.). *The Fourth Crusade. Philadelphia*: University of Pennsylvania Press, n.d. (Translations and Reprints from the Original Sources of History, vol. 3, no. 1).

Robert de Clari. *The Conquest of Constantinople.* New York: Columbia University Press, 1936 (Records of Civilization, vol. 23).

Three Old French Chronicles of the Crusades, trans. E. N. Stone. Seattle: University of Washington Press, 1939.

Topping, P. W. (trans.). *Feudal Institutions as Revealed in the Assizes of Romania.* Philadelphia: University of Pennsylvania Press, 1949 (Translations and Reprints from the Original Sources of History, 3d series, vol. 3).

3. Translations from Arabic

Ibn al-Qalanisi. *The Damscus Chronicle of the Crusades,* trans. Sir H. A. R. Gibb. London: Luzac, 1932.

Ibn Khaldun. *The Maqaddimah. An introduction*

to History, trans. Franz Rosenthal. 3 vols. New York: Pantheon, 1958.

Muhammed ibn 'Abd Allah (Ibn Battuta). *Travels in Asia and Africa, 1325-1354*, trans. Sir H. A. R. Gibb. New York: R. M. McBride, 1929.

Narashakhi. *The History of Bukhara*, trans. R. N. Frye. Cambridge, Mass.: Mediaeval Academy of America, 1954 (Mediaeval Academy of America, Publications, vol. 61).

Usamah ibn Munqidh. *An Arab-Syrian Gentleman and Warrior in the Period of the Crusades*, trans. P. K. Hitti. New York: Columbia University Press, 1929 (Records of Civilization).

II. SECONDARY WORKS

A. *General treatments of the Crusades*

Alphandéry, P. *La Chrétienté et l'idée de croisade*, ed. A. Dupront. 2 vols. Paris: Albin Miehel, 1954.

Bréhier, L. *L'Église et l'orient au moyen âge: Les Croisades*. 5th ed. Paris: J. Gabalda et fils, 1928.

Grousset, R. *Histoire des Croisades et du Royaume Franc de Jérusalem*. [= Grousset, *Croisades*] 3 vols. Paris: Plon, 1934-36.

Richard, Jean, *Le Royaume Latin de Jerusalem*. Paris: Presses Universitaires de France, 1953.

Runciman, Sir S. *A History of the Crusades*. [= Runciman, *Crusades*] 3 vols. Cambridge: Cambridge University Press, 1951-54.

Setton, K. M. (ed.). *A History of the Crusades*. [= Setton, *Crusades*] Philadelphia: University of Pennsylvania Press, 1955- (in progress; 1 vol. to date).

Waas, A. *Geschichte der Kreuzzüge*. 2 vols. Freiburg: Herder, 1956.

B. *Popular Accounts of the Crusades*

Barker, Sir E. *The Crusades*. London: Oxford University Press, 1939.

Belloc, H. *The Crusades: The World's Debate*. Milwaukee: Bruce, 1937.

Campbell, G. A. *The Crusades*. London: Duckworth, 1935.

Cox, G. W. *The Crusades*. New York: Scribners, 1926.

Lamb, Harold. *The Crusades: The Flame of Islam*. Garden City, N. Y.: Doubleday, 1931.

___. *The Crusades: Iron Men and Saints*. Garden City, N. Y.: Doubleday, 1930.

C. *General treatments of related topics*

1. Islam and the Muslims

Brockelmann, C. *History of the Islamic Peoples*. New York: G. P. Putnam's Sons, 1947.

Gibb, Sir H. A. R. *Mohammedanism. An Historical*

Survey. New York: New American Library, 1955.

Guillaume, A. *Islam.* London: Penguin, 1954.

Hitti, P. K. *History of the Arabs from the Earliest Times to the Present.* 5th ed. New York: Macmillan, 1951.

Lammens, H. *L'Islam. Croyances et institutions.* 2d ed. Beirut: Imprimerie Catholique, 1941.

Planhol, X. de. *The World of Islam.* Ithaca, N. Y.: Cornell University Press, 1959.

Rosenthal, E. I. J. *Political Thought in Medieval Islam.* Cambridge: Cambridge University Press, 1958.

2. Byzantium

Baynes, N. H., and H. St. L. B. Moss (ed.). *Byzantium. An Introduction of East Roman Civilization.* Oxford: Clarendon Press, 1948.

Bréhier, L. *Le Monde Byzantin.* 3 vols. Paris: Albin Michel, 1947-50.

Chalandon, F. *Les Comnènes. Études sur l'empire byzantin au XIe et XIIe siècle.* 2 vols. Paris: A. Picard, 1900-1921. (rp. New York: Burt Franklin, 1960).

Diehl, C. *History of the Byzantine Empire.* trans. George B. Ives. Princeton: Princeton University Press, 1925.

Goubert, P. *Byzance avant l'Islam.* Paris: Picard, 1951- (in progress; 2 vols. to date).

Lindsay, J. *Byzantium into Europe.* London: The Bodley Head, 1952.

Ostrogorsky, G. *History of the Byzantine Empire. trans.* George B. Ives. Princeton: Princeton University Press, 1957.

Runciman, Sir S. *Byzantine Civilization.* London: St. Martin's Press, 1933 (rp. New York: Clarendon Press, Meridian, 1956).

———.*The Eastern Schism.* Oxford: Clarendon Press, 1955.

Vasiliev, A. A. *History of the Byzantine Empire, 324-1453.* 2d English ed. Madison, Wis.: University of Wisconsin Press, 1952.

D. *Reference Works*

The American Historical Association's Guide to Historical Literature. New York: Macmillan, 1961.

The Cambridge Medieval History. 8 vols. Cambridge: Cambridge University Press, 1911-61.

Dictionnaire d'archéologie chrétienne et de liturgie. 15 vols. Paris: 1907-53.

Dictionnaire de droit canonique. Paris: Letouzey et Ané, 1935—(in progress; 6 vols. to date).

Dictionnaire d'histoire et de géographie ecclésiastique. Paris: Letouzey et Ané, 1913—(in progress; 80 fascicles to date).

Dictionnaire de théologie catholique 3d ed. 16 vols. Paris: Letouzey et Ané, 1923-50.

DuCange, C. du F. *Les Familles d'Outre-Mer,* ed. E.-G. Rey. Paris: Imprimerie Impiride, 1869.

———.*Glossarium mediae et infimae latinitatis.* Editio nova. 10 vols. Niort: L. Favre, 1837-87 (rp. in 5 vols., Graz: Akademische Druck-und Verlagsanstatt, 1954).

Encyclopedia of Islam. 4 vols. Leyden and London: Luzac, 1908-38.

Hazard, H. W. *Atlas of Islamic History.* 3d ed. Princeton: Princeton University Press, 1954.

Histoire de l'Église dupuis les origines jusqu' à nos jours, ed. A. Fliche and V. Martin. Paris: Bloud et Gay, 1934—(in progress; 19 vols. to date).

Lane-Pool, S. *The Mohammedan Dynasties.* Paris: Paul Geuthner, 1925.

Lexikon für Theologie und Kirche. 3d ed. Freiburg: Herder, 1957—(in progress; 4 vols. to date).

Mayer, H. E. *Bibliographie zur Geschichte der Kreuzzüge.* Hannover: Hahnsche Buchhandlanz, 1960.

Paetow, L. J. *A Guide to the Study of Mediaeval History.* Rev. ed. New York: F. S. Crofts, 1931.

E. *Monographs*
1. Books

Andressohn, J. C. *The Ancestry and Life of Godfrey*

of *Bouillon.* Bloomington: Indiana University Press, 1947.

Atiya, A. S. *The Crusade of Nicopolis.* London: Methuen, 1934.

———.*The Crusade in the Later Middle Ages.* London: Methuen, 1938.

Baldwin, M. W. *Raymond III of Tripolis and the Fall of Jerusalem (1140-1187).* Princeton: Princeton University Press, 1936.

Bridrey, E. *La Condition juridique des croisés et le privilège de la croix.* Paris: V. Giard et E. Brière, 1900.

Buckler, G. *Anna Comnena. A Study.* Oxford: Oxford University Press, 1929.

Campbell, G. A. *The Knights Templars, Their Rise and Fall.* New York: Robert McBride, n.d.

Chalandon, F. *Histoire de la première croisade.* Paris: Picard, 1925.

Cohn, N. *The Pursuit of the Millennium.* Fairlawn, N.J.: Essential Books, 1957.

Congar, Y. *The Background of the Schism Between the Eastern and Western Churches.* New York: Fordham University Press, 1959.

David, C. W. *Robert Curthose, Duke of Normandy.* Cambridge, Mass.: Harvard University Press, 1920.

Delisle, L. V. *Memoire sur les operations financières*

des Templiers. Paris: Imprimerie National, 1889.

Des Nersessian, S. *Armenia and the Byzantine Empire*. Cambridge, Mass.: Harvard University Press, 1945.

Donovan, J. P. *Pelagius and the Fifth Crusade*. Philadelphia: University of Pennsylvania Press, 1950.

Dussaud, R. *Topographie historique de la Syrie antique et médiévale*. Paris: Paul Geuthner, 1927.

Ebersolt, J. *Orient et occident. Recherches sur les influences byzantine et orientales en France*. 2 vols. Paris and Brussels: G. Van Dent, 1928-29.

Erdmann, C. *Die Entstehung des Kreuzzugsgedankens*. Stuttgart: W. Kohlhammer, 1935 (rp. 1955).

Fedden, R. *Crusader Castles. A Brief Study in the Military Architecture of the Crusades*. London: John Murray, 1950.

Flugi Van Aspermont, C. H. C. *De Johanniterorde in het Heilige Land, 1100-1292*. Asswn: Van Goroun, 1957.

Frolow, A. *Recherches sur la déviation de la IVe Croisade vers Constantinople*. Paris: Presses Universitaires de France, 1955.

Gay, J. *Les Papes du XIe siècle et la chrétienté*. Paris: V. Lecoffre, 1926.

Gottlob, A. *Die päpstlichen Kreuzzugssteuern des 13. Jahrhunderts. Ihre rechtliche Grundlage, politische Geschichte und technische Verwaltung*. Heiligenstadt: Franz Wilhelm Cordiet, 1892.

Gottschalk, H. L. *Al-Malik al-Kamīl von Egypten und seine Zeit*. Wiesbaden, Otto Harrassowitz, 1958.

Hagenmeyer, H. *Peter der Eremite. Ein kritischer Beitrag zur Geschichte des erstan Kreuzzuges*. Leipzig: Otto Harrassowitz, 1879.

Halecki, O. *The Crusade of Varna*. New York: Polish Institute of Arts and Sciences in America, 1943.

Hill, J. H. and L. L. *Raymond IV de Saint-Gilles, 1041 (1042)-1105*. Toulouse: Edouard Privat, 1959.

Hodgson, M. G. S. *The Order of Assassins. The Struggle of the Early Nizârî Ismâ 'îlîs Against the Islamic World*. The Hague: Mouton, 1955.

Hume, E. E. *Medical Work of the Knights Hospitallers of St. John of Jerusalem*. Baltimore: Johns Hopkins Press, 1940.

International Congress of Historical Sciences. *Relazioni del X Congresso Internazionale di Scienze Storice*. 6 vols. Firenze: G. C. Sansoni, 1955.

Kohler, C. *Mélanges pour servir à l'histoire de l'orient latin et des Croisades*.

Bibliography

2 vols. Paris: E. Leroux, 1906.

Lagenissiere, L. *Histoire de l'évêché de Bethléem.* Paris: Dumoulin, 1872.

Lamma, P. *Comneni e Staufer. Richerche sui rapporti fra Bisanzio e l'Occidente nel secolo XII.* Rome: Istitutio Storico Italiano per il Medio Evo, 1955.

LaMonte, J. L. *Feudal Monarchy in the Latin Kingdom of Jerusalem, 1100-1291.* Cambridge, Mass.: Mediaeval Academy of America, 1932 (Mediaeval Academy of America Publications, vol. 11).

LeFebvre, Y. *Pierre l'Ermite et la Croisade.* Amiens: Malfère, 1946.

Leib, B. *Rome, Kiev et Byzance à la fin du XIe siècle.* Paris: A. Picard, 1924.

Longnon, J. *L'empire latin de Constantinople et la principauté de Morée.* Paris: Perrin, 1949.

———.*Les Françaises d'Outre-Mer au moyen-âge.* Paris: Perrin, 1929.

McMahon, R. *The Story of the Hospitallers of St. John of God.* Westminster, Md.: Newman Press, 1959.

Michel, A. *Humbert and Kerullarios: Quellen und Studien sur Schisma des 11. Jahrhunderts.* 2 vols. Paderborn: F. Schöningh, 1925-30.

Minorski, V. *Studies in Caucasian History.* London:

Taylor's Foreign Press, 1953.

Mundo Lo, S. de. *Cruzados en Byzancio: La cuarta cruzada a la luz de las fuentes latinas y orientales.* Buenos Aires: Universidad de Buenos Aires, 1958.

[Munro, D. C.]. *The Crusades and Other Historical Essays Presented to Dana C. Munro by His Former Students,* ed. Louis J. Paetow. New York: F. S. Crofts, 1928.

———.*The Kingdom of the Crusaders.* New York: D. Appleton - Century,

Nicholson, R. L. *Joscelyn I, Prince of Edessa.* Urbana: University of Illinois Press, 1954.

Ohnsorge, W. *Abendland und Byzanz. Sammelte Aufsätze zur Geschichte der byzantinische - abendländischen Beziehungen und das Kaisertums.* Darmstadt: Hermann Gentner, 1958.

Painter, S. *The Scourge of the Clergy. Peter of Dreux, Duke of Brittany.* Baltimore: Johns Hopkins University Press, 1937.

Prescott, H. F. M. *Friar Felix at Large. A Fifteenth Century Pilgrimage to the Holy Land.* New Haven: Yale University Press, 1950 (rp. 1960).

———.*Once to Sinai. The Further Pilgrimage of Friar Fabri.* London: Eyre and Spottiswoode, 1957.

Prestage, E. (ed.). *Chivalry. A Series of Studies . . .*

By Members of King's College, London. New York: Knopf, 1928.

Prutz, H. *Kulturgeschichte der Kreuzzüge*. Berlin: Ernst Siegfried Mittler und Sohn, 1883.

Rey, E. G. *Les Colonies franques de Syrie aux XIIme et XIIIme siècles*. Paris: A. Picard, 1883.

Röhricht, R. *Geschichte des ersten Kreuzzuges*. Innsbruck: Wagner, 1901.

Rousset, P. *Les Origines et les charactères de la première Croisade*. Neuchatel: La Baconnnière, 1945.

Runciman, Sir S. *The Families of Outremer. The Feudal Nobility of the Crusader Kingdom of Jerusalem, 1099-1291*. London: Athlone Press, 1960.

_____.*The Sicilian Vespers. A History of the Mediterranean World in the Later Thirteenth Century*. Cambridge: Cambridge University Press, 1958 (r.p. London: Penguin, 1960).

Santifaller, L. *Beiträge zur Geschichte des lateinischen Patriarchats von Konstantinopel (1204-1261) und der venezianischen Urkunde*. Weimar: Hermann Böhlaus, 1938.

Schermerhorn, E. W. *Malta of the Knights*. New York: Houghton-Mifflin, 1929.

_____.*On the Trail of the Eight-Pointed Cross. A Study of the Heritage of the Knights Hospitallers in Feudal Europe*. New York: G. Putnam's Sons, 1940.

Schlumberger, G. *Récits de Byzance et des Croisades. ère série*. Paris: Plon, 1923.

Setton, K. M. *Catalan Domination of Athens, 1311-1388*. Cambridge, Mass.: Mediaeval Academy of America, 1948 (Mediaeval Academy of America, Publications, vol. 50).

Slaughter, G. *Saladin (1138-1193). A Biography*. New York: Exposition Press, 1955.

Slessarev, V. *Prester John: The Letter and the Legend*. Minneapolis: University of Minnesota Press, 1959.

Smail, R. C. *Crusading Warfare (1097-1193)*. Cambridge: Cambridge University Press, 1956.

Throop, P. A. *Criticism of the Crusade. A Study of Public Opinion and Crusade Propaganda*. Amsterdam: N. V. Swets and Zeitlinger, 1940.

Vincent, H., and F.-M. Abel. *Jérusalem. Recherches de topographie, d'archéologie et d'histoire*. 2 vols. Paris: V. Lecoffre, 1912-1926.

Wentzlaff-Eggebert, F.-W. *Kreuzzugsdichtung des Mittelalters. Studien zu ihrer geschichtlichen und dichterischen Wirklichkeit*. Berlin: Walter de Gruyter, 1960.

Bibliography

287

Wright, J. K. *The Geographical Lore of the Time of the Crusades.* New York: American Geographical Society, 1925.

2. Articles

Adolf, H. "Christendom and Islam in the Middle Ages: "New Light on 'Grail Stone' and 'Hidden Host,'" *Speculum*, XXXII (1957), 103-15.

Baldwin, M. W.: "Ecclesiastical Developments in the Twelfth Century Crusaders' State of Tripolis," *Catholic Historical Review*, XXII (1936-37), 149-71.

————."Some Recent Interpretations of Pope Urban II's Eastern Policy," *Catholic Historical Review*, XXV (1939-40), 459-66.

————."Western Attitudes Toward Islam," *Catholic Historical Review*, XXVII (1941-42), 403-11.

Beddie, J. "Some Notices of Books in the East in the Period of the Crusades," *Speculum*, VIII (1933), 240-42.

Benito Ruano, E. "Las ordenes militares espanõlas y la idea de cruzada," *Hispania*, XVI (1956), 3-15.

Berry, V. "Peter the Venerable and the Crusades," *Studia Anselmiana*, XL (1956), 141-62.

Bredero, A. "Studien zu den Kreuzzugsbriefen Bernhards von Clairvaux und seiner Reise nach Deutschlands im Jahre 1146," *Mitteilungen der Institut für Osterreichische Geschichtsforschungen*, LXVI (1958), 331-43.

Brown, E. A. R. "The Cistercians in the Latin Empire of Constantinople, 1204-1276," *Traditio*, XIV (1958), 63-120.

Brundage, J. A. "Adhemar of Puy: The Bishop and His Critics," *Speculum*, XXXIV (1959), 201-12.

————."An Errant Crusader: Stephen of Blois," *Tradito*, XVI (1960), 380-95.

Buckley, J. M. "The Problematical Octogenarianism of John of Brienne," *Speculum*, XXXII (1957), 315-22.

Burdach, K. "Walther von der Vogelweide und der vierte Kreuzzug," *Historische Zeitschrift*, CXLV (1932), 1-45.

Burns, R. I. "The Catalan Company and the European Powers, 1305-1311," *Speculum*, XXIX (1954), 751-71.

————."Journey from Islam: Incipient Cultural Transition in the Conquered Kingdom of Valencia (1240-1280)," *Speculum*, XXXV (1960), 337-56.

————."Social Riots on the Christian-Moslem Frontier: Thirteenth-Century Valencia," *American Historical Review*, LXVI (1961), 378-400.

Burr, G. L. "The Year 1000 and the Antecedents of the Crusaders," *American Historical Review,* VI (1900), 429-39.

Cartellieri, A. "Richard Löwenherz im Heiligen Lande," *Historische Zeitschrift,* CI (1908), 1-28.

Cazel, F. A. "The Tax of 1185 in Aid of the Holy Land," *Speculum,* XXX (1955), 385-92.

Charanis, P. "Aims of the Medieval Crusades and How They Were Viewed by Byzantium," *Church History,* XXI (1952), 3-14.

————."A Greek Source on the Origin of the First Crusade," *Speculum,* XXIV (1949), 93-94.

Cocheril, M. M. "Essai sur l'origine des ordres militaires dans la péninsule ibérique," *Collectanea Ordinis Cisterciensis,* XX (1958), 346-61.

Constable, G. "The Second Crusade as Seen by Contemporaries," *Traditio,* IX (1953), 213-79.

Crawford, R. W. "William of Tyre and the Maronites," *Speculum,* XXX (1955), 222-32.

Delaville le Roux, J. "La Suppression des Templiers," *Revue des Questions Historiques,* XLVIII (1890), 29-61.

Deschamps, P. "La Toponomastique en terre sainte au temps des croisades," *Mémoires et documents*

Publiés par la Société de l'École des Chartres, XXII, 1 (1955), 352-56.

Ehrenkreutz, A. S. "The Place of Saladin in the Naval History of the Mediterranean Sea in the Middle Agea," *Journal of the American Oriental Society,* LXXV (1955), 100-16.

Eidelberg, S. "The Solomon Bar Simeon Chronicle as a Source of the History of the First Crusade," *Jewish Quarterly Review,* XLIX (1959), 282-87.

Engreen, F. E. "Pope John the Eighth and the Arabs," *Speculum,* XX (1945), 318-30.

Flahiff, G. B. "*Deus non Vult:* A Critic of the Third Crusade," *Mediaeval Studies,* IX (1947), 162-88.

Fliche, A. "L'Élection d'Urbain II," *Le Moyen Âge,* XIX (1916), 356-94.

————."Les Origines de l'action de la papauté en vue da la Croisade," *Revue d'histoire ecclésiastique,* XXXIV (1938), 765-75.

Fotheringham, J. K. "Genoa and the Fourth Crusade," *English Historical Review,* XXV (1910), 26-57.

Geanakopolos, D. J. "The Council of Florence (1438-1439) and the Problem of Union Between the Greek and

Latin Churches," *Church History*, XXIV (1955), 2-23.

———."Michael VIII Palaeologus and the Union of Lyons (1274)," *Harvard Theological Review*, XLVI (1953), 79-89.

Gieysztor, A. "The Genesis of the Crusades: The Encyclical of Sergius IV (1009 - 1012)," *Medievalia et Humanistica*, V (1948), 3-23; VI (1950), 3-34.

Gibb, Sir H. A. R. "The Arabic Sources for the Life of Saladin," *Speculum*, XXV (1950), 58-72.

Grill, L. "Die Kreuzzugsepistel Sankt Bernhards: 'Ad peregrinantes Jerusalem,'" *Studien und Mitteilungen zur Geschichte des Benediktinerordens und seiner Zweige*, LXVII (1956), 237-53.

Grégoire, H. "The Question of the Diversion of the Fourth Crusade, or an Old Controversy Solved by a Latin Adverb," *Byzantion*, XV (1940-41), 158-66.

Hardy, E. R. "The Patriarchate of Alexandria: A Study in National Christianity," *Church History*, XV (1946), 81-100.

Hill, J. H. and L. L. "Contemporary Accounts and the Later Reputation of Adhemar, Bishop of Puy," *Medievalia et Humanistica*, IX (1955), 30-38.

———."The Convention of Alexius Commenus and Raymond of Saint Gilles," *American Historical Review*, LVIII (1952-53), 322-27.

Hill, J. H. "Raymond of Saint Gilles in Urban's Plan of Greek and Latin Friendship," *Speculum*, XXVI (1951), 265-76.

Holtzmann, W. "Studien zur Orientpolitik des Reformpapsttums und zur Entstehung des ersten Kreuzzuges," *Historische Vierteljahrschrift*, XXII (1924-25), 167-99.

———."Der Unionsverhandlung zwischen Alexius I und Urban II im Jahre 1089," *Byzantinische Zeitschrift*, XXVII (1928), 38-67.

John, E. "A Note on the Preliminaries of the Fourth Crusade," *Byzantion*, XXVIII (1958), 95-103.

Joranson, E. "The Problem of the Spurious Letter of Emperor Alexius to the Count of Flanders," *American Historical Review*, LV (1949-50), 811-32.

Kahl, H. D. "Zum Ereignis des Wendenkreuzzugs von 1147. Zugleich ein Beitrag zur Geschichte des sächsischen Frühchristentums," *Jarbuch für Kirchengeschichte im Bistum Berlin*, XI-XII (1957-58), 99-120.

Kohler, C. and C. V. Langlois. "Lettres inédites concernant les Croisades," *Bibliothèque de l'École* des Chartres, LII (1891), 46-63.

Krey, A. C. "Urban's Crusade —Success or Failure," American Historical Review, LIII (1947-48), 235-50.

———."William of Tyre," Speculum, XVI (1941), 149-66.

Labande, E.-R. "Recherches sur les pèlerins dans l'Europe des XIe et XIIe siècles," Cahiers de Civilization Médiévale, I, (1958), 159-69, 339-47.

Lair, J. "Encyclique de Sergius IV relative à une projet de Croisade," Bibliothèque de l'École des Chartres, XVIII 1856-57), 246-53.

Lalanne, L. "Des pèlerinages en terre sainte avant les croisades," Bibliothèque de l'École des Chartres, VII (1845-46), 1-31.

LaMonte, J. L. and N. Downs. "The Lords of Bethsan in the Kingdoms of Jerusalem and Cyprus," Medievalia et Humanistica, VI (1949), 57-75.

———."The Lords of Caesarea in the Period of the Crusales," Speculum, XII (1947), 145-61.

———."The Lords of Le Puiset on the Crusades," Speculum XVII (1942), 100-18.

———."The Significance of the Crusaders' States in Medieval History," Byzantion, XV (1940-41), 300-15.

———."Some Problems in Crusading Historiography," Speculum, XV (1940), 57-75.

Lecoy de la Marche, A. "La Prédication de la Croisade au trezième siècle," Revue des Questiones Historique, XLVIII (1890), 5-28.

Loomis, L. H. "Secular Dramatics in the Royal Palace, Paris, 1378, 1389, and Chaucer's 'Tregetoures,'" Speculum, XXXIII (1958), 242-55.

Lunt, W. E. "The Text of the Ordinance of 1184 Concerning an Aid for the Holy Land," English Historical Review, XXXVII (1922), 235-42.

Luttrell, A. T. "The Aragonese Crown and the Knights Hospitallers of Rhodes, 1291-1350," English Historical Review, LXXVI (1961), 1-19.

Mayer, H. E. "Zum Tode Wilhelms von Tyrus," Archiv für Diplomatik, Schriftgeschichte, Siegel- und Wappenkunde, V/VI (1959-60), 182-201.

———."Zur Beurteilung Adhémars van Le Puy," Deutsches Archiv, XVI (1960),547-52.

Morris, W. S. "A Crusader's Testament," Speculum, XXVII (1952), 197-98.

Munro, D. C. "The Children's Crusade," American Historical Review, XIX (1913-14), 516-24.

———."A Crusader: Seventh Presidential Address," *Speculum,* VII (1932), 321-35.

———."Did the Emperor Alexius I. Ask for Aid at the Council of Piacenza, 1095? *American Historical Review,* XXVII (1921-22), 731-33.

———."The Speech of Pope Urban II at Clermont," *American Historical Review,* XI (1905-06), 231-42.

———."The Western Attitude Toward Islam During the Crusades," *Speculum,* VI (1931), 329-43.

Nicol, D. M. "The Fourth Crusade and the Latin Empire of Constantinople," *History Today,* VI (1956), 486-94.

Nowell, C. E. "The Historical Prester John," *Speculum* XXVIII (1953) 435-45.

———."The Old Man of the Mountain," *Speculum* XXII (1947), 497-519.

O'Callaghan, J. F. "The Affiliation of the Order of Calatrava with the Order of Cîteaux," *Analecta Sacri Ordinis Cisterciensis,* XV (1959), 161-93; XVI (1960), 3-59, 255-92.

Painter, S. "The Houses of Lusignan and Chatellerault, 1150-1250," *Speculum,* XXX (1955,) 374-84.

———."The Lords of Lusignan in the Eleventh and Twelfth Centuries,"

Speculum, XXXIII (1957), 27-47.

Peeters, P. "Un Témoinage autographe sur le siège d'Antioche par les Croisés en 1098," *Miscellanea historica Alberti de Meyer,* 373-90.

Pelliot, P. "Mélanges sur l'epoque des Croisades," *Memoires de l'Académie des Inscriptions et Belles Lettres,* XLIV (1951), 1-97.

Perkins, C. "The Knights Hospitallers in England After the Fall of the Order of the Temple," *English Historical Review,* XLV (1930), 285-89.

———."The Knights Templars in the British Isles," *English Historical Review,* XXV (1910), 209-29.

———."The Trial of the Knight Templars in England," *English Historical Review,* XXIV (1909), 432-47.

———."The Wealth of the Knights Templars in England and the Disposition of it After Their Dissolution," *American Historical Review,* XV (1909-10), 252-63.

Pflaum, H. "A Strange Crusader's Song," *Speculum,* X (1935), 337-39.

Porges, W. "The Clergy, the Poor, and the Non-Combatants on the First Crusade," *Speculum,* XXI (1946), 1-21.

Prawer, J. "The Settlement of the Latins in Jerusalem," *Speculum*, XXVII (1952), 490-503.

Riant, P. "Inventaire critique des lettres histriques de croisades," *Archives de l'Orient Latin,* I (1881), 1-219.

———."Un dernier triomphe d'Urbain II," *Revue des Questions Historiques,* XXIV (1883), 247-55.

———."La Legende du martyre en orient de Thiemon, archévêque de Salzbourg (28 septembre 1102)," *Revue des Questiones Historiques,* XXXIX (1886), 218-37.

"Un Recit perdu de la première croisade," *Bibliothèque de l'École des Chartres,* XLIV (1883), 259-62.

Richard, J. "An Account of the Battle of Hattin Referring to the Frankish Mercenaries in Oriental Moslem States," *Speculum,* XXVII (1952), 168-77.

———."Quelques textes sur les premiers temps de l'église latine de Jérusalem," *Mémoires et Documents Publiés par la Société de l'École des Chartres,* XII, 2 (1955), 420-30.

Röhricht, R. "Der Kinderkreuzzug, 1212," *Historische Zeitschrift,* XXXVI (1876), 1-8.

———."Die Kreuzpredigten gegen den Islam. Ein Beitrag zur Geschichte der christlichen Predigt im 12. and 13. Jahrhundert," *Zeitschrift für Kirchengeschichte,* V I (1884), 550-72.

———."Die Pastorellen (1251)," *Zeitschrift für Kirchengeschichte,* V I (1884), 290-96.

———.Die Rüstungen des Abendlandes zum dritten grossen Kreuzzuge," *Historische Zeitschrift,* XXXIV (1875), 1-73.

Round, J. H. "The Saladin Tithe," *English Historical Review,* X X X I (1916), 447-50.

———."Some English Crusaders of Richard I," *English Historical Review,* XVIII (1903), 475-81.

Rowe, J. G. "The Papacy and the Ecclesiastical Province of Tyre (1100-1187)," *Bulletin of the John Rylands Library,* XLIII (1960), 160-68.

———."The Papacy and the Greeks (1122 - 1153)," *Church History,* XXVIII (1959), 310-27.

Runciman, Sir S. "The Holy Lance Found at Antioch," *Analecta Bollandiana,* LXVIII (1950), 197-209.

Savage, H. L. "Enguerrand de Coucy VII and the Campaign of Nicopolis," *Speculum,* XIV (1939), 423-42.

Setton, K. M. "Athens in the Later Twelfth Century," *Speculum,* XIX (1944), 179-207.

———."The Emperor John VIII Slept Here," *Speculum,* XXXIII (1958), 222-28.

————."A Note on Michael Choniates, Archbishop of Athens (1182-1204)," *Speculum,* XXI (1946), 234-36.

Throop, P. A. "Criticism of Papal Crusade Policy in Old French and Provençal," *Speculum,* XII (1938), 379-412.

Topping, P. W. "The Formation of the Assizes of Romania," *Byzantion,* XVII (1944-45), 304-14.

Tuleja, T. V. "Eugenius IV and the Crusade of Varna," *Catholic Historical Review,* XXV (1949-50), 257-75.

Ulhorn, G. "Die Anfänge des Johanniterordens," *Zeitschrift für Kirchengeschichte,* VI (1884), 46-59.

Vasiliev, A. A. "The Empire of Trebizond in History and Literature," *Byzantion,* XV (1940-41), 316-77.

————."The Foundation of the Empire of Trebizond (1204 - 1222)," *Speculum,* XI (1936), 3-37.

Waas, A. "Der heilige Krieg in Islam und Christentum in Vergangenheit und Gegenwart," *Welt als Geschichte,* XIX (1959), 211-25.

Walker, C. H. "Eleanor of Aquitaine and the Disaster at Cadmas Mountain on the Second Crusade," *American Historical Review,* LV (1949-50), 857-61.

Wentzlaff-Eggebert, F.-W. "Kreuzzugsidee und mittelalterliches Weltbild,' *Deutsche Vierteljahrschrift für Literaturwissenschaft und Geistesgeschichte,* XXX (1956), 71-88.

Willems, E. "Cîteaux" et la seconde Croisade," *Revue d'Histoire Ecclésiastique,* XLIX (1954), 116-51.

Witzel, H. J. "Le Problème de l'auteur des *Gesta Francorum et aliorum Hierosolymitanorum,*" *Le Moyen Âge,* LXI (1955), 319-28.

Wolff, R. L. "Baldwin of Flanders and Hainaut, First Latin Emperor of Constantinople: His Life, Death and Resurrection, 1172-1225," *Speculum,* XXVII (1952), 281-322.

————."Footnote to an Incident of the Latin Occupation of Constantinople," *Traditio,* VI (1948), 319-28.

————."Greeks and Latins Before and After 1204," *Revista di studi storici-religiosi,* I (1957), 320-34.

————."The Latin Empire of Constantinople and the Franciscans," *Traditio,* II (1944), 213-37.

————."Mortgage and Redemption of an Emperor's Son: Castile and the Latin Empire of Constantinople," *Speculum,* XXIX (1954), 45-84.

———."The Organization of the Latin Patriarchate of Constantinople, 1 2 0 4-1261: Social and Administrative Consequences of the Latin Conquest," *Traditio*, VI (1948), 33-60.

———."Politics in the Latin Patriarchate of Constantinople," *Dumbarton Oaks Papers*, VIII (1954), 225-303.

———."Romania: The Latin Empire of Constantinople," *Speculum*, XXIII (1948), 1-34.

———."The 'Second Bulgarian Empire.' Its Origin and History to 1204," *Speculum*, XXIV (1949), 167-206.

INDEX OF DOCUMENTS

The Letters of St. Bernard: See Bernard of Clairvaux, St., *The Letters of St. Bernard*

The Life of St. Louis: See Jean de Joinville, *The Life of St. Louis*

Ludolph of Suchem, *Description of the Holy Land and of the Way Thither* (trans. Aubrey Steward in Palestine Pilgrims' Text Society, *Publications*, XII, 54-61)   268-72

Mansi, J. D., *Sacrorum conciliorum nova et amplissima collectionem*, XXII, 1057-58   215-18

Massacre of the Crusaders: *See* Albert of Aachen, *Historia Hierosolymitana*, I, 17-22

Memoirs of the Crusades: See Geoffrey de Villehardouin, The Military Methods of the Mongols: *See* John of Plano Carpini, *History of the Mongols, VI*

The Mongol Mission: See Guyuk Khan; Innocent IV, Pope, Epist. 136; John of Plano Carpini, *History of the Mongols*

Moslem Hostages Slaughtered at Acre: *See Itinerarium peregrinorum et gesta regis Ricardi*, IV, 2, 4

Odo of Deuil, *La Croisade de Louis VII roi de France*, I (ed. H. Waquet in *Documents relatifs à l' histoire des Croisades*, II, 20-23)   89-90

Odo of Deuil, *La Croisade de Louis VII roi de France*, II-III (ed. H. Waquet in *Documents relatifs à l' histoire des Croisades*, II, 30-32, 35-37)   106-9

Odo of Deuil, *La Croisade de Louis VII roi de France*, IV (ed. H. Waquet in *Documents relatifs à l' histoire des Croisades*, II, 44-46)   109-11

Odo of Deuil, *La Croisade de Louis VII roi de France*, V (ed. H. Waquet in *Documents relatifs à l' histoire des Croisades*, II, 54-55)   111-12

Oliver of Paderborn, *The Capture of Damietta*, chaps. 27-29, 31-33 (trans. J. J. Gavigan, pp. 39-48)   219-24

The Organization of the Fourth Crusade: *See* Geoffrey de Villehardouin, *De la conqueste de Constantinople*, (trans. Marzials, pp. 1-2, 3-7, 15-17)

Osbernus, *De expugnatione Lyxbonensi* (ed. W. Stubbs in Rolls Series, *Chronicles and Memorials of the Reign of Richard I*, I, clv-clvi, clx-clxi, clxiv, clxvi, clxxviii-clxxx)   97-104

Otto of Freising, *Chronicon*, VII, 33 (ed. G. H. Pertz in *MGH, SSRG*, pp. 334-35)   83

Otto of Freising, *Gesta Friderici Imperatoris*, I, 35 (ed. G. H. Pertz in *MGH, SSRG*, pp. 55-58)   86-88

Index of Documents

301

INDEX OF TRANSLATORS

GENERAL INDEX

Auxonne, 233
Azymites, 54

Babylon; *See* Egypt, Cairo
Baghdad, 7, 78, 266
Baibars, Sultan, 266
Baladun; *See* Pons of Baladun
Baldwin of Boulogne; *See* Baldwin I, King of Jerusalem
Baldwin, Count of Flanders and Hainault, 201, 205-7
Baldwin d' Ibelin, 243
Baldwin I, King of Jerusalem, 41, 52, 72, 80
Baldwin II, King of Jerusalem, 79
Baldwin III, King of Jerusalem, 79, 115-16, 118-19, 126, 136
Baldwin IV, King of Jerusalem, 141-51
Baldwin V, King of Jerusalem, 150
Balian d' Ibelin, 154, 158, 162
Balistas, 100, 130, 176, 178
Balkans, 8, 14-15
Baltic Sea, 2
Bamberg; *See* Gunther, Bishop of Bamberg
Barbary, 234
Bari, 40, 42
Barneville; *See* Roger of Barneville
Bartholomew, Peter, 57
Bartholomew, Saint, 251
Batu, 258
Beatrice, Countess of Edessa, 126
Beauvais, 173
Beirut, 228-32
Beisan, 218
Belgrade, 26, 28-29, 107
Benedict, Saint, 179
Bernard, Saint, Abbot of Clairvaux, 88-92, 94-95, 122-24

Bernard of Tremelay, 132
Bernicles, 242-43
Bethany, 142, 154
Bethlehem, 2, 232
Bilbeis, 138
Blachernae, 109-10, 202, 205
Blecourt, 233
Bohemia, 2, 190
Bohemund of Taranto, 42, 47, 49, 53, 55-56, 61-62
Bohemund III, Prince of Antioch, 150
Boniface, Marquis of Montferrat, 205-7
Bouillon; *See* Godfrey of Bouillon
Boulogne; *See also* Eustace III, Count of Boulogne; *See also* Baldwin I, King of Jerusalem
Boulogne, 72
Bourges, 89
Bosporus, 30, 41, 44
Branicevo, 107
Branits, 105
Bremen, 104
Brindisi, 45, 214
Brittany, 45, 49
Bucoleon, 202, 205
Bulgaria, 26-28, 105-7
Bulgarians, 4, 44
Bulgars, 15, 210
Burgundy, 17, 45, 182, 236
Burel, Geoffrey, 28-29, 33-34
Byzantine Empire, 1, 7-8, 14-15, 105, 141, 124, 202, 219, 274-75

Caesar, C. Julius, 107
Caesarea, 5, 266
Cairo, 6-7, 136-37, 139, 151, 255, 248
Calabria, 45

Opium, 138
Orange, Bishop of, 61
Orontes River, 126
Otto, Bishop of Ratisbon, 3
Ottoman Turks, 273, 275

Pagan of Haifa, Knight, 172
Palermo, 226
Palestine, 2-3, 7, 52, 62, 78, 121, 166, 189, 218-19, 226, 230, 248, 266-67
Palmela, 98
Paradise, Ship, 204
Paris, 191, 237, 248-49
Passau, 106
Patrick, Thomas, 162
Paul, St., 9, 11, 95, 218
Paulicians, 50, 54
Pecheneg, Turks, 15, 44
Pedatica, 100
Pelagius, Cardinal, 219-21, 224
Pelecanum, 41-42, 46
Pelusium, 138
Persia, 18, 83, 254, 266
Persians, 50, 83
Peter, Archbishop of Tyre, 128
Peter, brother of Raynald of Ponts, 44
Peter, Count of Brittany, 243
Peter, St., 9-11, 50, 88, 95, 98, 154, 166, 218
Peter Bartholomew, 60-61
Peter de Montagu, Knight Templar, 231
Peter Desiderius, priest, 63
Peter of Capua, 191
Peter Raymond of Hautpul, 58
Peter the Hermit, 23-30, 32-33, 35-36, 46, 105
Petit Pont, 237
Phacusa, 136
Philip, Duke of Swabia, 199

Philip I, King of France, 39-40
Philip II, Augustus, King of France, 163-64, 166, 173, 175-77, 179-83, 185, 190
Philip d' Ibelin, 227
Philip of Montfort, 239
Philip of Nemours, 245, 247
Philip of Nablus, 81
Philippopolis, 27, 107-8
Philistines, 126
Piacenza, 213
Piacenza, Council of, 15-17
Pilgrim, Ship, 204
Pilgrimage, 3, 20, 75, 209, 249
Pilgrims, 5-7, 31, 120, 124, 129, 196-97, 234
Pisa, 78, 189, 221
Pisans, 220, 268, 275
Plato, 137
Poland, 2
Pons of Baladun, 61
Pontarlien, 45
Pontigny, Abbot of, 77
Portugal, 2, 97, 99
Pre-Crusades, 3
Prester, John, 82-83
Provence, 17, 49, 57

Rainald of Breis, 33-34
Ralph of Merencourt, Patriarch of Jerusalem, 221
Ramla, 6-7
Ranier d' Ibelin, 162
Ratisbon, 106
Ratisbon; *See also* Otto, Bishop of Ratisbon
Raymond II, Count of Tripoli, 126
Raymond III, Count of Tripoli, 144-45, 148-50, 153-58
Raymond, Prince of Antioch, 79, 81-82, 114. 126

General Index

315

3 5282 00710 4055

910.18
B89A